Vector Algebra

Abhijit Debnath

M.Sc, M.Phil

notionpress
.com

Publishing Year 2024
Composer : Palash Dhar
Email ID : dharpalash@gmail.com

Published and Printed by :
Notion Press Media Pvt. Ltd.
No. 50, Chettiyar Agaram Main Road,
Vanagaram, Chennai, Tamil Nadu 600095
Email ID : publish@notionpress.com
Phone Number: +91 44 46315631
Website : www.notionpress.com

Content:

1. Vector Algebra

2. Scalar product of two Vectors

VECTOR ALGEBRA

(i) DIRECTED LINE SEGMENT :

Any given portion of a given straight line where for the two end points are distinguished as Initial and Terminal is called a Directed line segment.

The directed line segment with initial point A and terminal point B is donoted by the symbol $\overrightarrow{AB}$.

The two end points of a directed line segment are not interchangeble and the directed line segments $\overrightarrow{AB}$ and $\overrightarrow{BA}$ must be thought of as different.

(ii) LENGTH SUPPORT AND SENSE OF A DIRECTED LINE SEGMENT :

Associated with every directed line segment $\overrightarrow{AB}$, we have its Length, Support and Sense.

(*a*) Length : The length of $\overrightarrow{AB}$ will be denoted by the symbol $|\overrightarrow{AB}|$.

Clearly, we have $|\overrightarrow{AB}|=|\overrightarrow{BA}|$.

(*b*) Support : The line of unlimited length of which a directed line segment is a part is called its line of support or simply the support.

(*c*) Sense : The sense of $\overrightarrow{AB}$ is from A to B and that of $\overrightarrow{BA}$ from B to A so that the sense of a directed line segment is from its initial to the terminal point.

The directed line segments $\overrightarrow{AB}$ and $\overrightarrow{BA}$ have the same lengths and supports but different senses.

The question of comparison of the senses of two directed line segments arises only when they have the same or parallel support.

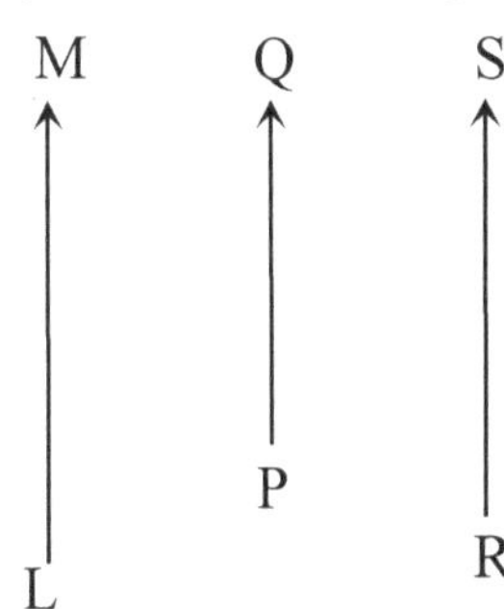

VECTOR : A vector is an object that has both a magnitude and a direction.

Geometrically, we can picture a vector as a directed line segment, where length is the magnitude of the vector and with an arrow indicating the direction.

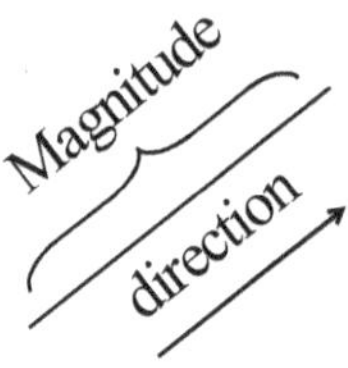

(iii) EQUALITY OF TWO VECTORS : Two vectors are said to be equal if they have :

(*a*) the same length.

(*b*) the same or parallel supports, and

(*c*) the same sense.

It may thus be seen that two different directed line segments may correspond to the same vectors.

Thus, the vectors $\overrightarrow{AB}, \overrightarrow{CD}, \overrightarrow{EF}$ are equal.

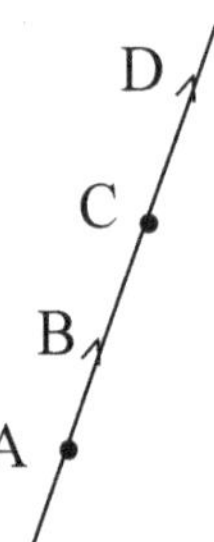

Two vectors will not be equal if they have different lengths or inclined supports or again, they will not be equal even if they have the same lengths and parallel supports but different senses.

If *ABCD* is a parallelogram, we have

$$\overrightarrow{AB} = \overrightarrow{DC}$$

and $\quad \overrightarrow{BC} = \overrightarrow{AD}$

Every vector belongs to a class of equal vectors.

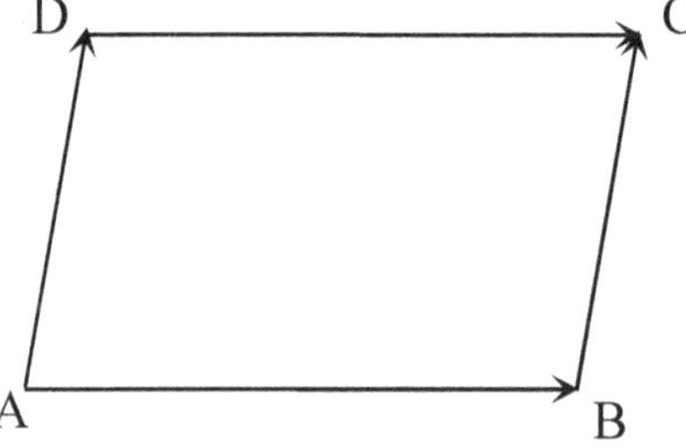

(iv) NOTATION FOR A VECTOR :

A Vector is also denoted by a single letter such that a, b, c etc. by using bold face type so that we may write.

$$a = \overrightarrow{AB}$$

Then the symbol $|a|$.

denotes the length of the vector, *a*, also called the Magnitude of the vector.

(v) DIFFERENT TYPES OF VECTORS :

(a) Zero Vector :   A vector which has zero length but no definite direction is called zero vector. It is denoted by $\vec{O}$ and $|\vec{O}| = 0$.

(b) Unit Vector :   A vector is said to be unit vector when it has unit length. This vector can be denoted by $\hat{a}$.

(c) Negative Vector :

A vector having direction opposite to that of the vector $\vec{a}$ but having same magnitude is denoted by $-\vec{a}$.

(d) Equal Vectors : Two or more vectors are equal when they have the same length and they point in the same direction.

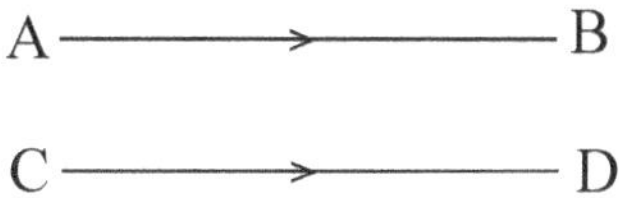

Here $\overrightarrow{AB}$ and $\overrightarrow{CD}$ vectors are same length and direction. So, they are equal vectors.

(e) Like and Unlike Vectors :

The vectors having the same direction are known as like vectors. On the contrary, the vectors having the opposite direction with respect to each other are termed to the unlike vector.

Here, $\overrightarrow{EF}$ and $\overrightarrow{GH}$ have the same direction. So, they are like vectors and $\overrightarrow{AB}$ and $\overrightarrow{CD}$ have the opposite direction, so thcy are unlike vectors.

(f) Co-initial Vectors :

The vectors which have the same starting point are called co-initial vectors.

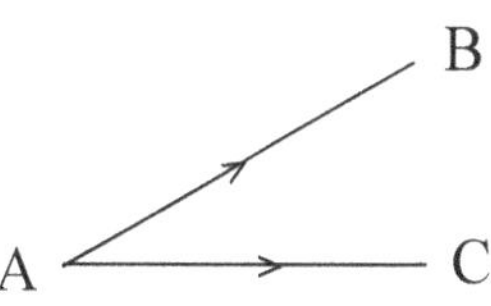

Here, $\overrightarrow{AB}$ and $\overrightarrow{AC}$ are co-initial vectors because they have the same starting point.

(g) Collinear Vectors or Parallel Vectors :

Vectors are said to be collinear or parallel vectors when they are parallel to the same line whatever be their magnitudes and directions.

$$A \xrightarrow{\hspace{3cm}} B$$

$$C \xleftarrow{\hspace{3cm}} D$$

Here, $\overrightarrow{AB}$ and $\overrightarrow{CD}$ are collinear vectors but their direction are opposite.

(*h*) Co-planar Vectors: Vectors are said to be co-planer when they are parallel to the same plane whatever be their magnitudes and direction.

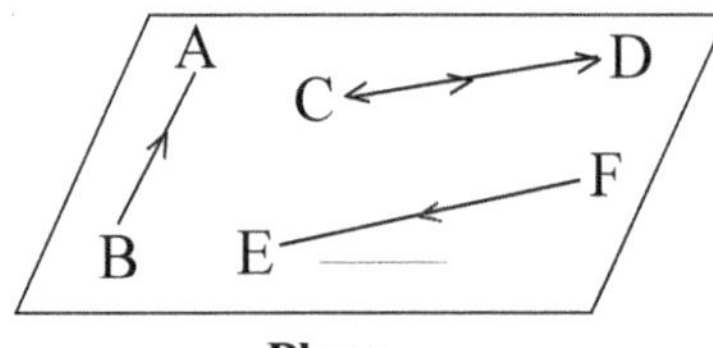

Plane

Here, and are co-planar vector because they lies on the same plane.

(*i*) Negative of a Vector :

If two vectors are the same in magnitude but exactly opposite in direction then both the vectors are negative of each other.

Assume there are two vectors a and b, such that these vectors are exactly the same in magnitude but opposite in direction then these vectors can be given by.

$$\vec{a} = -\vec{b}$$

(*j*) Position Vector of a Point :

Let, P be a point in space. The position vector of the point with respect to the origin O is denoted by $\overrightarrow{OP}$.

(*k*) Displacement Vector :

If a point is displaced from position A to B then the displacement AB represents a Vector AB, which is known as the displacement vector.

SCALARS : Scalar quantity is defined as the physical quantity with magnitude and no direction.

Some physical quantities can be described just by their numerical value without directions. The addition of these physical quantities follows the simple rules of the algebra.

Some of the Common examples of Scalars are Mass, Speed, Distance, Area, Volume etc.

(vi) ALGEBRA OF VECTORS :

(*a*) Addition of Vectors :

(*i*) Traingle law of Vector Addition :

Suppose two vectors $\vec{a}$ and $\vec{b}$ are represented by the two adjacent sides of a triangle such that the initial print of one coincides with the terminal point of the other (Say $\overrightarrow{AB}$ and $\overrightarrow{BC}$), then their sum is represented by the third side $\overrightarrow{AC}$ of $\triangle ABC$.

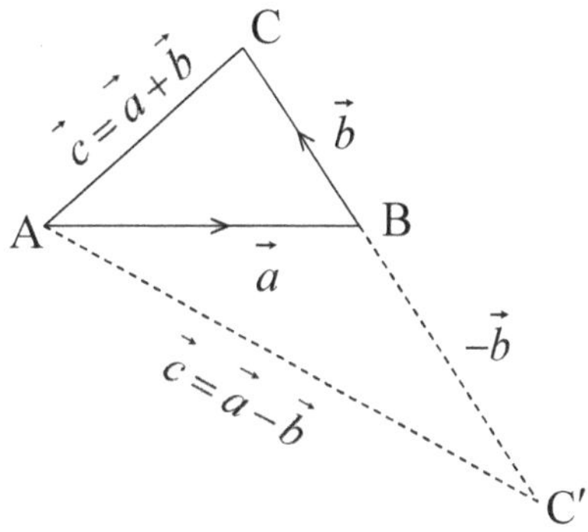

Thus, $\vec{a}+\vec{b}=\vec{c}$ or $\overrightarrow{AB}+\overrightarrow{BC}=\overrightarrow{AC}$.

This is known as the triangle law of vector addition.

Now, construct a vector $\overrightarrow{BC'}$ or $\vec{b}$, such that its magnitude is same as the vector $\overrightarrow{BC}$ and direction opposite to $\overrightarrow{BC}$.

i.e., $\quad\overrightarrow{BC'}=-\overrightarrow{BC}$ or $\vec{b'}=-\vec{b}$.

Then, by triangle law, we have

$$\overrightarrow{AC'}=\overrightarrow{AB}+\overrightarrow{BC'}$$

$$=\overrightarrow{AB}+(-\overrightarrow{BC})$$

$$=\overrightarrow{AB}-\overrightarrow{BC}$$

or, $\quad\overrightarrow{C'}=\vec{a}-\vec{b}$.

Here, the vector $\overrightarrow{AC'}$ or $\overrightarrow{C'}$ is said to be represent the difference of $\vec{a}$ and $\vec{b}$.

PARALLELOGRAM LAW OF VECTOR ADDITION :

Suppose two vectors $\vec{a}$ and $\vec{b}$ are represented by the two adjacent sides of a parallelogram then their sum $\vec{C}$ is represented by the diogonal of the parallelogram, which is comitial with the given vectors.

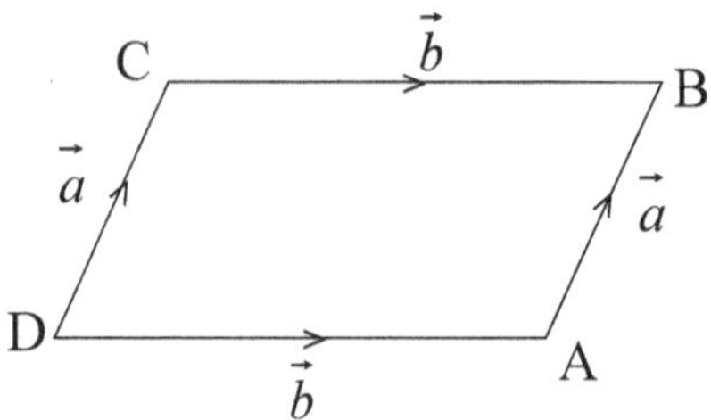

Mathematically, $\vec{C} = \vec{a} + \vec{b}$.

This is known as parallelogram law of vector addition.

Properties of Vector Addition :

Suppose, $\vec{a}, \vec{b}$ and $\vec{C}$ are any three vectors, then

(*i*) Vector addition is commutative,

i.e., $\quad \vec{a} + \vec{b} = \vec{b} + \vec{a}$

(*ii*) Vector addition is associative,

i.e., $\quad (\vec{a} + \vec{b}) + \vec{C} = \vec{a} + (\vec{b} + \vec{C})$

(*iii*) Existence of additive identity

$$\vec{a} + \vec{o} = \vec{a} = \vec{o} + \vec{a}$$

Where, $\vec{O}$ is called additive identity

MULTIPLICATION OF A VECTOR BY A SCALAR :

Let λ be a scalar and $\vec{a}$ be a vector, then $\lambda\vec{a}$ is defined as a vector whose magnitude is $|\lambda|$ times the magnitude of $\vec{a}$, i.e. $|\lambda\vec{a}| = |\lambda||\vec{a}|$ and the direction is same or opposite of $\vec{a}$, according as λ is positive or negative.

Example : When $\lambda = -2$, then $\lambda\vec{a} = -2\vec{a}$, which is a vector havifng magnitude double to the magnitude of $\vec{a}$ and direction opposite to that of the direction of $\vec{a}$.

PROPERTIES OF MULTIPLICATION OF A VECTOR BY A SCALAR :

The addition of vectors and the multiplication of a vector by a scalar, together constitute the following distribution law.

Let $\vec{a}$ and $\vec{b}$ be any two vectors and k and m be any two scalar, then

(*i*) $k\vec{a} + m\vec{a} = (k + m)\vec{a}$

(ii) $k(\vec{a} + \vec{b}) = k\vec{a} + k\vec{b}$

(iii) $k(m\vec{a}) = km(\vec{a})$

(vii) COMPONENTS OF A VECTOR :

Let a point P in a space has coordinate (x, y, z) and $\hat{i}, \hat{j}$ and $\hat{k}$ are unit vector along OX, OY and OZ axis, respectively. Then the position vector of P with respect to O is given by $\overrightarrow{OP}(\text{or } \vec{r}) = x\hat{i} + y\hat{j} + z\hat{k}$.

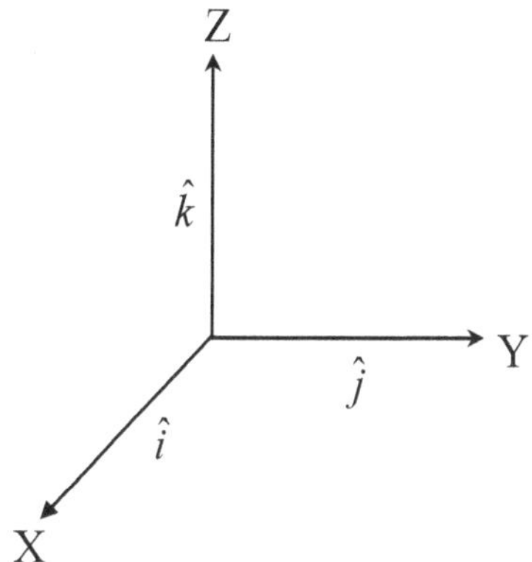

This form of vector $\overrightarrow{OP}$ is called component form. Here x, y and z are called the scalar components and $x\hat{i}, y\hat{j}$ and $z\hat{k}$ are called the vector components of $\overrightarrow{OP}(\text{or } \vec{r})$ along the respective axes.

Sometimes x, y and z are also formed as rectangular components. The length of any vector $\vec{r} = x\hat{i} + y\hat{j} + z\hat{k}$ is given by $|\vec{r}| = |x\hat{i} + y\hat{j} + z\hat{k}| = \sqrt{x^2 + y^2 + z^2}$.

(viii) DIRECTION RATIOS AND DIRECTION COSINES OF A VECTOR :

Consider a vector $\vec{r} = a\hat{i} + b\hat{j} + c\hat{k}$

Then, the numbers a, b, c are called the direction ratios of $\vec{r}$.

Direction cosines of $\vec{r}$ are given by

$$\frac{a}{\sqrt{a^2 + b^2 + c^2}}, \frac{b}{\sqrt{a^2 + b^2 + c^2}} \text{ and } \frac{c}{\sqrt{a^2 + b^2 + c^2}}$$

If, l, m, n are the direction cosines of a vector then we always have $l^2 + m^2 + n^2 = 1$.

(ix) VECTOR JOING TWO POINTS :

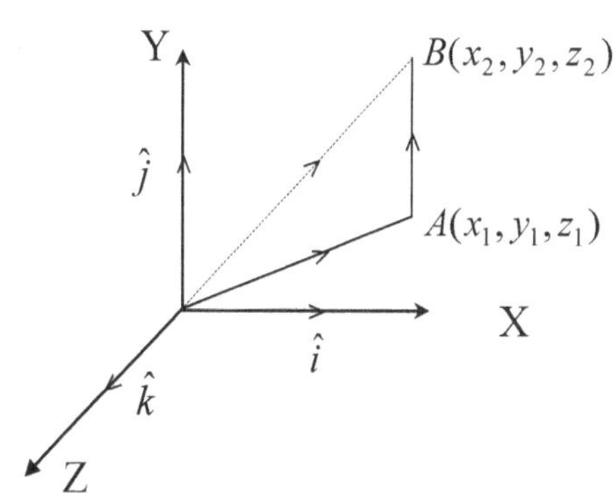

Let $A(x_1, y_1, z_1)$ and $B(x_2, y_2, z_2)$ be any two points on the plane. Then position vectors of A and B with respect to the origin O are $\overrightarrow{OA} = x_1\hat{i} + y_1\hat{j} + z_1\hat{k}$ and $\overrightarrow{OB} = x_2\hat{i} + y_2\hat{j} + z_2\hat{k}$ respectively.

In $\triangle OAB$, by applying triangle law of addition, we get

$$\overrightarrow{OA} + \overrightarrow{AB} = \overrightarrow{OB}$$

$$\therefore \quad \overrightarrow{AB} = \overrightarrow{OB} - \overrightarrow{OA}$$

$$= (x_2\hat{i} + y_2\hat{j} + z_2\hat{k}) - (x_1\hat{i} + y_1\hat{j} + z_1\hat{k})$$

$$= (x_2 - x_1)\hat{i} + (y_2 - y_1)\hat{j} + (z_2 - z_1)\hat{k}$$

and $|AB| = \sqrt{(x_2 - x_1)^2 + (y_2 - y_1)^2 + (z_2 - z_1)^2}$

EXAMPLE : Find the vector and its magnitude which joins the point A with co-ordinates $(4, 5, 6)$ to point B with co-ordinates $(10, 11, 12)$.

SOLUTION : The vector is directed from the point A to B and can be denoted by $\overrightarrow{AB}$. Thus,

$$\overrightarrow{AB} = \overrightarrow{OB} - \overrightarrow{OA}$$

$$= (10 - 4)\hat{i} + (11 - 5)\hat{j} + (12 - 6)\hat{k}$$

$$= 6\hat{i} + 6\hat{j} + 6\hat{k}$$

Magnitude can be given by

$$\overrightarrow{AB} = \sqrt{6^2 + 6^2 + 6^2} = \sqrt{108}$$

EXAMPLE : Find the vector joining the points $P(1, 2, 3)$ and $Q(6, 5, 4)$ directed to Q from P.

SOLUTION: The vector which is directed from the point P to Q can be written as $\overrightarrow{PQ}$.

$$\therefore \quad \overrightarrow{PQ} = (6 - 1)\hat{i} + (5 - 2)\hat{j} + (4 - 3)\hat{k}$$

$$= 5\hat{i} + 3\hat{j} + \hat{k}$$

(x) SECTION FORMULAE :

Let, A and B be two points represented by position vectors $\overrightarrow{OA} = x_1$ and $\overrightarrow{OB} = x_2$ respectiely, with respect to the origin.

Then the line segment joining the points A and B may be divided by a third point C (Say) in two ways which are given below.

(i) **Internal Division :** Let a point C divide the line joing A, B internally in the ratio $m : n$. Then, the position vector of point C is given by

$$\overrightarrow{OC} = \frac{m\overrightarrow{OB} + n\overrightarrow{OA}}{m + n}$$

$$= \frac{mx_2 + nx_1}{m + n}$$

Where, m and n are positive scalars.

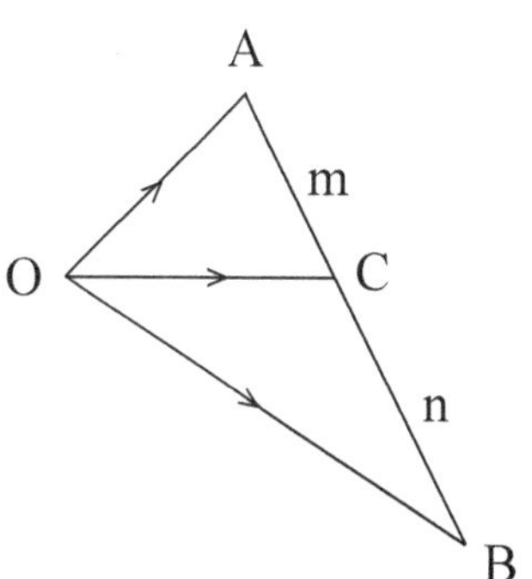

(ii) **External Division :** Let, a point C divide the line goining AB externally in the ratio of $m : n$. Then, the position vector of point C is given by

$$\overrightarrow{OC} = \frac{m\overrightarrow{OB} - n\overrightarrow{OA}}{m - n}$$

$$= \frac{mx_2 - nx_1}{m - n}$$

Where, m and n are positive scalars.

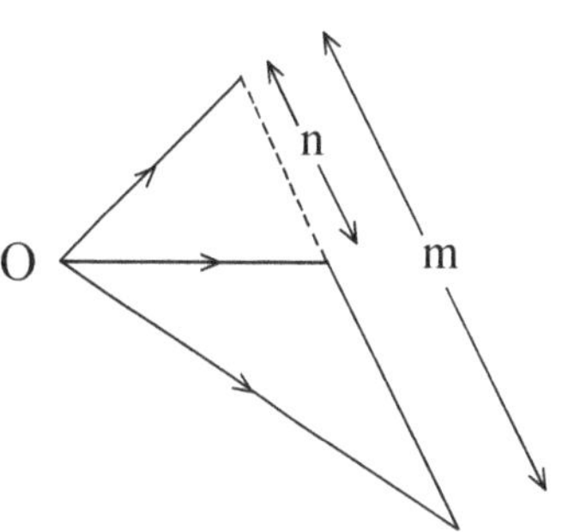

(xi) <u>SOLVED EXAMPLES</u>

EXAMPLE 1 : *If $\vec{a} = 2\hat{i} + 5\hat{j} - 2\hat{k}$ and $\vec{b} = \hat{i} - \hat{j} + \hat{k}$, then find*

(i) $\vec{a} + \vec{b}$ and $2\vec{a} - 3\vec{b}$

(ii) $|\vec{a} + \vec{b}|$ and $|\vec{a} - 2\vec{b}|$

(iii) a unit vector in the direction of $(\vec{a} + \vec{b})$

(iv) vector and scalar components of the vector $(2\vec{a} - 3\vec{b})$ along the coordinate axes.

SOLUTION : (i) We have, $\vec{a} + \vec{b} = 2\hat{i} + 5\hat{j} - 2\hat{k} + \hat{i} - \hat{j} + \hat{k} = 3\hat{i} + 4\hat{j} - \hat{k}$

and $2\vec{a} - 3\vec{b} = 2(2\hat{i} + 5\hat{j} - 2\hat{k}) - 3(\hat{i} - \hat{j} + \hat{k})$

$$= 4\hat{i} + 10\hat{j} - 4\hat{k} - 3\hat{i} + 3\hat{j} - 3\hat{k}$$

$$= \hat{i} + 13\hat{j} - 7\hat{k}$$

(ii) $|\vec{a} + \vec{b}| = |3\hat{i} + 4\hat{j} - \hat{k}| = \sqrt{3^2 + 4^2 + (-1)^2} = \sqrt{26}$

and $|\vec{a} - 2\vec{b}| = |(2\hat{i} + 5\hat{j} - 2\hat{k}) - 2(\hat{i} - \hat{j} + \hat{k})|$

$$= |(2\hat{i} + 5\hat{j} - 2\hat{k} - 2\hat{i} + 2\hat{j} - 2\hat{k}| = |7\hat{j} - 4\hat{k}|$$

$$= \sqrt{7^2 + (-4)^2} = \sqrt{49 + 16} = \sqrt{65}$$

(iii) The unit vector in the direction of $(\vec{a} + \vec{b})$ is

$$\frac{\vec{a} + \vec{b}}{|\vec{a} + \vec{b}|} = \frac{3\hat{i} + 4\hat{j} - \hat{k}}{\sqrt{26}}$$

(iv) Since, $2\vec{a} - 3\vec{b} = \hat{i} + 13\hat{j} - 7\hat{k}$, hence, the vector components of the vector $(2\vec{a} - 3\vec{b})$ along the coordinates axes are $\hat{i}$ and $13\hat{j}$ and $(-7\hat{k})$ respectively and its corresponding scalar components are 1, 13 and (-7).

EXAMPLE 2 : *If the position vectors of two given points A and B be $8\hat{i} + 3\hat{j} + 2\hat{k}$ and $2\hat{i} - 5\hat{j} + 3\hat{k}$ respectively, find the magnitude and direction of $\overrightarrow{AB}$.*

SOLUTION : We have,

$$\overrightarrow{AB} = (\text{position vector of } B) - (\text{position vector of } A)$$

$$= (2\hat{i} - 5\hat{j} + 3\hat{k}) - (8\hat{i} + 3\hat{j} + 2\hat{k})$$

$$= -6\hat{i} - 8\hat{j} + \hat{k}$$

$$\therefore \quad |\overrightarrow{AB}| = \sqrt{(-6)^2 + (-8)^2 + 1^2} = \sqrt{36 + 64 + 1} = \sqrt{101}$$

If $\overrightarrow{AB}$ makes an angle α with $\overrightarrow{OX}$ (*i.e.*, the positive direction of x-axis), then

$$\cos\alpha = \frac{\text{scalar component of } \overrightarrow{AB} \text{ along } \overrightarrow{OX}}{|\overrightarrow{AB}|} = \frac{-6}{\sqrt{101}}$$

$$\therefore \quad \alpha = \cos^{-1}\left(-\frac{6}{\sqrt{101}}\right)$$

Therefore, required magnitude of $\overrightarrow{AB}$ is $\sqrt{101}$ and its direction makes an angle $\cos^{-1}\left(-\frac{6}{\sqrt{101}}\right)$ with $\overrightarrow{OX}$ (*i.e*, the x-axis).

EXAMPLE 3 : *Let $\vec{a} = 3\hat{i} + 2\hat{j}$ and $\vec{b} = 2\hat{i} + 3\hat{j}$. Is $|\vec{a}| = |\vec{b}|\,3\hat{i} + 2\hat{j}$? Is $\vec{a} = \vec{b}$?*

SOLUTION : We have

$$|\vec{a}| = \sqrt{3^2 + 2^2} = \sqrt{13} \text{ and } |\vec{b}| = \sqrt{2^2 + 3^2} = \sqrt{13}$$

$$\therefore \quad |\vec{a}| = |\vec{b}|$$

But, $3\hat{i} + 2\hat{j} \neq 2\hat{i} + 3\hat{j}$ and therefore, $\vec{a} \neq \vec{b}$.

EXAMPLE 4 : *Find a unit vector in the direction of the vector $\vec{a} = \hat{i} + 2\hat{j} + 3\hat{k}$.*

SOLUTION : $\vec{a} = \hat{i} + 2\hat{j} + 3\hat{k} \;\Rightarrow\; |\vec{a}| = \sqrt{1^2 + 2^2 + 3^2} = \sqrt{14}$

Unit vector in the direction of $\vec{a}$ is given by

$$\hat{a} = \frac{\vec{a}}{|\vec{a}|} = \frac{(\hat{i} + 2\hat{j} + 3\hat{k})}{\sqrt{14}} = \left(\frac{1}{\sqrt{14}}\hat{i} + \frac{2}{\sqrt{14}}\hat{j} + \frac{3}{\sqrt{14}}\hat{k} \right)$$

EXAMPLE 5 : *Write a vector of magnitude **15** units in the direction of the vector $(\hat{i} - 2\hat{j} + 2\hat{k})$.*   *[CBSE 2010]*

SOLUTION : Let $\vec{a} = (\hat{i} - 2\hat{j} + 2\hat{k})$. Then,

a unit vector in the direction of $\vec{a}$ is given by

$$\hat{a} = \frac{\vec{a}}{|\vec{a}|} = \frac{(\hat{i} - 2\hat{j} + 2\hat{k})}{\sqrt{1^2 + (-2)^2 + 2^2}} = \frac{1}{3}(\hat{i} - 2\hat{j} + 2\hat{k})$$

$\therefore$ a vector of magnitude 15 in the direction of $\vec{a}$

$$= 15 \times \frac{1}{3}(\hat{i} - 2\hat{j} + 2\hat{k}) = (5\hat{i} - 10\hat{j} + 10\hat{k}).$$

EXAMPLE 6 : *Find a unit vector parallel to the sum of the vectors $(\hat{i} + \hat{j} + \hat{k})$ and $(2\hat{i} - 3\hat{j} + 5\hat{k})$.*   *[CBSE 2012]*

SOLUTION : Let $\vec{a} = (\hat{i} + \hat{j} + \hat{k})$ and $\vec{b} = (2\hat{i} - 3\hat{j} + 5\hat{k})$. Then,

$$(\vec{a} + \vec{b}) = (\hat{i} + \hat{j} + \hat{k}) + (2\hat{i} - 3\hat{j} + 5\hat{k}) = (3\hat{i} - 2\hat{j} + 6\hat{k}).$$

Required unit vectors parallel to $(\vec{a} + \vec{b})$ are

$$\pm \frac{(3\hat{i} - 2\hat{j} + 6\hat{k})}{\sqrt{3^2 + (-2)^2 + 6^2}} = \pm\frac{1}{7}(3\hat{i} - 2\hat{j} + 6\hat{k}).$$

EXAMPLE 7 : *If $\vec{a} = (\hat{i} + \hat{j} + \hat{k})$, $\vec{b} = (4\hat{i} - 2\hat{j} + 3\hat{k})$ and $\vec{c} = (\hat{i} - 2\hat{j} + \hat{k})$, find a vector of magnitude 6 units which is parallel to the vector $(2\vec{a} - \vec{b} + 3\vec{c})$.*

[CBSE 2011C]

SOLUTION : We have

$$(2\vec{a} - \vec{b} + 3\vec{c}) = 2(\hat{i} + \hat{j} + \hat{k}) - (4\hat{i} - 2\hat{j} + 3\hat{k}) + 3(\hat{i} - 2\hat{j} + \hat{k})$$

$$= (2 - 4 + 3)\hat{i} + (2 + 2 - 6)\hat{j} + (2 - 3 + 3)\hat{k}$$

$$= (\hat{i} - 2\hat{j} + 2\hat{k})$$

Unit vectors parallel to $(2\vec{a} - \vec{b} + 3\vec{c})$ are

$$\pm \frac{(\hat{i} - 2\hat{j} + 2\hat{k})}{\sqrt{1^2 + (-2)^2 + 2^2}} = \pm\frac{1}{3}(\hat{i} - 2\hat{j} + 2\hat{k})$$

Required vectors of magnitude 6 units are

$$\pm \left\{ 6 \times \frac{1}{3}(\hat{i} - 2\hat{j} + 2\hat{k}) \right\} = \pm 2(\hat{i} - 2\hat{j} + 2\hat{k})$$

EXAMPLE 8 : *Find a unit vector in the direction of $\overrightarrow{AB}$, where A(1, 2, 3) and B(4, 5, 6) are the given points.*

SOLUTION : We have

p.v. of $A = (\hat{i} + 2\hat{j} + 3\hat{k})$ and p.v. of $B = (4\hat{i} + 5\hat{j} + 6\hat{k})$

$\therefore \qquad \overrightarrow{AB} = $ (p.v. of B) $-$ (p.v. of A)

$$= (4\hat{i} + 5\hat{j} + 6\hat{k}) - (\hat{i} + 2\hat{j} + 3\hat{k}) = (3\hat{i} + 3\hat{j} + 3\hat{k}), \text{ and}$$

$$|\overrightarrow{AB}| = \sqrt{3^2 + 3^2 + 3^2} = \sqrt{27}$$

$\therefore \qquad$ unit vector in the direction of $\overrightarrow{AB}$

$$=\frac{\overrightarrow{AB}}{|\overrightarrow{AB}|}=\frac{(3\hat{i}+3\hat{j}+3\hat{k})}{\sqrt{27}}=\frac{3(\hat{i}+\hat{j}+\hat{k})}{3\sqrt{3}}=\frac{(\hat{i}+\hat{j}+\hat{k})}{\sqrt{3}}$$

$$=\left(\frac{1}{\sqrt{3}}\hat{i}+\frac{1}{\sqrt{3}}\hat{j}+\frac{1}{\sqrt{3}}\hat{k}\right)$$

EXAMPLE 9 : *For what value of a, the vectors $(2\hat{i}-3\hat{j}+4\hat{k})$ and $(a\hat{i}+6\hat{j}-8\hat{k})$ collinear?* **[CBSE 2011]**

SOLUTION : The given vectors ae collinear only when

$$(a\hat{i}+6\hat{j}-8\hat{k})=\lambda(2\hat{i}-3\hat{j}+4\hat{k})$$

for some nonzero scalar λ.

Now, $a\hat{i}+6\hat{j}-8\hat{k}=2\lambda\hat{i}-3\lambda\hat{j}+4\lambda\hat{k}$

$$\Leftrightarrow\ 2\lambda-a,-3\lambda=6\ \text{and}\ 4\lambda=-8$$

$$\Leftrightarrow\ \lambda=\frac{a}{2}\ \text{and}\ \lambda=-2\Leftrightarrow\frac{a}{2}=-2\Leftrightarrow a=-4.$$

Hence, the given vectors are collinear when $a=-4$.

EXAMPLE 10 : *Show that the points $A(-2\hat{i}-3\hat{j}+5\hat{k})$, $B(\hat{i}+2\hat{j}+3\hat{k})$ and $C(7\hat{i}-\hat{k})$ are collinear.* **[CBSE 2009]**

SOLUTION : Clearly, we have

$$\overrightarrow{AB}=(\text{position vector of }B)-(\text{position vector of }A)$$

$$=(\hat{i}+2\hat{j}+3\hat{k})-(-2\hat{i}+3\hat{j}+5\hat{k})=(3\hat{i}-\hat{j}-2\hat{k})$$

$$\overrightarrow{BC}=(\text{Position vector of }C)-(\text{position vector of }B)$$

$$=(7\hat{i}-3\hat{k})-(\hat{i}+2\hat{j}+3\hat{k})=(6\hat{i}-2\hat{j}-4\hat{k})$$

$\therefore\ \overrightarrow{AB}=2\overrightarrow{BC}$, which shows that $\overrightarrow{AB}$ and $\overrightarrow{BC}$ are parallel vectors, having a common end point B.

Hence, the points A, B and C are collinear.

EXAMPLE 11 : *Write the direction cosines of the vector $(-2\hat{i}+\hat{j}-5\hat{k})$.* **[CBSE 2011]**

SOLUTION : The given vector is $\vec{a}=(-2\hat{i}+\hat{j}-5\hat{k})$

Direction ratios of $\vec{a}$ are $-2, 1, -5$.

$$|\vec{a}| = \sqrt{(-2)^2 + 1^2 + (-5)^2} = \sqrt{30}$$

Hence, the direction cosines of $\vec{a}$ are $\dfrac{-2}{\sqrt{30}}, \dfrac{1}{\sqrt{30}}, \dfrac{-5}{\sqrt{30}}$.

EXAMPLE 12 : *What is the cosine of the angle which the vector $(\sqrt{2}\hat{i} + \hat{j} + \hat{k})$ makes with the y-axis?* **[CBSE 2010]**

SOLUTION : The given vector is $\vec{a} = (\sqrt{2}\hat{i} + \hat{j} + \hat{k})$.

Direction ratios of $\vec{a}$ are $\sqrt{2}, 1, 1$.

$$|\vec{a}| = \sqrt{(\sqrt{2})^2 + 1^2 + (1)^2} = \sqrt{4} = 2.$$

$\therefore$ Direction cosines of $\vec{a}$ are $\dfrac{\sqrt{2}}{2}, \dfrac{1}{2}, \dfrac{1}{2}$.

Let $\vec{a}$ make angle β with the y-axis.

Then, clearly $\beta = \dfrac{1}{2}$.

EXAMPLE 13 : *The position vectors of the points A, B and C are $2\hat{i} + 6\hat{j} - \hat{k}$, $\hat{i} + 2\hat{j} + 4\hat{k}$ and $3\hat{i} + 10\hat{j} - 6\hat{k}$ respectively. Show that the points A, B and C are collinear.*

SOLUTION : We have,

$$\overrightarrow{AB} = (\text{position vector of } B) - (\text{position vector of } A)$$

$$= \hat{i} + 2\hat{j} + 4\hat{k} - 2\hat{i} + 6\hat{j} + \hat{k} = -\hat{i} - 4\hat{j} + 5\hat{k}$$

and $\quad \overrightarrow{AC} = (\text{position vector of } C) - (\text{position vector of } A)$

$$= 3\hat{i} + 10\hat{j} - 6\hat{k} - 2\hat{i} - 6\hat{j} + \hat{k} = \hat{i} + 4\hat{j} - 5\hat{k}$$

$$= -(-\hat{i} - 4\hat{j} + 5\hat{k}) = -\overrightarrow{AB} \qquad [\because \overrightarrow{AB} = -\hat{i} - 4\hat{j} + 5\hat{k}]$$

Since $\overrightarrow{AC} = -\overrightarrow{AB}$ and the point A is common to both the vectors $\overrightarrow{AB}$ and $\overrightarrow{AC}$, it follows that $\overrightarrow{AB}$ and $\overrightarrow{AC}$ are collinear *i.e.*, the points A, B and C are collinear.

EXAMPLE 14 :   *Determine the values of p and q for which the vectors $p\hat{i} + 2\hat{j} + 6\hat{k}$ and $3\hat{i} - 3\hat{j} + q\hat{k}$ are collinear.*

SOLUTION :   Since the given vectors are collinear, hence we must have,

$$p\hat{i} + 2\hat{j} + 6\hat{k} = m(3\hat{i} - 3\hat{j} + q\hat{k}), \qquad \text{where } m(\neq 0) \text{ is a scalar,}$$

$$\therefore \qquad p = 3m, \ 2 = -3m \text{ or, } m = -\frac{2}{3} \text{ and } mq = 6$$

Hence $p = 3m = -2$ and $-\frac{2}{3}q = 6$ $\left[\because m = -\frac{2}{3} \right]$ or, $q = -9$

EXAMPLE 15 :   *The position vectors of the points A, B, C and D are $\hat{i} + \hat{j} + \hat{k}$, $2\hat{i} + 3\hat{j}$, $3\hat{i} + 5\hat{j} - 2\hat{k}$ and $-\hat{j} + \hat{k}$ respectively. Show that and are parallel $\overrightarrow{AB}$ and $\overrightarrow{CD}$ find the ratio of their moduli.*

SOLUTION :   We have,

$$\overrightarrow{AB} = \text{(position vector of the point } B) - \text{(position vector of the point } A)$$

$$= (2\hat{i} + 3\hat{j}) - (\hat{i} + \hat{j} + \hat{k}) = \hat{i} + 2\hat{j} - \hat{k}$$

$$\overrightarrow{CD} = \text{(position vector of the point } D) - \text{(position vector of the point } C)$$

$$= (-\hat{j} + \hat{k}) - (3\hat{i} + 5\hat{j} - 2\hat{k}) = -3\hat{i} - 6\hat{j} + 3\hat{k}$$

$$= -3(\hat{i} + 2\hat{j} - \hat{k}) = -3\overrightarrow{AB}$$

Clearly, $\overrightarrow{CD} = -3\overrightarrow{AB}$; hence, $\overrightarrow{AB}$ and $\overrightarrow{CD}$ are parallel.

Again, $|\overrightarrow{AB}| = \sqrt{1^2 + 2^2 + (-1)^2} = \sqrt{1 + 4 + 1} = \sqrt{6}$

and $|\overrightarrow{CD}| = \sqrt{(-3)^2 + (-6)^2 + 3^2} = 3\sqrt{1 + 4 + 1} = 3\sqrt{6}$

$$\therefore \qquad \frac{|\overrightarrow{AB}|}{|\overrightarrow{CD}|} = \frac{\sqrt{6}}{3\sqrt{6}} = \frac{1}{3} \ i.e., \text{ the ration of moduli of } \overrightarrow{AB} \text{ and } \overrightarrow{CD} \text{ is } 1 : 3.$$

EXAMPLE 16 :   *Show by vector method that the points (2, –1, 3), (3, –5, 1) and (–1, 11, 9) are collinear.*

SOLUTION :   Let $A(2, -1, 3), B(3, -5, 1)$ and $C(-1, 11, 9)$ be the given points;

Therefore, if $\hat{i}, \hat{j}, \hat{k}$ are unit vectors along $\overrightarrow{OX}$, $\overrightarrow{OY}$ and $\overrightarrow{OZ}$ respectively, then

$$\overrightarrow{OA} = 2\hat{i} - \hat{j} + 3\hat{k}, \overrightarrow{OB} = 3\hat{i} - 5\hat{j} + \hat{k} \text{ and}$$

$$\overrightarrow{OC} = -\hat{i} + 11\hat{j} + 9\hat{k}$$

$$\therefore \quad \overrightarrow{AB} = \overrightarrow{OB} - \overrightarrow{OA} = (3\hat{i} - 5\hat{j} + \hat{k}) - (2\hat{i} - \hat{j} + 3\hat{k})$$

$$= \hat{i} - 4\hat{j} - 2\hat{k}$$

and $\quad \overrightarrow{BC} = \overrightarrow{OC} - \overrightarrow{OB} = (-\hat{i} + 11\hat{j} + 9\hat{k}) - (3\hat{i} - 5\hat{j} + \hat{k})$

$$= -4\hat{i} + 16\hat{j} + 8\hat{k} = -4(\hat{i} - 4\hat{j} - 2\hat{k})$$

Since, $\overrightarrow{BC} = -4\overrightarrow{AB}$ and the point B is common to both the vectors $\overrightarrow{AB}$ and $\overrightarrow{BC}$, if follows that $\overrightarrow{AB}$ and $\overrightarrow{BC}$ are collinear $i.e.$, the points A, B and C are collinear.

EXAMPLE 17 :   *Using vector method show that the points (7, 9), (3, –7) and (–3, 3) form the sides of a right-angled isosceles traingle.*

SOLUTION :   If $A(7, 9)$, $B(3, -7)$ and $C(-3, 3)$ are the given points and $\hat{i}, \hat{j}$ are unit vectors along $\overrightarrow{OX}$ and $\overrightarrow{OY}$ respectively, then

$$\overrightarrow{OA} = 7\hat{i} + 9\hat{j}; \ \overrightarrow{OB} = 3\hat{i} - 7\hat{j} \text{ and } \overrightarrow{OC} = -3\hat{i} + 3\hat{j}$$

$$\therefore \quad \overrightarrow{AB} = \overrightarrow{OB} - \overrightarrow{OA} = (3\hat{i} - 7\hat{j}) - (7\hat{i} + 9\hat{j}) = -4\hat{i} - 16\hat{j}$$

$$\overrightarrow{BC} = \overrightarrow{OC} - \overrightarrow{OB} = (-3\hat{i} + 3\hat{j}) - (3\hat{i} - 7\hat{j}) = -6\hat{i} + 10\hat{j}$$

and $\quad \overrightarrow{CA} = \overrightarrow{OA} - \overrightarrow{OC} = (7\hat{i} + 9\hat{j}) - (-3\hat{i} + 3\hat{j}) = 10\hat{i} + 6\hat{j}$

Hence, $|\overrightarrow{AB}| = \sqrt{(-4)^2 + (-16)^2} = \sqrt{272}$

$$|\overrightarrow{BC}| = \sqrt{(-6)^2 + 10^2} = \sqrt{136}$$

and $\quad |\overrightarrow{CA}| = \sqrt{10^2 + 6^2} = 136$

Since, $|\overrightarrow{BC}| = |\overrightarrow{CA}|$ $i.e.$, the lengths of the two sides are equal, the triangle ABC is isosceles.

Again, $|\overrightarrow{BC}|^2 = |\overrightarrow{CA}|^2 = 136 + 136 = 272 = |\overrightarrow{AB}|^2$

Hence, the triangle ABC is right-angled.

Therefore, the given points form the sides of a right-angled isosceles triangle.

EXAMPLE 18 : *The position vectors of the points A, B and C are $2\hat{i} + 4\hat{j} - \hat{k}$, $4\hat{i} + 4\hat{j} + \hat{k}$ and $3\hat{i} + 6\hat{j} - 3\hat{k}$ respectively. Show that the points form a right-angled triangle.*

SOLUTION : We have,

$$\overrightarrow{AB} = \text{(position vector of the point } B) - \text{(position vector of the point } A)$$

$$= (4\hat{i} + 5\hat{j} + \hat{k}) - (2\hat{i} + 4\hat{j} - \hat{k}) = 2\hat{i} + \hat{j} + 2\hat{k}$$

Similarly, $\overrightarrow{BC} = (3\hat{i} + 6\hat{j} - 3\hat{k}) - (4\hat{i} + 5\hat{j} + \hat{k}) = -\hat{i} + \hat{j} - 4\hat{k}$

and $\overrightarrow{CA} = (2\hat{i} + 4\hat{j} - \hat{k}) - (3\hat{i} + 6\hat{j} - 3\hat{k}) = -\hat{i} - 2\hat{j} + 2\hat{k}$

$\therefore \quad |\overrightarrow{AB}| = \sqrt{2^2 + 1^2 + 2^2} = \sqrt{4 + 1 + 4} = \sqrt{9}$

$\therefore \quad |\overrightarrow{BC}| = \sqrt{(-1)^2 + 1^2 + (-4)^2} = \sqrt{1 + 1 + 16} = \sqrt{18}$

$\therefore \quad |\overrightarrow{CA}| = \sqrt{(-1)^2 + (-2)^2 + 2^2} = \sqrt{1 + 4 + 4} = \sqrt{9}$

Clearly, $AB^2 + CA^2 = 9 + 9 = 18 = BC^2$

Therefore, the points A, B, C form a right-angled triangle.

EXAMPLE 19 : *Write the direction ratios of the vector $2\hat{i} - \hat{j} - 2\hat{k}$ and hence find the values of direction cosines of the vector.*

SOLUTION : Let $\vec{r} = 2\hat{i} - \hat{j} - 2\hat{k}$; clearly, if the direction ratios of the vector $\vec{r}$ be a, b, c then $a = 2$, $b = -1$ and $c = -2$.

Again, if the direction cosines of the vector $\vec{r}$ be l, m, n then $l = \dfrac{a}{|\vec{r}|}$, $m = \dfrac{b}{|\vec{r}|}$

and $n = \dfrac{c}{|\vec{r}|}$.

Since, $a = 2$, $b = -1$, $c = -2$ and $|\vec{r}| = \sqrt{2^2 + (-1)^2 + (-2)^2} = \sqrt{9} = 3$,

hence the direction cosines of the vector $\vec{r}$ are $l = \dfrac{2}{3}$, $m = -\dfrac{1}{3}$, $n = -\dfrac{2}{3}$ i.e.,

$\dfrac{2}{3}, -\dfrac{1}{3}, -\dfrac{2}{3}$

EXAMPLE 20 : *Find the position vectors of the points which divide the line joining the two points $3\vec{a} - 2\vec{b}$ and $2\vec{a} - 5\vec{b}$ internally and externally in the ratio 3 : 2.*

SOLUTION : Let A and B the given points whose position vectors are $3\vec{a} - 2\vec{b}$ and $2\vec{a} - 5\vec{b}$ respectively, with respect to the origin O, *i.e.* $\overrightarrow{OA} = 3\vec{a} - 2\vec{b}$ and $\overrightarrow{OB} = 2\vec{a} - 5\vec{b}$.

Let P and Q be the points, which divides the line joining A and B internally and externally respectively, in the ration 3 : 2.

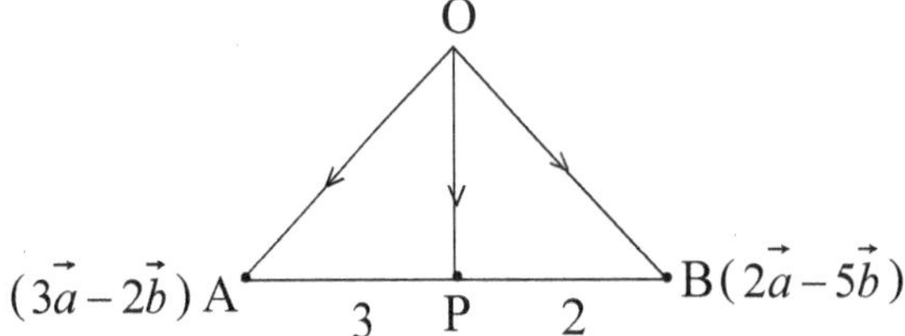

Then, by using section formula of internal division, we get

$$\overrightarrow{OP} = \frac{3\overrightarrow{OB} + 2\overrightarrow{OA}}{3+2} = \frac{3(2\vec{a} - 5\vec{b}) + 2(3\vec{a} - 2\vec{b})}{5}$$

$$= \frac{6\vec{a} - 15\vec{b} + 6\vec{a} - 4\vec{b}}{5} = \frac{12\vec{a} - 19\vec{b}}{5}$$

$$= \frac{12}{5}\vec{a} - \frac{19}{5}\vec{b}$$

Now, by using section formula of external division, we get

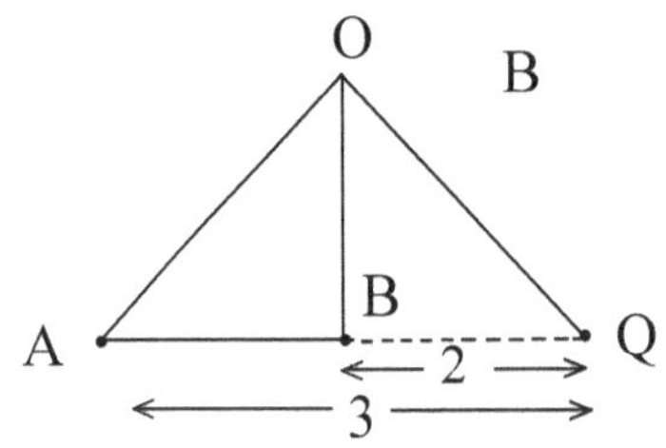

$$\overrightarrow{OQ} = \frac{3\overrightarrow{OB} - 2\overrightarrow{OA}}{3-2} = \frac{3(2\vec{a} - 5\vec{b}) - 2(3\vec{a} - 2\vec{b})}{1}$$

$$= \frac{6\vec{a} - 15\vec{b} - 6\vec{a} + 4\vec{b}}{1} = -11\vec{b}$$

EXAMPLE 21 : *Find the position vector of a point R which divides the line joining the points $P(\hat{i} + 2\hat{j} - \hat{k})$ and $Q(-\hat{i} + \hat{j} + \hat{k})$ in the ratio 2 : 1, (i) internally and (ii) externally.*

SOLUTION : Here $\vec{a} = (\hat{i} + 2\hat{j} - \hat{k})$ and $\vec{b} = (-\hat{i} + \hat{j} + \hat{k})$. Also, $m = 2$, $n = 1$.

(i) When R divides PQ internally in the ration $2 : 1$; then

$$\text{position vector of } R = \frac{(m\vec{b} + n\vec{a})}{(m + n)}$$

$$= \frac{2(-\hat{i} + \hat{j} + \hat{k}) + 1.(\hat{i} + 2\hat{j} - \hat{k})}{(2 + 1)}$$

$$= \frac{(-\hat{i} + 4\hat{j} + \hat{k})}{3}$$

(ii) When R divides PQ externally in the ratio $2 : 1$, then

$$\text{position vector of } R = \frac{(m\vec{b} - n\vec{a})}{(m - n)}$$

$$= \frac{2(-\hat{i} + \hat{j} + \hat{k}) + 1.(\hat{i} + 2\hat{j} - \hat{k})}{(2 - 1)}$$

$$= (-3\hat{i} + 3\hat{k}).$$

EXAMPLE 22 : *P and Q are two points with position vectors $(3\vec{a} - 2\vec{b})$ and $(\vec{a} + \vec{b})$ respectively. Write the position vector of a point R which divides the line segment PQ in the ratio 2 : 1 externally.* *[CBSE 2013]*

SOLUTION : The position vectors of the given points are

$$P(2\vec{a} - 2\vec{b}) \text{ and } Q(\vec{a} + \vec{b}).$$

We have to divide PQ in the ration $2 : 1$ externally at the point R.

The position vector of R is

$$\frac{2(\vec{a} + \vec{b}) - 1.(3\vec{a} - 2\vec{b})}{(2 - 1)}$$

$$= (-\vec{a} + 4\vec{b}).$$

Hence, the position vector of R is $(-\vec{a} + 4\vec{b})$.

EXAMPLE 23 : *Find the position vector of a point R which divides the line segment joining the points A(2, –3, 4) and B(3, 1, –2) externally in the ration 3 : 2.*

SOLUTION : The position vector of A is $(2\hat{i} - 3\hat{j} + 4\hat{k})$.

The position vector of B is $(3\hat{i} + \hat{j} - 2\hat{k})$.

Let R divide AB externally in the ration $3 : 2$

Then, position vector of R

$$= \left(\frac{3\vec{b} - 2\vec{a}}{3 - 2}\right) = \frac{3(3\hat{i} + \hat{j} - 2\hat{k}) - 2(2i - 3j + 4k)}{1}$$

$$= (5\hat{i} + 9\hat{j} - 14\hat{k}).$$

Hence, the position vector of R is $(5\hat{i} + 9\hat{j} - 14\hat{k})$.

EXAMPLE 24 : *Find the position vector of the mid-point of the vector joining the points P(2, 3, 4) and Q(4, 1, –2).* **[CBSE 2011]**

SOLUTION : The position vectors of the given points P and Q are

$$\vec{a} = (2\hat{i} + 3\hat{j} + 4\hat{k}) \text{ and } \vec{b} = (4\hat{i} + \hat{j} - 2\hat{k}) \text{ respectively.}$$

EXAMPLE 25 : *Show that the three points A(1, –2, –8), B(5, 0, –2) and C(11, 3, 7) are collinear and find the ration in which B divides AC.*

SOLUTION : The position vectors of A, B and C are $(\hat{i} - 2\hat{j} - 8\hat{k})$, $(5\hat{i} - 2\hat{k})$ and

$(11\hat{i} + 3\hat{j} + 7\hat{k})$ respectively.

$\therefore \quad \overrightarrow{AB} = (position\ vector\ of\ B) - (position\ vector\ of\ A)$

$$= (5\hat{i} - 2\hat{k}) - (\hat{i} - 2\hat{j} + 8\hat{k}) = (4\hat{i} + 2\hat{j} + 6\hat{k}).$$

$\overrightarrow{BC} = (position\ vector\ of\ C) - (position\ vector\ of\ B)$

$$= (11\hat{i} + 3\hat{j} + 7\hat{k}) - (5\hat{i} - 2\hat{k}) = (6\hat{i} + 3\hat{j} + 9\hat{k}), \text{ and}$$

$\overrightarrow{AC} = (position\ vector\ of\ C) - (position\ vector\ of\ A)$

$$= (11\hat{i} + 3\hat{j} + 7\hat{k}) - (\hat{i} - 2\hat{j} - 8\hat{k}) = (10\hat{i} + 5\hat{j} + 15\hat{k}).$$

Now, $\quad \overrightarrow{AB} = (4\hat{i} + 2\hat{j} + 6\hat{k}) = 2(2\hat{i} + \hat{j} + 3\hat{k})$

$$= \frac{2}{5}(10\hat{i} + 5\hat{j} + 15\hat{k}) = \frac{2}{5}\overrightarrow{AC}.$$

$\therefore \ \overrightarrow{AB}$ and $\overrightarrow{AC}$ are parallel vectors having same end point A.

Hence, the points A, B and C are collinear.

Also, $\overrightarrow{AB} = (4\hat{i} + 2\hat{j} + 6\hat{k}) = 2(2\hat{i} + \hat{j} + 3\hat{k})$

$$= \frac{2}{3}(6\hat{i} + 3\hat{j} + 9\hat{k}) = \frac{2}{3}\overrightarrow{BC}.$$

$$\therefore \quad \frac{|\overrightarrow{AB}|}{|\overrightarrow{BC}|} = \frac{2}{3}.$$

Hence, B divides AC in the ratio $2:3$.

EXAMPLE 26 : ***The position vectors of the points A, B and C are $2\hat{i} + 4\hat{j} - \hat{k}$, $4\hat{i} + 4\hat{j} + \hat{k}$ and $3\hat{i} + 6\hat{j} - 3\hat{k}$ respectively. Show that the points form a right-angled triangle.***

SOLUTION : We have,

$\overrightarrow{AB} = $ (*position vector of the point B*) $-$ (*position vector of the point A*)

$$= (4\hat{i} + 5\hat{j} + \hat{k}) - (2\hat{i} + 4\hat{j} - \hat{k}) = 2\hat{i} + \hat{j} + 2\hat{k})$$

Similarly, $\overrightarrow{BC} = (3\hat{i} + 6\hat{j} - 3\hat{k}) - (4\hat{i} + 5\hat{j} + \hat{k}) = -\hat{i} + \hat{j} - 4\hat{k}$

and $\overrightarrow{CA} = (2\hat{i} + 4\hat{j} - \hat{k}) - (3\hat{i} + 6\hat{j} - 3\hat{k}) = -\hat{i} - 2\hat{j} + 2\hat{k}$

$$\therefore \quad |\overrightarrow{AB}| = \sqrt{2^2 + 1^2 + 2^2} = \sqrt{4+1+4} = \sqrt{9}$$

$$\therefore \quad |\overrightarrow{BC}| = \sqrt{(-1)^2 + 1^2 + (-4)^2} = \sqrt{1+1+16} = \sqrt{18}$$

$$\therefore \quad |\overrightarrow{CA}| = \sqrt{(-1)^2 + (-2)^2 + 2^2} = \sqrt{1+4+4} = \sqrt{9}$$

Clearly, $AB^2 + CA^2 = 9 + 9 = 18 = BC^2$

Therefore, the points A, B, C form a right-angled triangle.

EXAMPLE 27 : ***Write the direction ratios of the vector $2\hat{i} - \hat{j} - 2\hat{k}$ and hence find the values of direction cosines of the vector.***

SOLUTION : Let $\vec{r} = 2\hat{i} - \hat{j} - 2\hat{k}$; clearly, if the direction ratios of the vector $\vec{r}$ be a, b, c then $a = 2, b = -1$ and $c = -2$. Again, if the direction cosines of the vector $\vec{r}$

be l, m, n then $l = \dfrac{a}{|\vec{r}|}$, $m = \dfrac{b}{|\vec{r}|}$ and $n = \dfrac{c}{|\vec{r}|}$.

Since, $a = 2$, $b = -1$, $c = -2$ and $|\vec{r}| = \sqrt{2^2 + (-1)^2 + (-2)^2} = \sqrt{9} = 3$, hence

the direction cosines of the vector $\vec{r}$ are $l = \dfrac{2}{3}$, $m = -\dfrac{b}{|\vec{r}|}$, $n = -\dfrac{2}{3}$

i.e., $\dfrac{2}{3}$, $-\dfrac{1}{3}$, $-\dfrac{2}{3}$

EXAMPLE 28 :   *For the vectors and show that*

(i) $|\vec{a} + \vec{b}| \le |\vec{a}| + |\vec{b}|$ *(ii)* $||\vec{a}| - |\vec{b}|| \le |\vec{a} - \vec{b}|$

SOLUTION :   (*i*) Let $\vec{a} = \overrightarrow{AB}$ and $\vec{b} = \overrightarrow{AB}$

where $|\vec{a}| = \overline{OA}$ and $|\vec{b}| = \overline{AB}$

Now, by the addition law of vectors we get,

$$\vec{a} + \vec{b} = \overrightarrow{OA} + \overrightarrow{AB} = \overrightarrow{OB}$$

$\therefore \qquad |\vec{a} + \vec{b}| = \overline{OB}$

Now, $\overline{OB} < \overline{OA} + \overline{AB}$

[when the points O, A and B form a triangle] and

$$\overline{OB} = \overline{OA} + \overline{AB}$$

[when the points O, A and B are collinear].

Hence, for all positions of the points A, B and O, we have,

$$\overline{OB} \le \overline{OA} + \overline{AB}$$

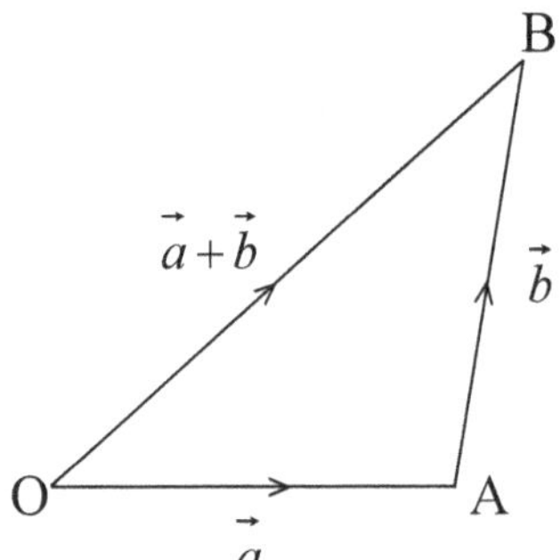

i.e., $|\vec{a} + \vec{b}| \le |\vec{a}| + |\vec{b}|$

(*ii*) $\because$ $|\vec{a}| = |(\vec{a} - \vec{b}) + \vec{b}| \le |\vec{a} - \vec{b}| + |\vec{b}|$ [using (*i*)]

$\therefore \qquad |\vec{a}| - |\vec{b}| \le |\vec{a} - \vec{b}|$ $\hspace{3cm}$ ... (1)

Similarly, $|\vec{b}| = |\vec{a} + (\vec{b} - \vec{a})| \le |\vec{a}| + |\vec{b} - \vec{a}|$

or, $|\vec{b}| - |\vec{a}| \le |\vec{a} - \vec{b}|$ $[\because |\vec{b} - \vec{a}| = |\vec{a} - \vec{b}|]$ ...(2)

Form (1) and (2) we get, $||\vec{a}| - |\vec{b}|| \le |\vec{a} - \vec{b}|$.

EXAMPLE 29 : *By vector method prove that the three medians of a triangle are concurrent.*

SOLUTION : Let $\vec{a}, \vec{b}$ and $\vec{c}$ be the position vectors of the vertices A, B and C respectively of the triangle ABC with respect to an arbitrary origin. Then, the position vectors of the middle points D, E and F of the sides $\overline{BC}$, $\overline{CA}$ and $\overline{AB}$ are $\dfrac{\vec{b}+\vec{c}}{2}$, $\dfrac{\vec{c}+\vec{a}}{2}$ and $\dfrac{\vec{a}+\vec{b}}{2}$ respectively.

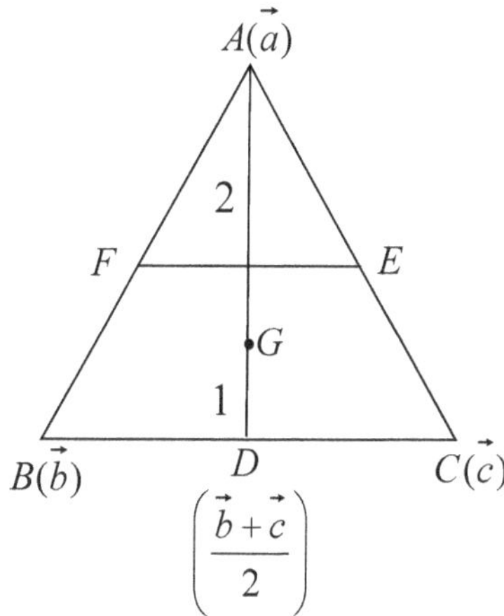

Now, the position vector of the point G which divides the median $\overline{AD}$ internally in the ration $2 : 1$ is,

$$\frac{2 \times \dfrac{\vec{b}+\vec{c}}{2} + 1 \times \vec{a}}{2+1} = \frac{1}{3}(\vec{a}+\vec{b}+\vec{c})$$

Similarly, we can show that the points which divide the medians $\overline{BE}$ and $\overline{CF}$ internally in the ratio $2 : 1$ will have the same position vector $\dfrac{1}{3}(\vec{a}+\vec{b}+\vec{c})$ *i.e.*, the three medians intersect at the common point G. Hence the three medians are concurrent and at the point of concurrence they are divided in the ration $2 : 1$.

The point of concurrence G is called the centroid of the triangle and its position vector is $\dfrac{1}{3}(\vec{a}+\vec{b}+\vec{c})$ (*Proved*).

EXAMPLE 30 : *If G be the centroid of the triangle ABC, then prove that $\overrightarrow{GA} + \overrightarrow{GB} + \overrightarrow{GC} = \vec{0}$.*

SOLUTION : Let, $\vec{a}, \vec{b}$ and $\vec{c}$ be the position vectors of the vertices A, B and C respectively of the triangle ABC with respect to an arbitrary origin [Fig. 19]. Then, the position vector of the centroid G of the triangle is $\dfrac{1}{3}(\vec{a}+\vec{b}+\vec{c})$.

$\therefore$ $\overrightarrow{GA} = (position\ vector\ of\ A) - (position\ vector\ of\ G)$

$$= \vec{a} - \frac{1}{3}(\vec{a} + \vec{b} + \vec{c}) = \frac{1}{3}(2\vec{a} - \vec{b} - \vec{c})$$

Similarly, $\overrightarrow{GB} = \frac{1}{3}(2\vec{b} - \vec{c} - \vec{a})$ and $\overrightarrow{GC} = \frac{1}{3}(2\vec{c} - \vec{a} - \vec{b})$

$$\therefore \qquad \overrightarrow{GA} + \overrightarrow{GB} + \overrightarrow{GC}$$

$$= \frac{1}{3}(2\vec{a} - \vec{b} - \vec{c}) + \frac{1}{3}(2\vec{b} - \vec{c} - \vec{a}) + \frac{1}{3}(2\vec{c} - \vec{a} - \vec{b})$$

$$= \frac{1}{3}[2(\vec{a} + \vec{b} + \vec{c}) - 2(\vec{a} + \vec{b} + \vec{c})] = \vec{0} \ (\textbf{\textit{Proved}}).$$

(xii) EXERCISE

1. If $\vec{a} = 2\hat{i} - 5\hat{j} + 3\hat{k}$ *and* $\vec{b} = \hat{i} - 2\hat{j} - 4\hat{k}$, *find the value of* $|3\vec{a} + 2\vec{b}|$.

Ans : $\sqrt{426}$

2. If $\vec{a} = 2\hat{i} + 3\hat{j} - 4\hat{k}$ *and* $\vec{b} = \hat{i} + 2\hat{j} + \hat{k}$, *then find* $(\vec{a} + \vec{b})$ *and* $|\vec{a} + \vec{b}|$.

Ans : $3\hat{i} + 5\hat{j} - 3\hat{k}$ *and* $\sqrt{43}$

3. Find a unit vector in the direction of the vector:

   (i) $(3\hat{i} - 2\hat{j} + 6\hat{k})$ *[CBSE 2012]*

   (ii) $(2\hat{i} + \hat{j} + 2\hat{k})$ *[CBSE 2009]*

Ans : (i) $\left(\frac{3}{7}\hat{i} - \frac{2}{7}\hat{j} + \frac{6}{7}\hat{k}\right)$ (ii) $\left(\frac{2}{3}\hat{i} + \frac{1}{3}\hat{j} - \frac{2}{3}\hat{k}\right)$

4. If $\vec{a} = (2\hat{i} - 4\hat{j} + 5\hat{k})$ *then find the value of* λ *so that* $\lambda\vec{a}$ *may be a unit vector.*

Ans : $\pm\dfrac{1}{3\sqrt{5}}$

5. If $\vec{a} = (-\hat{i} + \hat{j} - \hat{k})$ *and* $\vec{b} = (2\hat{i} - \hat{j} + 2\hat{k})$ *then find the unit vector in the direction of* $(\vec{a} + \vec{b})$.

Ans : $\dfrac{1}{\sqrt{2}}(\hat{i} + \hat{k})$

6. *If* $\vec{a} = (3\hat{i} + \hat{j} - 5\hat{k})$ *and* $\vec{b} = (\hat{i} + 2\hat{j} - \hat{k})$ *then find a unit vector in the direction of* $(\vec{a} - \vec{b})$.

Ans : $\dfrac{1}{\sqrt{21}}(2\hat{i} - \hat{j} - 4\hat{k})$

7. *If* $\vec{a} = (\hat{i} + 2\hat{j} - 3\hat{k})$ *and* $\vec{b} = (2\hat{i} + 4\hat{j} + 9\hat{k})$ *then find a unit vector parallel to* $(\vec{a} + \vec{b})$.

[CBSE 2008]

Ans : $\pm\dfrac{1}{3}(\hat{i} + 2\hat{j} + 2\hat{k})$

8. *Find a vector of magnitude* **9** *units in the direction of the vector* $(-2\hat{i} + \hat{j} + 2\hat{k})$. *[CBSE 2010]*

Ans : $(-6\hat{i} + 3\hat{j} + 6\hat{k})$

9. *Find a vector of magnitude* **8** *units in the direction of the vector* $(5\hat{i} - \hat{j} + 2\hat{k})$.

Ans : $\dfrac{8}{\sqrt{30}}(5\hat{i} - \hat{j} + 2\hat{k})$

10. *Find a vector of magnitude* **21** *units in the direction of the vector* $(2\hat{i} - 3\hat{j} + 6\hat{k})$.

[CBSE 2014]

Ans : $(6\hat{i} - 9\hat{j} + 18\hat{k})$

11. *If* $\vec{a} = (\hat{i} - 2\hat{j})$, $\vec{b} = (2\hat{i} - 3\hat{j})$ *and* $\vec{c} = (2\hat{i} + 3\hat{k})$, *find* $(\vec{a} + \vec{b} + \vec{c})$. *[CBSE 2012]*

Ans : $(5\hat{i} - 5\hat{j} + 3\hat{k})$

12. *If* $\vec{a} = x\hat{i} + 2\hat{j} - z\hat{k}$ *and* $\vec{b} = 3\hat{i} - y\hat{j} + \hat{k}$ *are two equal vectors, then find the value of* $x+y+z$.

[Delhi 2013]

Ans : 0

13. *Write a vector in the direction of the vector* $\hat{i} - 2\hat{j} + 2\hat{k}$ *that has magnitude* **9** *units.*

[Delhi 2014C]

Ans : $(3\hat{i} - 6\hat{j} + 6\hat{k})$

14. *Find a vector in the direction of* $\vec{a} = 2\hat{i} - \hat{j} + 2\hat{k}$ *which has magnitude* **6** *units.*

[NCERT Exemplar]

Ans : $4\hat{i} - 2\hat{j} + 4\hat{k}$

15. *Find the sum of the vectors* $\vec{a} = \hat{i} - 2\hat{j} + \hat{k}$, $\vec{b} = -2\hat{i} + 4\hat{j} + 5\hat{k}$ *and* $\vec{c} = \hat{i} - 6\hat{j} - 7\hat{k}$.

[Delhi 2012]

Ans : $-4\hat{j}-\hat{k}$

16. *Write a unit vector in the direction of the sum of the vectors* $\vec{a}=2\hat{i}+2\hat{j}-5\hat{k}$ *and* $\vec{b}=2\hat{i}+\hat{j}-7\hat{k}$.

[Delhi 2014 C]

Ans : $\dfrac{4}{13}\hat{i}+\dfrac{3}{13}\hat{j}-\dfrac{12}{13}\hat{k}$

17. *Find the unit vector in the direction of the sum of the vectors* $\vec{a}=2\hat{i}-\hat{j}+2\hat{k}$ *and* $\vec{b}=-\hat{i}+\hat{j}+3\hat{k}$.

[NCERT Exemplar]

Ans : $\dfrac{1}{\sqrt{26}}\hat{i}+\dfrac{5}{\sqrt{26}}\hat{k}$

18. *If* $\vec{a}=4\hat{i}-\hat{j}+\hat{k}$ *and* $\vec{b}=2\hat{i}-2\hat{j}+\hat{k}$, *then find a unit vector parallel to the vector* $\vec{a}+\vec{b}$.

[All India 2016]

Ans : $\dfrac{6\hat{i}-3\hat{j}+2\hat{k}}{7}$

19. *Find the value of p for which the vectors* $3\hat{i}+2\hat{j}+9\hat{k}$ *and* $\hat{i}-2p\hat{j}+3\hat{k}$ *are parallel.*

[All India 2014]

Ans : $-\dfrac{1}{3}$

20. *If A(–2, 1, 2) and B(2, –1, 6) are two given points, find a unit vector in the direction of* $\overrightarrow{AB}$.

Ans : $\dfrac{2}{3}\hat{i}-\dfrac{1}{3}\hat{j}+\dfrac{2}{3}\hat{k}$

21. *Fidn the direction ratios and direction cosines of the vector* $\vec{a}=(5\hat{i}-3\hat{j}+4\hat{k})$.

Ans : $(5,-3,4);\ \left(\dfrac{1}{\sqrt{2}},\dfrac{-3}{5\sqrt{2}},\dfrac{4}{5\sqrt{2}}\right)$

22. *Find the direction ratios and the direction cosines of the vector joining the points A(2, 1, –2) and B(3, 5, –4).*

Ans : $(1,4,-2);\ \left(\dfrac{1}{\sqrt{21}},\dfrac{4}{\sqrt{21}},\dfrac{-2}{\sqrt{21}}\right)$

23. *Show that the points A, B and C having position vectors* $(\hat{i}+2\hat{j}+7\hat{k})$, $(2\hat{i}+6\hat{j}+3\hat{k})$ *and* $(3\hat{i}+10\hat{j}-3\hat{k})$ *respectively, are collinear.*

24. *The position vectors of the points A, B and C are $(2\hat{i} + \hat{j} - \hat{k})$, $(3\hat{i} - 2\hat{j} + \hat{k})$ and $(\hat{i} + 4\hat{j} - 3\hat{k})$ respectively. Show that the points A, B and C are collinear.*

25. *If the position vectors of the vertices A, B and C of a $\triangle ABC$ be $(\hat{i} + 2\hat{j} + 3\hat{k})$, $(2\hat{i} + 3\hat{j} + \hat{k})$ and $(3\hat{i} + \hat{j} + 2\hat{k})$ respectively, prove that is equilateral.*

26. *Show that the points A, B and C having position vectors $(3\hat{i} - 4\hat{j} - 4\hat{k})$, $(2\hat{i} - \hat{j} + \hat{k})$ and $(\hat{i} - 3\hat{j} - 5\hat{k})$ respectively, form the vertices of a right-angled triangle.*

27. *Using vector method, show that the points $A(1, -1, 0)$, $B(4, -3, 1)$ and $C(2, -4, 5)$ are the vertices of a right-angled triange.*

28. *Find the position vector of the point which divides the join of the points $(2\vec{a} - 3\vec{b})$ and $(3\vec{a} - 2\vec{b})$ (i) internally and (ii) exrternally in the ration 2 : 3.*

Ans : (i) $\dfrac{12}{5}\vec{a} - \dfrac{13}{5}\vec{b}$ *(ii)* $-5\vec{b}$

29. *The position vectors of two points A and B are $(2\vec{a} + \vec{b})$ and $(\vec{a} - 3\vec{b})$ respectively. Find the position vector of a point C which divides AB externally in the ratio 1 : 2. Also, show that A is the mid-point of the line segment CB.*   *[CBSE 2010]*

Ans : $(3\vec{a} + 5\vec{b})$

30. *Find the position vector of the mid-point of the vector joining the points*

    $A(3\hat{i} + 2\hat{j} + 6\hat{k})$ *and* $B(\hat{i} + 4\hat{j} - 2\hat{k})$.

Ans : $P(2\hat{i} + 3\hat{j} + 2\hat{k})$

31. *If $\overrightarrow{AB} = (2\hat{i} + \hat{j} - 3\hat{k})$ and $A(1, 2, -1)$ is the given point, find the coordinates of B.*

Ans : $(3, 3, -4)$

32. *Write a unit vector in the direction of $\overrightarrow{PQ}$, where P and Q are the points $(1, 3, 0)$ and $(4, 5, 6)$ respectively.*   *[CBSE 2014]*

Ans : $\dfrac{1}{7}(3\hat{i} + 2\hat{j} + 6\hat{k})$

33. *Write the value of cosine of the angle which the vector $\vec{a} = \hat{i} + \hat{j} + \hat{k}$ makes with Y-axis.*

[Delhi 2014C]

Ans : $\dfrac{1}{\sqrt{3}}$

34. Find the angle between X-axis and the vector $\hat{i} + \hat{j} + \hat{k}$. *[All India 2014C]*

Ans : $\cos^{-1}\left(\dfrac{1}{\sqrt{3}}\right)$

35. Write the direction cosines of vector $-2\hat{i} + \hat{j} - 5\hat{k}$. *[Delhi 2011]*

Ans : $\left(\dfrac{-2}{\sqrt{30}}, \dfrac{1}{\sqrt{30}}, \dfrac{-5}{\sqrt{30}}\right)$

36. If A, B, P, Q and R be the five points in a plane, then show that the sum of the vectors $\overrightarrow{AP}$, $\overrightarrow{AQ}$, $\overrightarrow{AR}$, $\overrightarrow{PB}$, $\overrightarrow{QB}$ and $\overrightarrow{RB}$ is $\overrightarrow{AB}$.

37. If O be the centre of a regular hexagon PQRSTU, then prove that $\overrightarrow{OP} + \overrightarrow{OQ} + \overrightarrow{OR} + \overrightarrow{OS} + \overrightarrow{OT} + \overrightarrow{OU} = \vec{0}$.

38. If $\vec{a} = \hat{i} + \hat{j} + 2\hat{k}$ and $\vec{b} = 2\hat{i} + \hat{j} - 2\hat{k}$, then find the unit vector in the direction $2\vec{a} - \vec{b}$.

[NCERT Exemplar]

Ans : $\dfrac{\hat{j} + 6\hat{k}}{\sqrt{37}}$

39. Find a vector of magnitude 5 units and parallel to the resultant of $\vec{a} = 2\hat{i} + 3\hat{j} - 3\hat{k}$ and $\vec{b} = \hat{i} - 2\hat{j} + 3\hat{k}$. *[NCERT]*

Ans : $\dfrac{15}{\sqrt{10}}\hat{i} + \dfrac{5}{\sqrt{10}}\hat{j}$

40. Show that the vector $\hat{i} + \hat{j} + \hat{k}$ is equally inclined to the axes, OX, OY and OZ.

41. A vector $\vec{r}$ is inclined at equal angles to the three axes. If the magnitude of $\vec{r}$ is $2\sqrt{3}$ untis, then find the value of $\vec{r}$.

Ans : $\pm 2(\hat{i} + \hat{j} + \hat{k})$

42. Show that the vectors $\vec{a} = 3\hat{i} - 2\hat{j} + \hat{k}$, $\vec{b} = \hat{i} - 3\hat{j} + 5\hat{k}$ and $\vec{c} = 2\hat{i} + \hat{j} - 4\hat{k}$ form a right angled triangle.

43. If a vector $\vec{r}$ has magnitude 14 and direction ratios 2, 3 and −6. Then, find the direction cosines and components of $\vec{r}$, given that $\vec{r}$ makes an acute angle with X-axis.

[NCERT Exemplar]

Ans : $4\hat{i}, 6\hat{j}$ and $-12\hat{k}$

44. *If the position vectors of the points A, B, C are* $3\hat{i} - 4\hat{j} - 4\hat{k}$, $2\hat{i} - \hat{j} + \hat{k}$ *and* $\hat{i} - 3\hat{j} - 5\hat{k}$ *respectively. Show that ABC is a right-angled triangle.* **[NCERT]**

45. *If* $\vec{a}, \vec{b}, \vec{c}$ *are three given vectors, shwo that the points having position vectors* $7\vec{a} - \vec{c}$, $\vec{a} + 2\vec{b} + 3\vec{c}$ *and* $-2\vec{a} + 3\vec{b} + 5\vec{c}$ *are collinear.*

46. *If* $\vec{a} = \hat{i} + \hat{j} - 4\hat{k}$ *and* $\vec{b} = 4\hat{i} - \hat{j} - 2\hat{k}$, *then find*

> *(i) a unit vector in the direction of the vector* $(2\vec{a} - \vec{b})$ *and*

> *(ii) vector and scalar components of the vector* $(2\vec{a} - \vec{b})$ *along coordinate axes.*

Ans :   *(i)* $\dfrac{1}{7}(-2\hat{i} + 3\hat{j} - 6\hat{k})$

> *(ii)* $-2\hat{i},\ 3\hat{j},\ -6\hat{k}$ *and* $-2, 3, -6$

47. *If the position vectors of the points A, B, C are* $-2\hat{i} + 2\hat{j} + 2\hat{k}$, $2\hat{i} + 3\hat{j} + 3\hat{k}$ *and* $-\hat{i} - 2\hat{j} + 3\hat{k}$ *respectively, show that ABC is an isosceles triangle.*

48. *(i) If the coordinates of the points A, B and C are (2, 6, 3), (1, 2, 7) and (3, 10, –1) respectively, show by vector method that the points A, B and C are collinear.*

> *(ii) The position vectors of three points are*

In each case show that the three points are collinear.

> *(a)* $-2\hat{i} + 3\hat{j} + 5\hat{k}, \hat{i} + 2\hat{j} + 3\hat{k}, 7\hat{i} - \hat{k}$

> *(b)* $\hat{i} - 2\hat{j} + 3\hat{k}, 2\hat{i} + 3\hat{j} - 4\hat{k}, -7\hat{j} + 10\hat{k}$

49. *The position vectors of three points are* $\hat{i} + 3\hat{j} - 2\hat{k}$, $3\hat{i} - 2\hat{j} + \hat{k}$ *and* $-2\hat{i} + \hat{j} + 3\hat{k}$; *show that the points are the vertices of an equilateral triangle.*

50. *If the vectors* $p\hat{i} - 5\hat{j} + 6\hat{k}$ *and* $2\hat{i} - 3\hat{j} - q\hat{k}$ *are collinear, find p and q.*

Ans : $p = \dfrac{10}{8},\ q = \dfrac{18}{5}$

51. *If the points having position vectors* $\hat{i} + b\hat{j} + c\hat{k}$, $7\hat{i} + 2\hat{j} + 6\hat{k}$ *and* $5\hat{i} + 2\hat{j} + 5\hat{k}$ *are collinear, find the values of b and c.*

Ans : $b = 2;\ c = 3$

52. *If* $\overrightarrow{AB} = 2\hat{i} - 4\hat{j} + 5\hat{k}$ *and* $\overrightarrow{BC} = \hat{i} - 2\hat{j} - 3\hat{k}$ *in parallelogram ABCD, find a unit vector in direction parallel to the diagonal* $\overrightarrow{AC}$ *of the parallelogram.*

Ans : $\dfrac{1}{7}(3\hat{i} - 6\hat{j} + 2\hat{k})$

53. *Find the diection cosines of the vector joining the points $A(1, 2, -3)$ and $B(-1, -2, 1)$ directed from B to A.* **[All India 2016C]**

Ans : $\dfrac{1}{3}, \dfrac{2}{3}, \dfrac{-2}{3}$

54. *Find the scalar components of* $\overrightarrow{AB}$ *with initial point $A(2, 1)$ and terminal point $B(-5, 7)$.*

[All India 2012]

Ans : $-7, 6$

55. *If* $\vec{a}$ *and* $\vec{b}$ *denote the position vectors of points A and B respectively and C is a point on AB such that $AC = 2CB$, then write the position vector of C.* **[Delhi 2016C]**

Ans : $\dfrac{2\vec{b} + \vec{a}}{3}$

56. *A and B are two points with position vectors* $2\vec{a} - 3\vec{b}$ *and* $6\vec{b} - \vec{a}$, *respectively.*

Write the position vector of a point P which divides the line segment AB internally in the ratio 1 : 2.

[All India 2013]

Ans : $\vec{a}$

57. *L and M are two points with position vectors* $2\vec{a} - \vec{b}$ *and* $\vec{a} + 2\vec{b}$, *respectively.*

Write the position vector of a point N which divides the line segment LM in the ratio 2 : 1 externally.

[All India 2013]

Ans : $5\vec{b}$

58. *Find the position vector of a point which divides the join of points with position vectors* $\vec{a} - 2\vec{b}$ *and* $2\vec{a} + \vec{b}$ *externally in the ratio 2 : 1.* **[Delhi 2016]**

Ans : $3\vec{a} + 4\vec{b}$

59. *If* $\overrightarrow{PO} + \overrightarrow{OQ} = \overrightarrow{QO} + \overrightarrow{OR}$, *then show that the points P, Q and R are collinear.*

60. *Find the scalar and vector component of* $\overrightarrow{QP}$ *with initial point $Q(2, 3, 5)$ and terminal point $P(7, 1, 5)$.* **[NCERT Exemplar]**

Ans : $(5, -2, 0);\ (5\hat{i}, -2\hat{j}, 0\hat{k})$

SCALAR PRODUCT OF TWO VECTORS :

Multiplication or product of two vectors is defined in two ways, namely scalar (or dot) product where the result is scalar and vector (or cross) product where the result is a vector.

(i) SCALAR (OR DOT) PRODUCT OF TWO VECTORS :

Let $\vec{a}$ and $\vec{b}$ be two non-zero vectors inclined at an angle θ. Then, the scalar product or dot product of $\vec{a}$ and $\vec{b}$ is denoted by $\vec{a} \cdot \vec{b}$ and defined as

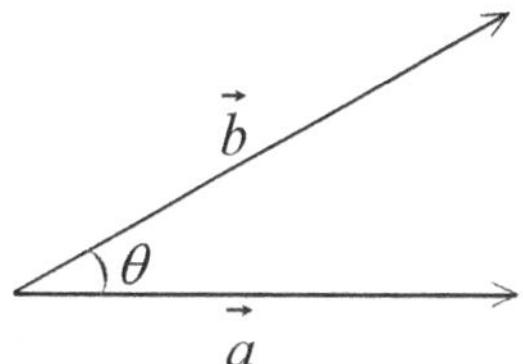

$$\vec{a} \cdot \vec{b} = |\vec{a}||\vec{b}|\cos\theta,\ 0 \le \theta \le \pi$$

or, $\vec{a} \cdot \vec{b} = ab\cos\theta,\ 0 \le \theta \le \pi$

Where, $a = |\vec{a}|$ and $b = |\vec{b}|$.

(ii) PROPERTIES OF SCALAR PRODUCT OF TWO VECTORS :

(i) Scalar product of two vector sis commutative, *i.e.* for vectors $\vec{a}$ and $\vec{b}$, we have $\vec{a} \cdot \vec{b} = \vec{b} \cdot \vec{a}$.

(ii) Scalar product of vector is distributive over addition, *i.e.* for vectors $\vec{a}, \vec{b}$ and $\vec{c}$, we have

$$\vec{a} \cdot (\vec{b} + \vec{c}) = \vec{a} \cdot \vec{b} + \vec{a} \cdot \vec{c}.$$

(iii) If m is any scalar and $\vec{a}$ and $\vec{b}$ be two non-zero vectors. Then, $(m\vec{a}) \cdot (\vec{b}) = m(\vec{a} \cdot \vec{b}) = \vec{a} \cdot m(\vec{b})$

(iv) If $\vec{a}$ and $\vec{b}$ be two non-zero vectors, then $\vec{a} \cdot \vec{b} = 0$ if and only if $\vec{a}$ and $\vec{b}$ are perpendicular to each other, *i.e.* $\vec{a} \cdot \vec{b} = 0 \Leftrightarrow \vec{a} \perp \vec{b}.$

(v) If, $\theta = 0$, then $\vec{a} \cdot \vec{b} = |\vec{a}| \cdot |\vec{b}|$. Also, $\vec{a} \cdot \vec{a} = |\vec{a}|^2$.

(vi) If, $\theta = \pi$, then $\vec{a} \cdot \vec{b} = -|\vec{a}||\vec{b}|$.

Also, $\vec{a} \cdot (-\vec{a}) = -|\vec{a}|^2$.

(vii) For mutually perpendicular unit vectors $\hat{i}, \hat{j}$ and $\hat{k}$, $\hat{i} \cdot \hat{i} = \hat{j} \cdot \hat{j} = \hat{k} \cdot \hat{k} = 1$ and $\hat{i} \cdot \hat{j} = \hat{j} \cdot \hat{k} = \hat{k} \cdot \hat{i} = 0.$

($viii$) The angle between two non-zero vectors $\vec{a}$ and $\vec{b}$ is given by

$$\cos\theta = \frac{\vec{a} \cdot \vec{b}}{|\vec{a}||\vec{b}|}$$

or, $\theta = \cos^{-1}\left(\dfrac{\vec{a}\cdot\vec{b}}{|\vec{a}||\vec{b}|}\right)$.

(iii) PROJECTION OF A VECTOR ON A LINE :

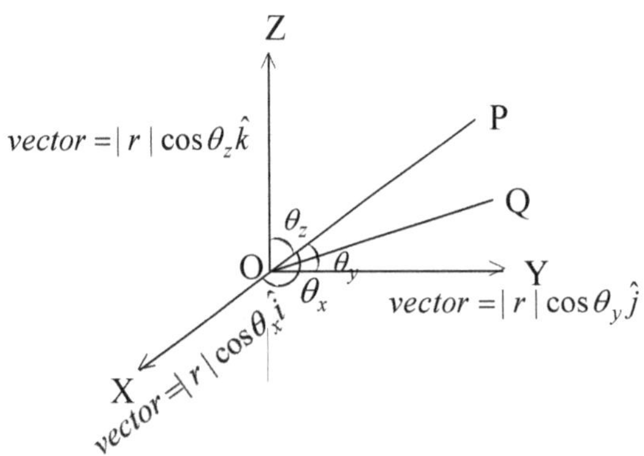

Suppose, a vector $\overrightarrow{AB}$ makes an angle θ with a given directed line l(say). Then the projection of on l is a vector $\vec{P}$ (Say) with magnitude $|AB|\cos\theta$, and the direction of $\vec{P}$ being the same (or opposite) to that of the line l, depending upon whether $\cos\theta$ is positive or negative.

The vector $\vec{P}$ is called the projection vector and its magnitude $|\vec{P}|$ is called as the projection of the vector $\overrightarrow{AB}$ on line l.

In each of the following figures (i) to (iv), projection vector of $\overrightarrow{AB}$ along the line l is vector $\overrightarrow{AC}$.

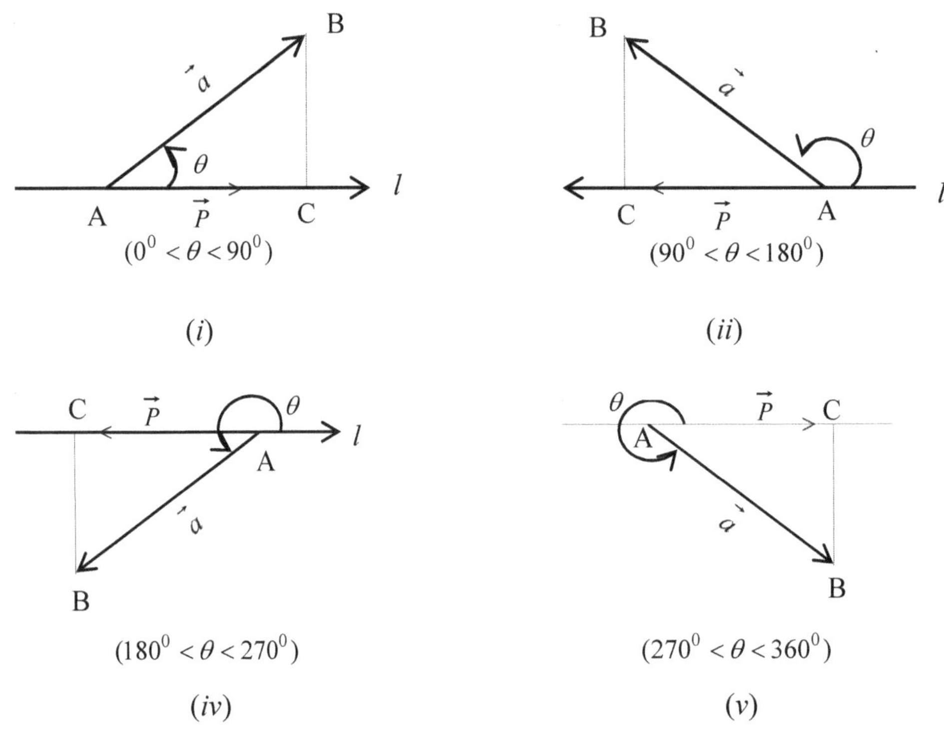

(iv) SOME RESULTS ON PROJECTION OF A VECTOR :

(i) If is the unit vector $\hat{p}$ along a line l, then the projection of a vector $\vec{a}$ on the line l is given by $\vec{a} \cdot \vec{p}$.

(ii) Projection of vector $\vec{a}$ on $\vec{b}$ is given by $\vec{a} \cdot \hat{b}$ or $\dfrac{\vec{a} \cdot \vec{b}}{|\vec{b}|}$ and projection of vector $\vec{b}$ on $\vec{a}$ is given by $\vec{b} \cdot \hat{a}$ or $\dfrac{\vec{a} \cdot \vec{b}}{|\vec{a}|}$.

(iii) If $\theta = \dfrac{\pi}{2}$ or $\theta = \dfrac{3\pi}{2}$, then the projection vector of $\overrightarrow{AB}$ will be zero vector.

(iv) Let α, β and r be the direction angles of vector $\vec{a} = a_1 \hat{i} + a_2 \hat{j} + a_3 \hat{k},$ then its direction cosines may be given as

$$\cos\alpha = \frac{\vec{a} \cdot \hat{i}}{|\vec{a}||\hat{i}|} = \frac{a_1}{|\vec{a}|}, \quad \cos\beta = \frac{\vec{a} \cdot \hat{j}}{|\vec{a}||\hat{j}|} = \frac{a_2}{|\vec{a}|}$$

$$\text{and } \cos r = \frac{\vec{a} \cdot \hat{k}}{|\vec{a}||\hat{k}|} = \frac{a_3}{|\vec{a}|}.$$

EXAMPLE : *Find the angle between two vectors $\vec{a}$ and $\vec{b}$ with magnituds $\sqrt{3}$ and 2, having $(\vec{a} \cdot \vec{b}) = \sqrt{6}$.*

SOLUTION : It is given that

$$|\vec{a}| = \sqrt{3}, \ |\vec{b}| = 2 \ \text{ and } (\vec{a} \cdot \vec{b}) = \sqrt{6}$$

$$(\vec{a} \cdot \vec{b}) = |\vec{a}||\vec{b}|\cos\theta$$

Now we know that,

$$\sqrt{6} = \sqrt{3} \times 2 \times \cos\theta$$

$$\Rightarrow \cos\theta = \frac{\sqrt{6}}{\sqrt{3} \times 2}$$

$$\Rightarrow \cos\theta = \frac{1}{\sqrt{2}}$$

$$\Rightarrow \cos\theta = \left(\frac{\pi}{4}\right)$$

$$\Rightarrow \theta = \left(\frac{\pi}{4}\right).$$

Hence, the angle between the given vectors $\vec{a}$ and $\vec{b}$ is $\left(\frac{\pi}{4}\right)$.

EXAMPLE :   *Find the angle between the vectors $(\hat{i} - 2\hat{j} + 3\hat{k})$ and $(3\hat{i} - 2\hat{j} + \hat{k})$.*

SOLUTION :   The given vectors are $\vec{a} = (\hat{i} - 2\hat{j} + 3\hat{k})$ and $\vec{b} = (3\hat{i} - 2\hat{j} + \hat{k})$.

$$\therefore \quad |\vec{a}| = \sqrt{(1)^2 + (-2)^2 + (3)^2} = \sqrt{14}$$

$$\therefore \quad |\vec{b}| = \sqrt{(3)^2 + (-2)^2 + (3)^2} = \sqrt{14}$$

$$\text{Now } (\vec{a} \cdot \vec{b}) = (\hat{i} - 2\hat{j} + 3\hat{k}) \cdot (3\hat{i} - 2\hat{j} + \hat{k})$$

$$= 1 \times 3 + (-2)(-2) + 3 \cdot 1$$

$$= 10$$

Also, we know that $(\vec{a} \cdot \vec{b}) = |\vec{a}||\vec{b}| \cos\theta$

$$\therefore \quad 10 = \sqrt{14}\sqrt{14} \cos\theta$$

$$\text{or,} \quad \cos\theta = \left(\frac{10}{14}\right)$$

$$\text{or,} \quad \theta = \cos^{-1}\left(\frac{5}{7}\right).$$

(v) <u>SOLVED EXAMPLES</u>

EXAMPLE 1 :   *Find the projection of the vector $(\hat{i} + 3\hat{j} + 7\hat{k})$ on the vector $(2\hat{i} - 3\hat{j} + 6\hat{k})$.*

[CBSE 2014]

SOLUTION :   Let $\vec{a} = (\hat{i} + 3\hat{j} + 7\hat{k})$ and $\vec{b} = (2\hat{i} - 3\hat{j} + 6\hat{k})$. Then,

$$\text{projection of } \vec{a} \text{ on } \vec{b} = \frac{(\vec{a} \cdot \vec{b})}{|\vec{b}|}$$

$$= \frac{(\hat{i} + 3\hat{j} + 7\hat{k}) \cdot (2\hat{i} - 3\hat{j} + 6\hat{k})}{\sqrt{4 + 9 + 36}}$$

$$= \frac{(2 - 9 + 42)}{\sqrt{49}} = \frac{35}{7} = 5.$$

EXAMPLE 2 : *Write the projection of $(\vec{b} + \vec{c})$ on $\vec{a}$, where $\vec{a} = (2\hat{i} - 2\hat{j} + \hat{k})$, $\vec{b} = (\hat{i} + 2\hat{j} - 2\hat{k})$ and $\vec{c} = (2\hat{i} - \hat{j} + 4\hat{k})$.* **[CBSE 2013C]**

SOLUTION : We have

$$(\vec{b} + \vec{c}) = (\hat{i} + 2\hat{j} - 2\hat{k}) + (2\hat{i} - \hat{j} + 4\hat{k})$$

$$= (1 + 2)\hat{i} + (2 - 1)\hat{j} + (-2 + 4)\hat{k} = (3\hat{i} + \hat{j} + 2\hat{k}).$$

$$\therefore \text{ projection of } (\vec{b} + \vec{c}) \text{ on } \vec{a} = \frac{(\vec{b} + \vec{c}) \cdot \vec{a}}{|\vec{a}|}$$

$$= \frac{(3\hat{i} + \hat{j} + 2\hat{k}) \cdot (2\hat{i} - 2\hat{j} + \hat{k})}{\sqrt{2^2 + (-2)^2 + 1^2}}$$

$$= \frac{(6 - 2 + 2)}{\sqrt{9}} = \frac{6}{3} = 2.$$

EXAMPLE 3 : *Find λ when the projection of $\vec{a} = \lambda\hat{i} + \hat{j} + 4\hat{k}$ on $\vec{b} = (2\hat{i} + 6\hat{j} + 3\hat{k})$ is 4 units.* **[CBSE 2012]**

SOLUTION : Projection of $\vec{a}$ on $\vec{b} = \frac{(\vec{a} \cdot \vec{b})}{|\vec{b}|}$

$$= \frac{(\lambda\hat{i} + \hat{j} + 4\hat{k}) \cdot (2\hat{i} + 6\hat{j} + 3\hat{k})}{\sqrt{2^2 + 6^2 + 3^2}}$$

$$= \frac{(2\lambda + 6 + 12)}{\sqrt{4 + 36 + 9}} = \frac{(2\lambda + 18)}{\sqrt{49}} = \frac{2(\lambda + 9)}{7}$$

$$\therefore \quad \frac{2(\lambda+9)}{7} = 4 \Rightarrow 2(\lambda+9) = 28 \Rightarrow \lambda+9 = 14 \Rightarrow \lambda = 5.$$

Hence, $\lambda = 5$.

EXAMPLE 4 : *Write the value of λ so that the vectors $\vec{a} = 2\hat{i} + \lambda\,\hat{j} + \hat{k}$ and $\vec{b} = \hat{i} - 2\hat{j} + 3\hat{k}$ are perpendicular to each other.* **[CBSE 2013C]**

SOLUTION :

$$\vec{a} \perp \vec{b} \Leftrightarrow \vec{a}\cdot\vec{b} = 0$$

$$\Leftrightarrow (2\hat{i} + \lambda\hat{j} + \hat{k})\cdot(\hat{i} - 2\hat{j} + 3\hat{k}) = 0$$

$$\Leftrightarrow (2 - 2\lambda + 3) = 0 \Leftrightarrow 2\lambda = 5 \Leftrightarrow \lambda = \frac{5}{2}$$

Hence, $\lambda = \dfrac{5}{2}$

EXAMPLE 5 : *The scalar product of the vector $(\hat{i} + \hat{j} + \hat{k})$ with the unit vector along the sum of the vectors $(2\hat{i} + 4\hat{j} - 5\hat{k})$ and $(\lambda\hat{i} + 2\hat{j} + 3\hat{k})$ is equal to 1. Find the value of λ.* **[CBSE 2009, '14]**

SOLUTION :

Let $\vec{a} = (\hat{i} + \hat{j} + \hat{k})$, $\vec{b} = (2\hat{i} + 4\hat{j} - 5\hat{k})$ and $\vec{c} = (\lambda\hat{i} + 2\hat{j} + 3\hat{k})$.

Then, $(\vec{b} + \vec{c}) = (2\hat{i} + 4\hat{j} - 5\hat{k}) + (\lambda\hat{i} + 2\hat{j} + 3\hat{k}) = (2+\lambda)\hat{i} + 6\hat{j} - 2\hat{k}$

$$\text{Unit vector along } (\vec{b} + \vec{c}) = \frac{(\vec{b} + \vec{c})}{|\vec{b} + \vec{c}|} = \frac{(2+\lambda)\hat{i} + 6\hat{j} - 2\hat{k}}{\sqrt{(2+\lambda)^2 + 6^2 + (-2)^2}}$$

$$= \frac{(2+\lambda)\hat{i} + 6\hat{j} - 2\hat{k}}{\sqrt{\lambda^2 + 4\lambda + 44}}$$

But, $\dfrac{(\vec{b} + \vec{c})}{|\vec{b} + \vec{c}|}\cdot\vec{a} = 1$ (given).

$$\therefore \quad \frac{(2+\lambda)\hat{i} + 6\hat{j} - 2\hat{k}}{\sqrt{\lambda^2 + 4\lambda + 44}}\cdot(\hat{i} + \hat{j} + \hat{k}) = 1$$

$$\Rightarrow (2+\lambda)(\hat{i} + 6\hat{j} - 2\hat{k})\cdot(\hat{i} + \hat{j} + \hat{k}) = \sqrt{\lambda^2 + 4\lambda + 44}$$

$$\Rightarrow (2+\lambda) + 6 - 2 = \sqrt{\lambda^2 + 4\lambda + 44}$$

$$\Rightarrow (6 + \lambda) = \sqrt{\lambda^2 + 4\lambda + 44}$$

$$\Rightarrow \lambda^2 + 4\lambda + 44 = (6 + \lambda)^2$$

$$\Rightarrow \lambda^2 + 4\lambda + 44 = 36 + \lambda^2 + 12\lambda$$

$$\Rightarrow 8\lambda \Rightarrow 8 \Rightarrow \lambda = 1.$$

Hence, the required value of λ is 1.

EXAMPLE 6 :   *Dot products of a vector with the vectors* $(\hat{i} - \hat{j} + \hat{k}), (2\hat{i} + \hat{j} - 3\hat{k})$ *and* $(\hat{i} + \hat{j} + \hat{k})$ *are respectively* **4, 0** *and* **2.** *Find the vector.*   *[CBSE 2013C]*

SOLUTION :   Let the required vector be $(x\hat{i} + y\hat{j} + z\hat{k})$. Then,

$$(x\hat{i} + y\hat{j} + z\hat{k}) \cdot (\hat{i} - \hat{j} + \hat{k}) = 4 \Rightarrow x - y + z = 4 \qquad \dots \text{(i)}$$

$$(x\hat{i} + y\hat{j} + z\hat{k}) \cdot (2\hat{i} + \hat{j} - 3\hat{k}) = 0 \Rightarrow 2x + y - 3z = 0 \qquad \dots \text{(ii)}$$

$$(x\hat{i} + y\hat{j} + z\hat{k}) \cdot (\hat{i} + \hat{j} + \hat{k}) = 2 \Rightarrow x + y + z = 2 \qquad \dots \text{(iii)}$$

On subtracting (i) from (iii) we get $2y = -2 \Rightarrow y = -1$

On adding (i) and (ii), we get $3x - 2z = 4$ $\qquad \dots \text{(iv)}$

On adding (i) and (iii), we get $2x + 2z = 6$ $\qquad \dots \text{(v)}$

On solving (iv) and (v), we get $x = 2$ and $z = 1$.

$$\therefore \qquad x = 2, y = -1 \text{ and } z = 1.$$

Hence, the required vector is $(2\hat{i} - \hat{j} + \hat{k})$.

EXAMPLE 7 :   *Let* $\vec{a} = \hat{i} + 4\hat{j} + 2\hat{k},\ \vec{b} = 3\hat{i} - 2\hat{j} + 7\hat{k}$ *and* $\vec{c} = 2\hat{i} - \hat{j} + 4\hat{k}$. *Find a vector* $\vec{p}$ *which is perpendicular to both* $\vec{a}$ *and* $\vec{b}$ *and* $\vec{p} \cdot \vec{c} = 18$.   *[CBSE 2012]*

SOLUTION :   Let $\vec{p} = (x\hat{i} + y\hat{j} + z\hat{k})$. Then,

$$\vec{p} \perp \vec{a},\ \vec{p} \perp \vec{b} \text{ and } \vec{p} \cdot \vec{c} = 18$$

$$\Rightarrow \vec{p} \cdot \vec{a} = 0,\ \vec{p} \cdot \vec{b} = 0 \text{ and } \vec{p} \cdot \vec{c} = 18$$

$$\Rightarrow \begin{cases} (x\hat{i} + y\hat{j} + z\hat{k}) \cdot (\hat{i} + 4\hat{j} + 2\hat{k}) = 0 \Rightarrow x + 4y + 2z = 0 & \dots\text{(i)} \\ (x\hat{i} + y\hat{j} + z\hat{k}) \cdot (3\hat{i} - 2\hat{j} + 7\hat{k}) = 0 \Rightarrow 3x - 2y + 7z = 0 & \dots\text{(ii)} \\ (x\hat{i} + y\hat{j} + z\hat{k}) \cdot (2\hat{i} - \hat{j} + 4\hat{k}) = 18 \Rightarrow 2x - y + 4z = 18 & \dots\text{(iii)} \end{cases}$$

On solving (i) and (ii) by cross multiplication, we get

$$\frac{x}{(28+4)} = \frac{y}{(6-7)} = \frac{z}{(-2-12)} = k \ \ (\text{say})$$

$$\Rightarrow x = 32k, \ y = -k \text{ and } z = -14k.$$

Substituting these values in (iii), we get :

$$64k + k - 56k = 18 \Rightarrow 9k = 18 \Rightarrow k = 2.$$

$$\therefore \quad x = (32 \times 2) = 64, \ y = -2 \text{ and } z = (-14) \times 2 = -28$$

Hence, the requied vector is $(64\hat{i} - 2\hat{j} - 28\hat{k})$.

EXAMPLE 8 : *Find a vector whose magnitude is 3 units and which is perpendicular to each of the vectors* $\vec{a} = 3\hat{i} + \hat{j} - 4\hat{k}$ *and* $\vec{b} = 6\hat{i} + 5\hat{j} - 2\hat{k}$. *[CBSE 2000C]*

SOLUTION : Let the required vector be $\vec{c} = c_1\hat{i} + c_2\hat{j} + c_3\hat{k}$

Then, $|\vec{c}| = 3 \Leftrightarrow \sqrt{c_1^2 + c_2^2 + c_3^2} = 3 \Leftrightarrow c_1^2 + c_2^2 + c_3^2 = 9$ ... (i)

Also, $\vec{c} \perp \vec{a} \Rightarrow \vec{c} \cdot \vec{a} = 0$

$$\Rightarrow (c_1\hat{i} + c_2\hat{j} + c_3\hat{k}) \cdot (3\hat{i} + \hat{j} - 4\hat{k}) = 0 \quad \text{... (ii)}$$

$$\Rightarrow 3c_1 + c_2 - 4c_3 = 0.$$

And, $\vec{c} \perp \vec{b} \Rightarrow \vec{c} \cdot \vec{b} = 0$

$$\Rightarrow (c_1\hat{i} + c_2\hat{j} + c_3\hat{k}) \cdot (6\hat{i} + 5\hat{j} - 2\hat{k}) = 0 \quad \text{... (iii)}$$

$$\Rightarrow 6c_1 + 5c_2 - 2c_3 = 0.$$

From (ii) and (iii), by cross multiplication, we get

$$\frac{c_1}{(-2+20)} = \frac{c_2}{(-24+6)} = \frac{c_3}{(15-6)} = k \ \ (\text{say})$$

$$\Rightarrow \frac{c_1}{18} = \frac{c_2}{-18} = \frac{c_3}{9} = k$$

$$\Rightarrow \frac{c_1}{2} = \frac{c_2}{-2} = \frac{c_3}{1} = k$$

$$\Rightarrow c_1 = 2k, \ c_2 = -2k \text{ and } c_3 = k.$$

Substituting these values in (i), we get

$$4k^2 + 4k^2 + k^2 = 9 \Rightarrow k^2 = 1 \Rightarrow k = 1.$$

$\therefore \qquad c_1 = 2, \ c_2 = -2 \ \text{and} \ c_3 = 1.$

Hence, $\vec{c} = (2\hat{i} - 2\hat{j} + \hat{k})$ is the required vector.

EXAMPLE 9 : *Find the cosine of the angle between the vectors $\vec{a} = 3\hat{i} + \hat{j} + 2\hat{k}$ and $\vec{b} = 2\hat{i} - 2\hat{j} + 4\hat{k}$.*

SOLUTION : We have, $|\vec{a}| = \sqrt{3^2 + 1^2 + 2^2} = \sqrt{14}$

$$|\vec{b}| = \sqrt{2^2 + (-2)^2 + 4^2} = \sqrt{24} = 2\sqrt{6}$$

and $\vec{a} \cdot \vec{b} = (3\hat{i} + \hat{j} + 2\hat{k}) \cdot (2\hat{i} - 2\hat{j} + 4\hat{k})$

$$= 6\hat{i}\cdot\hat{i} - 6\hat{i}\cdot\hat{j} + 12\hat{i}\cdot\hat{k} + 2\hat{j}\cdot\hat{i} - 2\hat{j}\cdot\hat{j} + 4\hat{j}\cdot\hat{k} + 4\hat{k}\cdot\hat{i} - 4\hat{k}\cdot\hat{j} + 8\hat{k}\cdot\hat{k}$$

$$= 6 - 2 + 8$$

$$[\because \ \hat{i}\cdot\hat{i} = \hat{j}\cdot\hat{j} = \hat{k}\cdot\hat{k} = 1 \ \text{and} \ \hat{i}\cdot\hat{j} = \hat{j}\cdot\hat{k} = \hat{k}\cdot\hat{i} = 0 \ ]$$

$$= 12$$

If θ is the angle between vectors $\vec{a}$ and $\vec{b}$ then,

$$\therefore \qquad \cos\theta = \frac{\vec{a}\cdot\vec{b}}{|\vec{a}||\vec{b}|} = \frac{12}{\sqrt{14} \times 2\sqrt{6}} = \frac{12}{4\sqrt{21}} = \sqrt{\frac{3}{7}}$$

EXAMPLE 10 : *If the vectors $3\hat{i} - 2\hat{j} + m\hat{k}$ and $-2\hat{i} + \hat{j} + 4\hat{k}$ are perpendicular to each other, find the value of m.*

SOLUTION : Let $\vec{a} = 3\hat{i} - 2\hat{j} + m\hat{k}$ and $\vec{b} = -2\hat{i} + \hat{j} + 4\hat{k}$

By problem, the vectors $\vec{a}$ and $\vec{b}$ are perpendicular to each other; hence, we must have,

$$\vec{a}\cdot\vec{b} = 0$$

or, $\qquad (3\hat{i} - 2\hat{j} + m\hat{k}) \cdot (-2\hat{i} + \hat{j} + 4\hat{k}) = 0$

or, $\qquad -6 - 2 + 4m = 0$

$$[\because \ \hat{i}\cdot\hat{i} = \hat{j}\cdot\hat{j} = \hat{k}\cdot\hat{k} = 1 \ \text{and} \ \hat{i}\cdot\hat{j} = \hat{j}\cdot\hat{k} = \hat{k}\cdot\hat{i} = 0]$$

or, $\qquad 4m = 8$ or, $m = 2$

EXAMPLE 11 :   *If $\vec{a}$ and $\vec{b}$ are vectors such that $|\vec{a}| = 2, |\vec{b}| = 3$ and $\vec{a} \cdot \vec{b} = 4$, find $|\vec{a} - \vec{b}|$.*

SOLUTION :   We have

$$|\vec{a} - \vec{b}|^2 = (\vec{a} - \vec{b}) \cdot (\vec{a} - \vec{b})$$

$$= \vec{a} \cdot \vec{a} - \vec{a} \cdot \vec{b} - \vec{b} \cdot \vec{a} + \vec{b} \cdot \vec{b} \qquad \text{(by distributive law)}$$

$$= |\vec{a}|^2 - 2\vec{a} \cdot \vec{b} + |\vec{b}|^2 \qquad [\because \ \vec{a} \cdot \vec{b} = \vec{b} \cdot \vec{a}]$$

$$= (2^2 - 2 \times 4 + 3^2) = 5$$

Hence, $|\vec{a} - \vec{b}| = \sqrt{5}$

EXAMPLE 12 :   *If $\vec{a}$ makes equal angles with the coordinate axes and has magnitude 3, find the angle between $\vec{a}$ and each of the three coordinate axes.*

SOLUTION :   Let $\vec{a} = a_1 \hat{i} + a_2 \hat{j} + a_3 \hat{k}$ and let α be the angle between $\vec{a}$ and each of the coordinate axes.

Then, α is the angle between $\vec{a}$ and each one of $\hat{i}, \hat{j}$ and $\hat{k}$.

$$\therefore \ \cos\alpha = \frac{\vec{a} \cdot \hat{i}}{|\vec{a}||\hat{i}|} = \frac{a_1}{3} \Rightarrow a_1 = 3\cos\alpha \ [\because \ \vec{a} \cdot \hat{i} = a_1, |\vec{a}| = 3, |\hat{i}| = 1]$$

Similarly, $a_2 = 3\cos\alpha$ and $a_3 = 3\cos\alpha$

Now, $|\vec{a}| = 3 \Rightarrow |\vec{a}|^2 = 9$

$$\Rightarrow a_1^2 + a_2^2 + a_3^2 = 9$$

$$\Rightarrow 9\cos^2\alpha + 9\cos^2\alpha + 9\cos^2\alpha = 9$$

$$\Rightarrow 27\cos^2\alpha = 9 \Rightarrow \cos^2\alpha = \frac{1}{3}$$

$$\Rightarrow \cos\alpha = \frac{1}{\sqrt{3}} \Rightarrow \alpha = \cos^{-1}\left(\frac{1}{\sqrt{3}}\right)$$

Hence, the required angle is $\cos^{-1}\left(\frac{1}{\sqrt{3}}\right)$.

EXAMPLE 13 :   *If a unit vector $\vec{a}$ makes angles $\dfrac{\pi}{4}$ with $\hat{i}, \dfrac{\pi}{3}$ with $\hat{j}$ and an acute angle*

θ *with $\hat{k}$ then find the value of θ. Also, find the scalar and vector components of $\vec{a}$ along the axes.*   *[CBSE 2013]*

SOLUTION :   Let $\vec{a} = (a_1\hat{i} + a_2\hat{j} + a_3\hat{k})$. Then, $\vec{a}$ being a unit vector, we have

$$(a_1^2 + a_2^2 + a_3^2) = 1.$$

Now, $\vec{a}\cdot\hat{i} = a_1 \Rightarrow |\vec{a}||\hat{i}|\cos\dfrac{\pi}{4} = a_1 \Rightarrow a_1 = \dfrac{1}{\sqrt{2}}$ $[\because |\vec{a}|=1, |\hat{i}|=1\,]$

$\vec{a}\cdot\hat{j} = a_2 \Rightarrow |\vec{a}||\hat{j}|\cos\dfrac{\pi}{3} = a_2 \Rightarrow a_2 = \dfrac{1}{2}$ $[\because |\vec{a}|=1, |\hat{j}|=1\,]$

$\vec{a}\cdot\hat{k} = a_3 \Rightarrow |\vec{a}||\hat{k}|\cos\theta = a_3 \Rightarrow a_2 = \cos\theta$ $[\because |\vec{a}|=1, |\hat{k}|=1\,]$

Now, $|\vec{a}|=1 \Rightarrow |\vec{a}|^2 = 1$

$$\Rightarrow a_1^2 + a_2^2 + a_3^2 = 1$$

$$\Rightarrow \frac{1}{2} + \frac{1}{4} + \cos^2\theta = 1 \qquad [\because a_1 = \frac{1}{\sqrt{2}},\ a_2 = \frac{1}{2}, a_3 = \cos\theta\,]$$

$$\Rightarrow \cos^2\theta = \frac{1}{4} \Rightarrow \cos\theta = \frac{1}{2} \Rightarrow \theta = \frac{\pi}{3}$$

Hence, the scalar components of $\vec{a}$ are $\dfrac{1}{\sqrt{2}}, \dfrac{1}{2}$ and $\dfrac{1}{2}$.

And, the vector components of $\vec{a}$ are $\dfrac{1}{\sqrt{2}}\hat{i}, \dfrac{1}{2}\hat{j}$ and $\dfrac{1}{2}\hat{k}$.

EXAMPLE 14 :   *If $\vec{a}$ and $\vec{b}$ are two unit vectors such that $\vec{a}+\vec{b}$ is also a unit vector, then find the angle between $\vec{a}$ and $\vec{b}$.*   *[CBSE 2014]*

SOLUTION :   Let θ be the angle between the unit vectors $\vec{a}$ and $\vec{b}$.

Since $\vec{a}$ and $\vec{b}$ are unit vectors, we have $|\vec{a}|=1$ and $|\vec{b}|=1$.

Again, since $(\vec{a}+\vec{b})$ is a unit vector, we have

$$|\vec{a}+\vec{b}|^2 = 1$$

$$\Rightarrow (\vec{a}+\vec{b})\cdot(\vec{a}+\vec{b}) = 1 \Rightarrow \vec{a}\cdot\vec{a} + \vec{a}\cdot\vec{b} + \vec{b}\cdot\vec{a} + \vec{b}\cdot\vec{b} = 1$$

$$\Rightarrow |\vec{a}|^2 + 2(\vec{a}\cdot\vec{b}) + |\vec{b}|^2 = 1 \qquad [\because \vec{b}\cdot\vec{a} = \vec{a}\cdot\vec{b}]$$

$$\Rightarrow 2(\vec{a}\cdot\vec{b}) = -1 \Rightarrow \vec{a}\cdot\vec{b} = \frac{-1}{2} \qquad\qquad [\because |\vec{a}|^2 = 1,\ |\vec{b}|^2 = 1]$$

$$\Rightarrow |\vec{a}||\vec{b}|\cos\theta = \frac{-1}{2} \Rightarrow \cos\theta = \frac{-1}{2} \Rightarrow \theta = \frac{2\pi}{3} \qquad [\because |\vec{a}| = 1,\ |\vec{b}| = 1]$$

Hence, the angle between $\vec{a}$ and $\vec{b}$ is $\dfrac{2\pi}{3}$.

EXAMPLE 15 : *If the sum of two unit vectors $\hat{a}$ and $\hat{b}$ is a unit vector, show that the magnitude of their difference is $\sqrt{3}$.* **[CBSE 2012C]**

SOLUTION : Let $\hat{a} + \hat{b} = \hat{c}$, where $\hat{c}$ is a unit vector. Then,

$$\hat{a} + \hat{b} = \hat{c} \Rightarrow (\hat{a} + \hat{b})\cdot(\hat{a} + \hat{b}) = \hat{c}\cdot\hat{c}$$

$$\Rightarrow \hat{a}\cdot\hat{a} + \hat{a}\cdot\hat{b} + \hat{b}\cdot\hat{a} + \hat{b}\cdot\hat{b} = \hat{c}\cdot\hat{c}$$

$$\Rightarrow |\hat{a}|^2 + 2(\hat{a}\cdot\hat{b}) + |\hat{b}|^2 = |\hat{c}|^2 \qquad\qquad [\because \hat{b}\cdot\hat{a} = \hat{a}\cdot\hat{b}]$$

$$\Rightarrow 1 + 2(\hat{a}\cdot\hat{b}) + 1 = 1 \qquad\qquad [\because |\hat{a}| = |\hat{b}| = |\hat{c}| = 1]$$

$$\Rightarrow 2(\hat{a}\cdot\hat{b}) = -1 \qquad\qquad ...(i)$$

Now, $|\hat{a} - \hat{b}|^2 = (\hat{a} - \hat{b})\cdot(\hat{a} - \hat{b})$

$$= \hat{a}\cdot\hat{a} - \hat{a}\cdot\hat{b} - \hat{b}\cdot\hat{a} + \hat{b}\cdot\hat{b}$$

$$= |\hat{a}|^2 - 2(\hat{a}\cdot\hat{b}) + |\hat{b}|^2 \qquad\qquad [\because \hat{b}\cdot\hat{a} = \hat{a}\cdot\hat{b}]$$

$$= 1 - 2(\hat{a}\cdot\hat{b}) + 1 = 1 + 1 + 1 = 3 \qquad\qquad [\text{using (i)}]$$

Hence, $|\hat{a} - \hat{b}| = \sqrt{3}$.

EXAMPLE 16 : *If $\vec{a}, \vec{b}$ and $\vec{c}$ are three vectors such that $|\vec{a}| = 5$, $|\vec{b}| = 12$, $|\vec{c}| = 13$ and $\vec{a} + \vec{b} + \vec{c} = \vec{0}$, find the value of $(\vec{a}\cdot\vec{b} + \vec{b}\cdot\vec{c} + \vec{c}\cdot\vec{a})$.* **[CBSE 2012]**

SOLUTION :

$$\vec{a} + \vec{b} + \vec{c} = \vec{0} \Rightarrow \vec{a} + \vec{b} = -\vec{c}$$

$$\Rightarrow (\vec{a} + \vec{b})\cdot\vec{c} = (-\vec{c})\cdot\vec{c} \Rightarrow \vec{a}\cdot\vec{c} + \vec{b}\cdot\vec{c} = -|\vec{c}|^2$$

$$\Rightarrow \vec{c}\cdot\vec{a} + \vec{b}\cdot\vec{c} = -169 \qquad\qquad ...\ (i)$$

$$[\because \vec{a}\cdot\vec{c} = \vec{c}\cdot\vec{a} \ \text{ and } |\vec{c}| = 13]$$

Again, $\vec{a}+\vec{b}+\vec{c}=\vec{0} \Rightarrow \vec{b}+\vec{c}=-\vec{a}$

$$\Rightarrow (\vec{b}+\vec{c})\cdot\vec{a}=(-\vec{a})\cdot\vec{a}$$

$$\Rightarrow \vec{b}\cdot\vec{a}+\vec{c}\cdot\vec{a}=-|\vec{a}|^2$$

$$\Rightarrow \vec{a}\cdot\vec{b}+\vec{c}\cdot\vec{a}=-25 \qquad\qquad \text{... (ii)}$$

$$[\because \ \vec{b}\cdot\vec{a}=\vec{a}\cdot\vec{b} \ \text{and} \ |\vec{a}|=5\,]$$

Also, $\vec{a}+\vec{b}+\vec{c}=\vec{0} \Rightarrow \vec{a}+\vec{c}=-\vec{b}$

$$\Rightarrow (\vec{a}+\vec{c})\cdot\vec{b}=(-\vec{b})\cdot\vec{b}$$

$$\Rightarrow \vec{a}\cdot\vec{b}+\vec{c}\cdot\vec{b}=-|\vec{b}|^2$$

$$\Rightarrow \vec{a}\cdot\vec{b}+\vec{b}\cdot\vec{c}=-144 \ ... \qquad\qquad \text{(iii)}$$

$$[\because \ \vec{c}\cdot\vec{b}=\vec{b}\cdot\vec{c} \ \text{and} \ |\vec{b}|=12\,]$$

Adding the corresponding sides of (i), (ii) and (iii), we get

$$2(\vec{a}\cdot\vec{b}+\vec{b}\cdot\vec{c}+\vec{c}\cdot\vec{a})=-(169+25+144)$$

$$\Rightarrow (\vec{a}\cdot\vec{b}+\vec{b}\cdot\vec{c}+\vec{c}\cdot\vec{a})=\frac{-338}{2}=-169.$$

Hence, $(\vec{a}\cdot\vec{b}+\vec{b}\cdot\vec{c}+\vec{c}\cdot\vec{a})=-169.$

EXAMPLE 17 : *If $\vec{a},\vec{b},\vec{c}$ are three vectors such that $|\vec{a}|=3, |\vec{b}|=4$ and $|\vec{c}|=5$ and each one of them is perpendicular to the sum of the two then find $|\vec{a}+\vec{b}+\vec{c}|$.*

[CBSE 2011C]

SOLUTION : Let $\vec{a},\vec{b},\vec{c}$ be the given vectors such that

$$\{|\vec{a}|=3, |\vec{b}|=4, |\vec{c}|=5\}, \qquad\qquad \text{... (i)}$$

$$\left.\begin{array}{l} \vec{a}\cdot(\vec{b}+\vec{c})=0 \\ \vec{b}\cdot(\vec{c}+\vec{a})=0 \\ \vec{c}\cdot(\vec{a}+\vec{b})=0 \end{array}\right\} \qquad\qquad \text{...(ii)}$$

$$\therefore \ |\vec{a}+\vec{b}+\vec{c}|^2=(\vec{a}+\vec{b}+\vec{c})\cdot(\vec{a}+\vec{b}+\vec{c})$$

$$=\vec{a}\cdot\vec{a}+\vec{a}\cdot(\vec{b}+\vec{c})+\vec{b}\cdot(\vec{c}+\vec{a})+\vec{b}\cdot\vec{b}+\vec{c}\cdot(\vec{a}+\vec{b})+\vec{c}\cdot\vec{c}$$

$$= |\vec{a}|^2 + |\vec{b}|^2 + |\vec{c}|^2 \qquad \text{[using (ii)]}$$

$$= (3^2 + 4^2 + 5^2) = (9 + 16 + 25) = 50$$

Hence, $|\vec{a} + \vec{b} + \vec{c}| = \sqrt{50} = 5\sqrt{2}$.

EXAMPLE 18 : *If $\vec{a}, \vec{b}$ and $\vec{c}$ are three mutually perpendicular vectors of the same magnitude, prove that $(\vec{a} + \vec{b} + \vec{c})$ is equally inclined to the vectors, $\vec{a}, \vec{b}$ and $\vec{c}$. Also find this angle,* **[CBSE 2006C, '11C, '13C]**

SOLUTION : It is given that

$$|\vec{a}| = |\vec{b}| = |\vec{c}| = a \ \text{(say)} \qquad \text{... (i)}$$

Since $\vec{a}, \vec{b}$ and $\vec{c}$ are mutually perpendicular vectors, we have

$$\vec{a} \cdot \vec{b} = \vec{b} \cdot \vec{c} = \vec{c} \cdot \vec{a} = 0. \qquad \text{... (ii)}$$

Now, $|\vec{a} + \vec{b} + \vec{c}|^2 = (\vec{a} + \vec{b} + \vec{c}) \cdot (\vec{a} + \vec{b} + \vec{c})$

$$= \vec{a} \cdot \vec{a} + \vec{b} \cdot \vec{b} + \vec{c} \cdot \vec{c} + 2(\vec{a} \cdot \vec{b} + \vec{b} \cdot \vec{c} + \vec{c} \cdot \vec{a})$$

$$= |\vec{a}|^2 + |\vec{b}|^2 + |\vec{c}|^2 \qquad \text{[using (ii)]}$$

$$= 3a^2 \qquad \text{[using (i)]}$$

$$\therefore \qquad |\vec{a} + \vec{b} + \vec{c}| = \sqrt{3}\,a \qquad \text{... (iii)}$$

Let $(\vec{a} + \vec{b} + \vec{c})$ make angles α, β and γ with $\vec{a}, \vec{b}$ and $\vec{c}$ respectively.

Then $(\vec{a} + \vec{b} + \vec{c}) \cdot \vec{a} = |\vec{a} + \vec{b} + \vec{c}||\vec{a}| \cos\alpha$

$$= (\sqrt{3}\,a \times a \times \cos\alpha) = \sqrt{3}\,a^2 \cos\alpha$$

$$\Rightarrow (\vec{a} \cdot \vec{a} + \vec{b} \cdot \vec{a} + \vec{c} \cdot \vec{a}) = \sqrt{3}\,a^2 \cos\alpha$$

$$\Rightarrow |\vec{a}|^2 = \sqrt{3}\,a^2 \cos\alpha \Rightarrow a^2 = \sqrt{3}\,a^2 \cos\alpha$$

$$\Rightarrow \cos\alpha = \frac{1}{\sqrt{3}} \Rightarrow \alpha = \cos^{-1}\left(\frac{1}{\sqrt{3}}\right)$$

Similarly, $\beta = \cos^{-1}\left(\dfrac{1}{\sqrt{3}}\right)$ and $\gamma = \cos^{-1}\left(\dfrac{1}{\sqrt{3}}\right)$

$$\therefore \qquad \alpha = \beta = \gamma = \cos^{-1}\left(\frac{1}{\sqrt{3}}\right)$$

Hence, $(\vec{a}+\vec{b}+\vec{c})$ is equally inclined to $\vec{a},\vec{b}$ and $\vec{c}$ and the required angle is $\cos^{-1}\left(\dfrac{1}{\sqrt{3}}\right)$.

EXAMPLE 19 : *If $\vec{a},\vec{b},\vec{c}$ are unit vectors such that $\vec{a}+\vec{b}+\vec{c}=\vec{0}$ then find the value of $(\vec{a}\cdot\vec{b}+\vec{b}\cdot\vec{c}+\vec{c}\cdot\vec{a})$.*

SOLUTION : Since, $\vec{a},\vec{b},\vec{c}$ are unit vectors, we have

$$|\vec{a}|=1, |\vec{b}|=1 \text{ and } |\vec{c}|=1.$$

Now, $\quad \vec{a}+\vec{b}+\vec{c}=\vec{0}$

$$\Rightarrow (\vec{a}+\vec{b}+\vec{c})\cdot(\vec{a}+\vec{b}+\vec{c})=0 \qquad [\because \ \vec{0}\cdot\vec{0}=0]$$

$$\Rightarrow (\vec{a}\cdot\vec{a}+\vec{b}\cdot\vec{b}+\vec{c}\cdot\vec{c})+2(\vec{a}\cdot\vec{b}+\vec{b}\cdot\vec{c}+\vec{c}\cdot\vec{a})=0$$

$$\Rightarrow |\vec{a}|^2+|\vec{b}|^2+|\vec{c}|^2+2(\vec{a}\cdot\vec{b}+\vec{b}\cdot\vec{c}+\vec{c}\cdot\vec{a})=0$$

$$\Rightarrow (\vec{a}\cdot\vec{b}+\vec{b}\cdot\vec{c}+\vec{c}\cdot\vec{a})=-\frac{3}{2} \qquad [\because \ |\vec{a}|^2=1,|\vec{b}|^2=1,|\vec{c}|^2=1]$$

Hence, $(\vec{a}\cdot\vec{b}+\vec{b}\cdot\vec{c}+\vec{c}\cdot\vec{a})=-\dfrac{3}{2}$

EXAMPLE 20 : *If $\vec{a}\cdot\vec{b}=\vec{a}\cdot\vec{c}$, show that $\vec{a}=\vec{0}$ or $\vec{b}=\vec{c}$ or $\vec{a}\perp(\vec{b}-\vec{c})$.*

SOLUTION : $\vec{a}\cdot\vec{b}=\vec{a}\cdot\vec{c} \Rightarrow \vec{a}\cdot\vec{b}-\vec{a}\cdot\vec{c}=0 \Rightarrow \vec{a}\cdot(\vec{b}-\vec{c})=0$

$$\Rightarrow \vec{a}=\vec{0} \text{ or } (\vec{b}-\vec{c})=0 \text{ or } \vec{a}\perp(\vec{b}\ \ \vec{c})$$

$$\Rightarrow \vec{a}=\vec{0} \text{ or } \vec{b}=\vec{c} \text{ or } \vec{a}\perp(\vec{b}-\vec{c})$$

Hence, $\vec{a}\cdot\vec{b}=\vec{a}\cdot\vec{c} \Rightarrow \vec{0}$ or $\vec{b}=\vec{c}$ or $\vec{a}\perp(\vec{b}-\vec{c})$

EXAMPLE 21 : *Let $\vec{a}$ and $\vec{b}$ be two nonzero vectors. Prove that $\vec{a}\perp\vec{b} \Leftrightarrow |\vec{a}+\vec{b}|=|\vec{a}-\vec{b}|$.*

SOLUTION : Let $\vec{a}\perp\vec{b}$. Then, $(\vec{a}\cdot\vec{b})=0$ $\qquad\qquad$ ... (i)

Now, $|\vec{a}+\vec{b}|^2=(\vec{a}+\vec{b})\cdot(\vec{a}+\vec{b})$

$$= \vec{a} \cdot \vec{a} + \vec{a} \cdot \vec{b} + \vec{b} \cdot \vec{a} + \vec{b} \cdot \vec{b}$$

$$= |\vec{a}|^2 + |\vec{b}|^2 \qquad \{\because \ \vec{a} \cdot \vec{b} = 0 \text{ and } \vec{b} \cdot \vec{a} = \vec{a} \cdot \vec{b} = 0\}$$

Also, $\quad |\vec{a} - \vec{b}|^2 = (\vec{a} - \vec{b}) \cdot (\vec{a} - \vec{b})$

$$= \vec{a} \cdot \vec{a} - \vec{a} \cdot \vec{b} - \vec{b} \cdot \vec{a} + \vec{b} \cdot \vec{b}$$

$$= |\vec{a}|^2 + |\vec{b}|^2 \qquad \{\because \ \vec{a} \cdot \vec{b} = 0 \text{ and } \vec{b} \cdot \vec{a} = \vec{a} \cdot \vec{b} = 0\}$$

Thus, $|\vec{a} + \vec{b}|^2 = |\vec{a} - \vec{b}|^2$, and therefore, $|\vec{a} + \vec{b}| = |\vec{a} - \vec{b}|$

$$\therefore \quad \vec{a} \perp \vec{b} \Rightarrow |\vec{a} + \vec{b}| = |\vec{a} - \vec{b}|$$

Conversely, suppose that $|\vec{a} + \vec{b}| = |\vec{a} - \vec{b}|$. Then,

$$|\vec{a} + \vec{b}| = |\vec{a} - \vec{b}| \Rightarrow |\vec{a} + \vec{b}|^2 = |\vec{a} - \vec{b}|^2$$

$$\Rightarrow (\vec{a} + \vec{b}) \cdot (\vec{a} + \vec{b}) = (\vec{a} - \vec{b}) \cdot (\vec{a} - \vec{b})$$

$$\Rightarrow \vec{a} \cdot \vec{a} + \vec{a} \cdot \vec{b} + \vec{b} \cdot \vec{a} + \vec{b} \cdot \vec{b}$$

$$= \vec{a} \cdot \vec{a} - \vec{a} \cdot \vec{b} - \vec{b} \cdot \vec{a} + \vec{b} \cdot \vec{b}$$

$$\Rightarrow 2(\vec{a} \cdot \vec{b} + \vec{b} \cdot \vec{a}) = 0$$

$$\Rightarrow 4(\vec{a} \cdot \vec{b}) = 0 \qquad [\because \ \vec{b} \cdot \vec{a} = \vec{a} \cdot \vec{b}]$$

$$\Rightarrow \vec{a} \cdot \vec{b} = 0 \Rightarrow \vec{a} \perp \vec{b}$$

Thus, $|\vec{a} + \vec{b}| = |\vec{a} - \vec{b}| \Rightarrow \vec{a} \perp \vec{b}$

Hence, $|\vec{a} + \vec{b}| = |\vec{a} - \vec{b}| \Leftrightarrow \vec{a} \perp \vec{b}$

EXAMPLE 22 : *Express the vector $\vec{a} = (5\hat{i} - 2\hat{j} + 5\hat{k})$ as sum of two vectors such that one is parallel to the vector $\vec{b} = (3\hat{i} + \hat{k})$ and the other is perpendicular to $\vec{b}$.*

[CBSE 2005]

SOLUTION : Any vector parallel to $\vec{b}$ is of the form $\lambda \vec{b}$ for some scalar λ.

Let $\vec{a} = \lambda \vec{b} + \vec{c}$, where $\vec{c} \perp \vec{b}$. Then, $\vec{c} = (\vec{a} - \lambda \vec{b}) \perp \vec{b}$

$$\Leftrightarrow (\vec{a} - \lambda \vec{b}) \cdot \vec{b} = 0 \Leftrightarrow (\vec{a} \cdot \vec{b}) - \lambda (\vec{b} \cdot \vec{b}) = 0$$

$$\Leftrightarrow (5\hat{i} - 2\hat{j} + 5\hat{k}) \cdot (3\hat{i} + \hat{k}) - \lambda(3\hat{i} + \hat{k}) \cdot (3\hat{i} + \hat{k}) = 0$$

$$\Leftrightarrow (15 - 0 + 5) - \lambda(9 + 1) = 0 \Leftrightarrow 10\lambda = 20 \Leftrightarrow \lambda = 2.$$

$$\therefore \quad \lambda \vec{b} = 2\vec{b} = (6\hat{i} + 2\hat{k})$$

And, $\quad \vec{c} = (\vec{a} - 2\vec{b}) = (5\hat{i} - 2\hat{j} + 5\hat{k}) - 2(3\hat{i} + \hat{k}) = (-\hat{i} - 2\hat{j} + 3\hat{k})$

Hence, the required vectors are $(6\hat{i} + 2\hat{k})$ and $(-\hat{i} - 2\hat{j} + 3\hat{k})$.

EXAMPLE 23 : *Find the values of λ for which the angle between the vectors $\vec{a} = 2\lambda^2\hat{i} + 4\lambda\hat{j} + \hat{k}$ and $\vec{b} = 7\hat{i} - 2\hat{j} + \lambda\hat{k}$ is obtuse.* *[CBSE 2013C]*

SOLUTION : Let θ be the angle between $\vec{a}$ and $\vec{b}$. Then,

$$\cos\theta = \frac{\vec{a} \cdot \vec{b}}{|\vec{a}||\vec{b}|} \qquad \qquad \ldots (i)$$

Clearly, θ is obtuse $\Leftrightarrow \cos\theta < 0 \Leftrightarrow \vec{a} \cdot \vec{b} < 0$ $\qquad$ [form (i)]

$$\Leftrightarrow 14\lambda^2 - 8\lambda + \lambda < 0 \Leftrightarrow 14\lambda^2 - 7\lambda < 0$$

$$\Leftrightarrow 2\lambda^2 - \lambda < 0 \Leftrightarrow \lambda(2\lambda - 1) < 0.$$

Now, $\lambda(2\lambda - 1) < 0 \Rightarrow$ either $\{\lambda < 0 \text{ and } (2\lambda - 1) > 0\}$

$$\text{or } \{\lambda > 0 \text{ and } (2\lambda - 1) < 0\}$$

$$\Rightarrow \left\{\lambda < 0 \text{ and } \lambda > \frac{1}{2}\right\} \text{ or } \left\{\lambda > 0 \text{ and } \lambda < \frac{1}{2}\right\}$$

$$\Rightarrow \left\{\frac{1}{2} < \lambda < 0\right\} \text{ or } \left\{0 < \lambda < \frac{1}{2}\right\}$$

$$\Rightarrow 0 < \lambda < \frac{1}{2} \left[\quad \frac{1}{2} < \lambda < 0 \text{ is not possible} \right]$$

$$\Rightarrow \lambda \in \left]0, \frac{1}{2}\right[$$

$\therefore$ the required values of λ are all real values in $\left]0, \dfrac{1}{2}\right[$

EXAMPLE 24 : *Let $(\hat{i} + \hat{j} + \hat{k})$, $(2\hat{i} + 5\hat{j})$, $(3\hat{i} + 2\hat{j} - 3\hat{k})$ and $(\hat{i} - 6\hat{j} - \hat{k})$ be the position vectors of points A, B, C, D respectively. Find the angle between AB and CD. Hence, show that AB| |CD.* *[CBSE 2008]*

SOLUTION : Let the angle between $\overrightarrow{AB}$ and $\overrightarrow{CD}$ be θ.

Now, $\overrightarrow{AB} = $ (p.v. of B) $-$ (p.v. of A)

$$= (2\hat{i} + 5\hat{j}) - (\hat{i} + \hat{j} + \hat{k}) = (\hat{i} + 4\hat{j} - \hat{k})$$

and, $\overrightarrow{CD} = $ (p.v. of D) $-$ (p.v. of C)

$$= (\hat{i} - 6\hat{j} - \hat{k}) - (3\hat{i} + 2\hat{j} - 3\hat{k}) = (-2\hat{i} - 8\hat{j} + 2\hat{k})$$

$\therefore \qquad |\overrightarrow{AB}| = \sqrt{1^2 + 4^2 + (-1)^2} = \sqrt{18} = 3\sqrt{2}$

and, $\qquad |\overrightarrow{CD}| = \sqrt{(-2)^2 + (-8)^2 + 2^2} = \sqrt{72} = 6\sqrt{2}$

Now, $\quad \overrightarrow{AB} \cdot \overrightarrow{CD} = (\hat{i} + 4\hat{j} - \hat{k}) \cdot (-2\hat{i} - 8\hat{j} + 2\hat{k})$

$$= (-2 - 32 - 2) = -36$$

$\therefore \qquad \cos\theta = \dfrac{\overrightarrow{AB} \cdot \overrightarrow{CD}}{|\overrightarrow{AB}||\overrightarrow{CD}|} = \dfrac{-36}{(3\sqrt{2} \times 6\sqrt{2})} = \dfrac{-36}{36} = -1 \Rightarrow \theta = \pi$

Hence, $AB \,||\, CD$.

(vi) EXERCISE

1. Find the scalar product of the following pair of vectors and the angle between them:

(i) $\hat{i} + \hat{j}$ *and* $\hat{j} + \hat{k}$

(ii) $2\hat{i} - \hat{j} + 2\hat{k}$ *and* $\hat{i} + \hat{j} + m\hat{k}$

(iii) $\vec{a} = 2\hat{i} + 3\hat{j} - 4\hat{k}$ *and* $\vec{b} = \hat{i} + 2\hat{j} + \hat{k}$

(iv) $\vec{a} = 2\hat{i} - 5\hat{j} + 3\hat{k}$ *and* $\vec{b} = \hat{i} - 2\hat{j} - 4\hat{k}$

2. Show that the vectors

(i) $\vec{a} = 2\hat{i} + \hat{j} - \hat{k}$ *and* $\vec{b} = \hat{i} + \hat{j} + 3\hat{k}$

(ii) $\vec{a} = (3, 2, -1)$ *and* $\vec{b} = (-2, 0, -6)$

(iii) $\vec{\alpha} = -3\hat{i} - 2\hat{j} + \hat{k}$ *and* $\vec{\beta} = -2\hat{i} + \hat{j} - 4\hat{k}$ *are perpendicular to each other.*

3. Show that the vectors

(i) $\hat{i} + 2\hat{j} + \hat{k}$, $\hat{i} + \hat{j} - 3\hat{k}$ *and* $7\hat{i} - 4\hat{j} + \hat{k}$

(ii) $a = 2\hat{i} + 3\hat{j} + 6\hat{k}$, $b = 3\hat{i} - 6\hat{j} + 2\hat{k}$ and $c = 6\hat{i} + 2\hat{j} - 3\hat{k}$ are mutually perpendicular.

4. Find the value of λ for which $\vec{a}$ and $\vec{b}$ are perpendicular, where

(i) $\vec{a} = 2\hat{i} + \lambda\hat{j} + \hat{k}$ and $\vec{b} = (\hat{i} - 2\hat{j} + 3\hat{k})$ *[CBSE 2012C]*

Ans: $\lambda = \dfrac{5}{2}$

(ii) $\vec{a} = 3\hat{i} - \hat{j} + 4\hat{k}$ and $\vec{b} = -\lambda\hat{i} + 3\hat{j} + 3\hat{k}$

Ans: $\lambda = 3$

(iii) $\vec{a} = 2\hat{i} + 4\hat{j} - \hat{k}$ and $\vec{b} = 3\hat{i} - 2\hat{j} + \lambda\hat{k}$ *[CBSE2003C]*

Ans: $\lambda = -2$

(iv) $\vec{a} = 3\hat{i} + 2\hat{j} - 5\hat{k}$ and $\vec{b} = -5\hat{i} + \lambda\hat{k}$

Ans: $\lambda = -2$

5. *(i) If $\vec{a} = \hat{i} + 2\hat{j} - 3\hat{k}$ and $\vec{b} = 3\hat{i} - \hat{j} + 2\hat{k}$, show that $(\vec{a} + \vec{b})$ is perpendicular $(\vec{a} - \vec{b})$.*

[CBSE2002]

(ii) If $\vec{a} = (5\hat{i} - \hat{j} - 3\hat{k})$ and $\vec{b} = (\hat{i} + 3\hat{j} - 5\hat{k})$ then show that $(\vec{a} + \vec{b})$ and $(\vec{a} - \vec{b})$ are orthogonal.

[CBSE2004]

6. If $\vec{a} = (\hat{i} - \hat{j} + 7\hat{k})$ and $\vec{b} = (5\hat{i} - \hat{j} + \lambda\hat{k})$ then find the value of λ so that $(\vec{a} + \vec{b})$ and $(\vec{a} - \vec{b})$ are orthogonal vectors.   *[CBSE 2013]*

Ans: $\lambda = \pm 5$

7. Show that the vectors

$$\frac{1}{7}(2\hat{i} + 3\hat{j} + 6\hat{k}), \ \frac{1}{7}(3\hat{i} - 6\hat{j} + 2\hat{k}) \ and \ \frac{1}{7}(6\hat{i} + 2\hat{j} - 3\hat{k})$$

are mutually perpendicular unit vectors.

8. Write the projection of vector $(\hat{i} + \hat{j} + \hat{k})$ along the vector $\hat{j}$.   *[CBSE 2014]*

Ans: $\lambda = 1$

9. (i) Find the projection of $\vec{a}$ on $\vec{b}$ if $\vec{a} \cdot \vec{b} = 8$ and $\vec{b} = (2\hat{i} + 6\hat{j} + 3\hat{k})$.   *[CBSE 2009]*

Ans: $\dfrac{8}{7}$

(ii) Write the projection of the vector $(\hat{i} + \hat{j})$ on the vector $(\hat{i} - \hat{j})$.   *[CBSE 2011]*

Ans: 0

10. Find the angle between the vectors $\vec{a}$ and $\vec{b}$, when

(i) $\vec{a} = \hat{i} - 2\hat{j} + 3\hat{k}$ and $\vec{b} = 3\hat{i} - 2\hat{j} + \hat{k}$

Ans: $\cos^{-1}\left(\dfrac{5}{7}\right)$

(ii) $\vec{a} = 3\hat{i} + \hat{j} + 2\hat{k}$ and $\vec{b} = 2\hat{i} - 2\hat{j} + 4\hat{k}$

Ans: $\cos^{-1}\left(\sqrt{\dfrac{3}{7}}\right)$

11. **If** $\vec{a} = (\hat{i} + 2\hat{j} - 3\hat{k})$ *and* $\vec{b} = (3\hat{i} - \hat{j} + 2\hat{k})$ *then calculate the angle between* $(2\vec{a} + \vec{b})$ *and* $(\vec{a} + 2\vec{b})$.

Ans: $\cos^{-1}\left(\dfrac{31}{50}\right)$

12. **If** $\vec{a}$ *is a unit vector such that* $(\vec{x} - \vec{a}) \cdot (\vec{x} + \vec{a}) = 8$, *find* $|\vec{x}|$.

Ans: 3

13. **Show that the vector** $\vec{a} = (\hat{i} + \hat{j} + \hat{k})$ *is equally inclined to the coordinate axes.*

14. **Find a vector** $\vec{a}$ *of magnitude* $5\sqrt{2}$, *making an angle* $\pi/4$ *with x-axis,* $\pi/2$ *with y-axis and an acute angle* θ *with z-axis.* **[CBSE 2014]**

Ans: $5(\hat{i} + \hat{k})$

15. **Find the angle between** $(\vec{a} + \vec{b})$ *and* $(\vec{a} - \vec{b})$, *if* $\vec{a} = (2\hat{i} - \hat{j} + 3\hat{k})$ *and* $\vec{b} = (3\hat{i} + \hat{j} + 2\hat{k})$. **[CBSE 2006]**

Ans: $\dfrac{\pi}{2}$

16. **Express the vector** $\vec{a} = (6\hat{i} - 3\hat{j} - 6\hat{k})$ *as sum of two vectors such that one is parallel to the vector* $\vec{b} = (\hat{i} + \hat{j} + \hat{k})$ *and the other is perpendicular to* $\vec{b}$.

Ans: $\vec{a} = -(\hat{i} + \hat{j} + \hat{k}) + (7\hat{i} - 2\hat{j} - 5\hat{k})$

17. **The dot products of a vector with the vectors** $(\hat{i} + \hat{j} - 3\hat{k})$, $(\hat{i} + 3\hat{j} - 2\hat{k})$ *and* $(2\hat{i} + \hat{j} + 4\hat{k})$ *are* **0, 5** *and* **8** *respectively. Find the vector.* **[CBSE 2003]**

Ans: $(\hat{i} + 2\hat{j} + \hat{k})$

18. **If** $\overrightarrow{AB} = (3\hat{i} - \hat{j} + 2\hat{k})$ *and the coordinates of* A *are* $(0, -2, -1)$, *find the coordinates of* B.

Ans: $B(3, -3, 1)$

19. If $A(2,3,4)$, $B(5,4,-1)$, $C(3,6,2)$ and $D(1,2,0)$ be four points, show that $\overrightarrow{AB}$ is perpendicular to $\overrightarrow{CD}$.

20. Find the value of λ for which the vectors $(2\hat{i} + \lambda\hat{j} + 3\hat{k})$ and $(3\hat{i} + 2\hat{j} - 4\hat{k})$ are perpendicular to each other. *[CBSE 2010]*

Ans: $\lambda = 3$

21. Show that the vectors $\vec{a} = (3\hat{i} - 2\hat{j} + \hat{k})$, $\vec{b} = (\hat{i} - 3\hat{j} + 5\hat{k})$ and $\vec{c} = (2\hat{i} + \hat{j} - 4\hat{k})$ form a right-angled triangle. *[CBSE 2005]*

22. If the position vectors of the vertices A, B and C of a $\triangle ABC$ be $(1,2,3)$, $(-1,0,0)$ and $(0,1,2)$ respectively then find $\angle ABC$.

Ans: $\cos^{-1}\left(\dfrac{10}{\sqrt{102}}\right)$

23. If $\vec{a}$ and $\vec{b}$ are two unit vectors such that $|\vec{a} + \vec{b}| = \sqrt{3}$, find $(2\vec{a} - 5\vec{b}) \cdot (3\vec{a} + \vec{b})$.

Ans: $\dfrac{-11}{2}$

24. If $\vec{a}$ and $\vec{b}$ are two vectors such that $|\vec{a} + \vec{b}| = |\vec{a}|$ then prove that vector $(2\vec{a} + \vec{b})$ is perpendicular to vector $\vec{b}$. *[CBSE 2013]*

25. If $\vec{a} = (3\hat{i} - \hat{j})$ and $\vec{b} = (2\hat{i} + \hat{j} - 3\hat{k})$ then express $\vec{b}$ in the form $\vec{b} = (\vec{b}_1 + \vec{b}_2)$, where $\vec{b}_1 \parallel \vec{a}$ and $\vec{b}_2 \perp \vec{a}$. *[CBSE 2013C]*

Ans: $\vec{b}_1 = \left(\dfrac{3}{2}\hat{i} - \dfrac{1}{2}\hat{j}\right)$ and $\vec{b}_2 = \left(\dfrac{1}{2}\hat{i} + \dfrac{3}{2}\hat{j} - 3\hat{k}\right)$

26. Let $\vec{a}, \vec{b}$ and $\vec{c}$ be three vectors of magnitudes $3, 4$ and 5, respectively. If each one is perpendicular to the sum of the other two vectors, then prove that $|\vec{a} + \vec{b} + \vec{c}| = 5\sqrt{2}$.

[NCERT; Delhi 2013]

27. If $\vec{a} = (2\hat{i} - \hat{j} - 2\hat{k})$ and $\vec{b} = (7\hat{i} + 2\hat{j} - 3\hat{k})$, then express $\vec{b}$ in the form of $\vec{b} = \vec{b}_1 + \vec{b}_2$, where $\vec{b}_1$ is parallel to $\vec{a}$ and $\vec{b}_2$ is prependicular to $\vec{a}$. *[All India 2017]*

Ans: $\vec{b}_1 = 4\hat{i} - 2\hat{j} - 4\hat{k}$, $\vec{b}_2 = 3\hat{i} + 4\hat{j} + \hat{k}$

28. Prove that for any two vectors $\vec{a}$ and $\vec{b}$, $|\vec{a} + \vec{b}| \le |\vec{a}| + |\vec{a}|$.

29. Find the value of p for which the vectors $\vec{a} = 3\hat{i} + 2\hat{j} + 9\hat{k}$ and $\vec{b} = \hat{i} + p\hat{j} + 3\hat{k}$ are

(i) perpendicular. (ii) parallel.

Ans: (i) -15 (ii) $\dfrac{2}{3}$

30. **If $\vec{a}, \vec{b}$ and $\vec{c}$ are three mutually perpendicular vectors of equal magnitude, then find the angle between $\vec{a}$ and $(\vec{a} + \vec{b} + \vec{c})$.** *[Foreign 2011]*

Ans: $\cos^{-1}\left(\dfrac{1}{\sqrt{3}}\right)$

31. **If $\vec{a}, \vec{b}$ and $\vec{c}$ are three mutually perpendicular vectors of the same magnitude, then prove that $\vec{a} + \vec{b} + \vec{c}$ is equally inclined with the vectors $\vec{a}, \vec{b}$ and $\vec{c}$. Also, find the angle which $\vec{a} + \vec{b} + \vec{c}$ makes with $\vec{a}$ or $\vec{b}$ or $\vec{c}$.** *[Delhi 2017, 2013C, 2011]*

(i) VECTOR (OR CROSS) PRODUCT OF TWO VECTORS :

The vector product or cross product of two vectors A and is denoted by $A \times B$, and its resultant vector is perpendicular to the vectors A and B. The cross product is mostly used to determine the vector which is perpendicular to the plane surface spanned by two vectors, whereas the dot product is used to find the angle between two vectors or the length of the vector. The cross product of two vectors, say $A \times B$, is equal to another vector at right angles to both, and it happens in the three dimensions.

If θ is the angle between the given two vectors A and B, then the formula for the cross product of vecters is given by:

$$A \times B = |A||B|\sin\theta$$

or

$$\vec{A} \times \vec{B} = ||\vec{A}|| \, ||\vec{B}||\sin\theta \, \hat{n}.$$

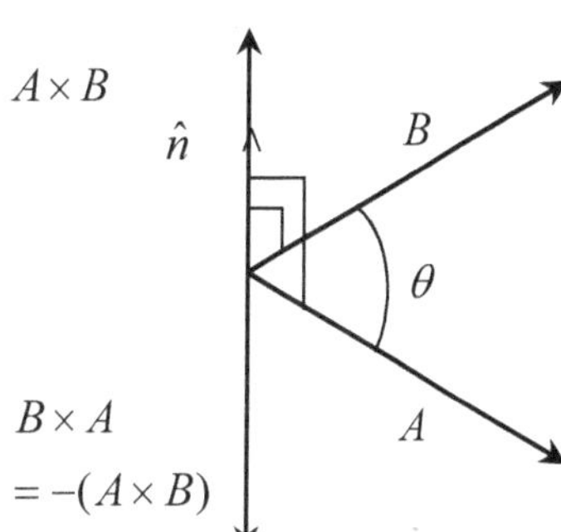

Here, $\vec{A}, \vec{B}$ are the two vectors and $|\vec{A}||, ||\vec{B}|$ are the magnitudes of given vectors. Also θ is the angle between two vectors and $\hat{n}$ is the unit vector perpendicular to the plane containing the given two vectors, in the direction given by the right-hand rule.

(ii) PROPERTIES OF VECTOR PRODUCT OF TWO VECTORS:

(*i*) Vector product is not commutative, for vectors $\vec{a}$ and $\vec{b}$, we have $(\vec{a} \times \vec{b}) = -(\vec{b} \times \vec{a})$.

(*ii*) Vector product is distributive over additions *i.e* for vectors $\vec{a}, \vec{b}$ and $\vec{c}$, we have

$$\vec{a} \times (\vec{b} + \vec{c}) = \vec{a} \times \vec{b} + \vec{a} \times \vec{c}$$

(*iii*) If m is any scalar and $\vec{a}$ and $\vec{b}$ be the two non-zero vectors, then

$$(m\vec{a}) \times \vec{b} = m(\vec{a} \times \vec{b}) = \vec{a} \times (m\vec{b})$$

(*iv*) If $\vec{a}$ and $\vec{b}$ be two non-zero vectors. Then, $\vec{a} \times \vec{b} = 0$ if $\vec{a}$ and $\vec{b}$ only if and are parallel to each other, *i.e.*

$$\vec{a} \times \vec{b} = \vec{0} \Leftrightarrow \vec{a} \parallel \vec{b}.$$

(*v*) If $\vec{a} \times \vec{a} = \vec{0}$, as $\theta = 0^0$ and $\vec{a} \times (-\vec{a}) = \vec{0}$, as $\theta = \pi$

(*vi*) If, $\theta = \dfrac{\pi}{2}$, then $\vec{a} \times \vec{b} = |\vec{a}| \, |\vec{b}|$

(*vii*) For mutually perpendicular unit vectors $\hat{i}, \hat{j}$ and $\hat{k}$,

$$\hat{i} \times \hat{i} = \hat{j} \times \hat{j} = \hat{k} \times \hat{k} = \vec{0}$$

and $\qquad \hat{i} \times \hat{j} = \hat{k}, \ \hat{j} \times \hat{k} = \hat{i}, \ \hat{k} \times \hat{i} = \hat{j};$

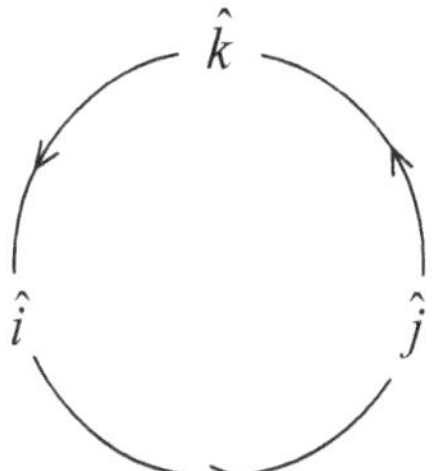

$$\hat{j} \times \hat{i} = -\hat{k}, \ \hat{k} \times \hat{j} = -\hat{i}, \ \hat{i} \times \hat{k} = -\hat{j}$$

($viii$) The angle between two non-zero vectors $\vec{a}$ and $\vec{b}$ in terms of vector products is given by

$$\sin\theta = \frac{|\vec{a} \times \vec{b}|}{|\vec{a}||\vec{b}|}$$

(ix) Vectors of magnitude λ normal to the plane of $\vec{a}$ and $\vec{b}$ are given as $\dfrac{\pm \lambda(\vec{a} \times \vec{b})}{|\vec{a} \times \vec{b}|}$.

(iii) VECTOR PROUCT OF TWO VECTORS IN COMPONENT FORM :

Suppose two vectors $\vec{a}$ and $\vec{b}$ are given in component form, say $\vec{a} = a_1\hat{i} + a_2\hat{j} + a_3\hat{k}$ and $\vec{b} = b_1\hat{i} + b_2\hat{j} + b_3\hat{k}$, then their vector product is given by

$$\vec{a} \times \vec{b} = \begin{vmatrix} \hat{i} & \hat{j} & \hat{k} \\ a_1 & a_2 & a_3 \\ b_1 & b_2 & b_3 \end{vmatrix}$$

EXAMPLE : *Find $\vec{a} \times \vec{b}$ if $\vec{a} = 2\hat{i} + \hat{k}$ and $\vec{b} = \hat{i} + \hat{j} + \hat{k}$*

SOLUTION : Given $\vec{a} = 2\hat{i} + 0\hat{j} + \hat{k}$

$$\vec{b} = \hat{i} + \hat{j} + \hat{k}$$

So, $\vec{a} \times \vec{b} = \begin{vmatrix} \hat{i} & \hat{j} & \hat{k} \\ 2 & 0 & 1 \\ 1 & 1 & 1 \end{vmatrix}$

$$= \hat{i}(0-1) - \hat{j}(2-1) + \hat{k}(2-0)$$

$$= -\hat{i} - \hat{j} + 2\hat{k}$$

EXAMPLE : *Given $\vec{a} = (\hat{i} + 3\hat{j} - 2\hat{k}) \times (-\hat{i} + 3\hat{k})$. Find the magnitude of $\vec{a}$.*

SOLUTION : Here, $\vec{a} = (\hat{i} + 3\hat{j} - 2\hat{k}) \times (-\hat{i} + 3\hat{k})$

$$\therefore \quad \vec{a} = \begin{vmatrix} \hat{i} & \hat{j} & \hat{k} \\ 1 & 3 & -2 \\ -1 & 0 & 3 \end{vmatrix}$$

$$= \hat{i}(9-0) - \hat{j}(3-2) + \hat{k}(0+3)$$

$$= 9\hat{i} - \hat{j} + 3\hat{k}$$

$$\therefore \quad |\vec{a}| = \sqrt{(9)^2 + (-1)^2 + (3)^2} = \sqrt{81+1+9} = \sqrt{91}$$

(iv) APPLICATIONS OF VECTOR PRODUCT OF TWO VECTORS:

Vector product of two vectors can be used to find the area of some geometrical figures which are given below.

(*i*) Area of a triangle : The area of tri-angle having adjacent sides $\vec{a}$ and $\vec{b}$ is given by

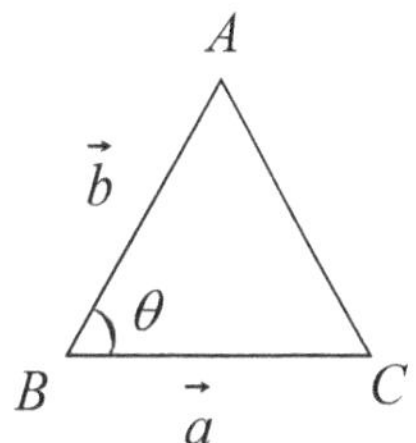

$$Area = \frac{1}{2}|\vec{a} \times \vec{b}|$$

(*ii*) Area of a parallelogram : The area of a parallelogram having diagonals $\vec{d_1}$ and $\vec{d_2}$ is given by

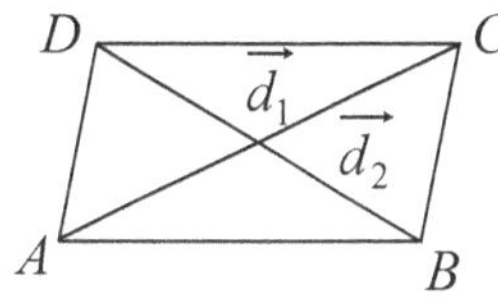

$$Area = \frac{1}{2}|\vec{d_1} \times \vec{d_2}|$$

(v) <u>SOLVED EXAMPLES</u>

EXAMPLE 1 : *If $\vec{a} = (3\hat{i} + \hat{j} - 4\hat{k})$ and $\vec{b} = (6\hat{i} + 5\hat{j} - 2\hat{k})$, find $(\vec{a} \times \vec{b})$ and $|\vec{a} \times \vec{b}|$.*

SOLUTION : We have

$$(\vec{a} \times \vec{b}) = \begin{vmatrix} \hat{i} & \hat{j} & \hat{k} \\ 3 & 1 & -4 \\ 6 & 5 & -2 \end{vmatrix}$$

$$= (-2 + 20)\,\hat{i} - (-6 + 24)\,\hat{j} + (15 - 6)\,\hat{k}$$

$$= (18\,\hat{i} - 18\,\hat{j} + 9\,\hat{k}).$$

$$|\vec{a} \times \vec{b}|^2 = \{(18)^2 + (-18)^2 + 9^2\} = 729$$

$$\Rightarrow |\vec{a} \times \vec{b}| = \sqrt{729} = 27.$$

EXAMPLE 2 : *By vector method find the area of the triangle whose vertices are (1, 1, 1), (2, 0, 1) and (3, − 2, 0).*

SOLUTION : Assume that the vertices of the triangle are $A(1,1,1), B(2,0,1)$ and $C(3,-2,0)$.

If $\hat{i}, \hat{j}$ and $\hat{k}$ are unit vectors along OX, OY and OZ respectively, then the position vectors of A, B and C with respect to O as origin are $\hat{i} + \hat{j} + \hat{k}$, $2\hat{i} + \hat{k}$ and $3\hat{i} - 2\hat{j}$ respectively.

$$\overrightarrow{AB} = (2\hat{i} + \hat{k}) - (\hat{i} + \hat{j} + \hat{k}) = \hat{i} - \hat{j}$$

$$\overrightarrow{AC} = (3\hat{i} - 2\hat{j}) - (\hat{i} + \hat{j} + \hat{k}) = 2\hat{i} - 3\hat{j} - \hat{k}$$

$$\overrightarrow{AB} \times \overrightarrow{AC} = \begin{vmatrix} \hat{i} & \hat{j} & \hat{k} \\ 1 & -1 & 0 \\ 2 & -3 & -1 \end{vmatrix}$$

$$= \hat{i}(1 - 0) - \hat{j}(-1 - 0) + \hat{k}(-3 + 2)$$

$$= \hat{i} + \hat{j} - \hat{k}$$

Hence, the area of the traingle ABC.

$$= \frac{1}{2}|\overrightarrow{AB} \times \overrightarrow{AC}| = \frac{1}{2}\sqrt{1^2 + 1^2 + (-1)^2} = \frac{\sqrt{3}}{2} \text{ squre units.}$$

EXAMPLE 3 : *If $\vec{a} = a_1\hat{i} + a_2\hat{j} + a_3\hat{k},\ \ \vec{b} = b_1\hat{i} + b_2\hat{j} + b_3\hat{k}$ and $\vec{c} = c_1\hat{i} + c_2\hat{j} + c_3\hat{k},$ prove that $\vec{a} \times (\vec{b} + \vec{c}) = \vec{a} \times \vec{b} + \vec{a} \times \vec{c}.$* **[NCERT]**

SOLUTION :   We have,

$$\vec{b} + \vec{c} = b_1\hat{i} + b_2\hat{j} + b_3\hat{j} + c_2\hat{j} + c_3\hat{j}$$

$$= (b_1 + c_1)\hat{i} + (b_2 + c_2)\hat{j} + (b_3 + c_3)\hat{k}$$

$$\therefore \quad \vec{a} \times (\vec{b} + \vec{c}) = \begin{vmatrix} \hat{i} & \hat{j} & \hat{k} \\ a_1 & a_2 & a_3 \\ b_1 + c_1 & b_2 + c_2 & b_3 + c_3 \end{vmatrix}$$

$$= \hat{i}[a_2(b_3 + c_3) - a_3(b_2 + c_2)] - \hat{j}[a_1(b_3 + c_3) - a_3(b_1 + c_1)]$$

$$+ \hat{k}[a_1(b_2 + c_2) - a_2(b_1 + c_1)]$$

$$= [\hat{i}(a_2 b_3 - a_3 b_2) - \hat{j}(a_1 b_3 - a_3 b_1) + \hat{k}(a_1 b_2 - a_2 b_1)] + [\hat{i}(a_2 c_3 - a_3 c_2)$$

$$- \hat{j}(a_1 c_3 - a_3 c_1) + \hat{k}(a_1 c_2 - a_2 c_1)]$$

$$= \begin{vmatrix} \hat{i} & \hat{j} & \hat{k} \\ a_1 & a_2 & a_3 \\ b_1 & b_2 & b_3 \end{vmatrix} + \begin{vmatrix} \hat{i} & \hat{j} & \hat{k} \\ a_1 & a_2 & a_3 \\ c_1 & c_2 & c_3 \end{vmatrix}$$

$$= \vec{a} \times \vec{b} + \vec{a} \times \vec{c} \quad \text{(Proved)}.$$

EXAMPLE 4 :   *Find the vector α which is perpendicular to both $4\hat{i} + 4\hat{j} - \hat{k}$ and $\hat{i} - 4\hat{j} + 5\hat{k}$ and which satisfies the relation $\alpha \cdot \beta = 21$ where $\beta = 3\hat{i} + 5\hat{j} - \hat{k}$.*

SOLUTION :   Let $\vec{a} = 4\hat{i} + 5\hat{j} - \hat{k}$ and $\vec{b} = \hat{i} - 4\hat{j} + 5\hat{k}$

$$\therefore \quad \vec{a} \times \vec{b} = \begin{vmatrix} \hat{i} & \hat{j} & \hat{k} \\ 4 & 5 & -1 \\ 1 & -4 & 5 \end{vmatrix}$$

$$= \hat{i}(25 - 4) - \hat{j}(20 + 1) + \hat{k}(-16 - 5)$$

$$= 21\hat{i} - 21\hat{j} - 21\hat{k}$$

By problem, the required vector α is perpendicular to both $\vec{a}$ and $\vec{b}$; again, the vector $\vec{a} \times \vec{b}$ is also perpendicular to both $\vec{a}$ and $\vec{b}$. Hence, the vector α

must be parallel to $\vec{a} \times \vec{b} = 21\hat{i} - 21\hat{j} - 21\hat{k}$.

Accordingly we assume, $\alpha = m(21\hat{i} - 21\hat{j} - 21\hat{k})$ where m is a scalar.

Again, $\vec{\alpha} \cdot \vec{\beta} = 21$

or, $\qquad (21m\hat{i} - 21m\hat{j} - 21m\hat{k}) \cdot (3\hat{i} + 5\hat{j} - \hat{k}) = 21$

or, $\qquad 63m - 105m + 21m = 21$

or, $\qquad -21m = 21 \qquad$ or, $m = -1$

Hence, $\alpha = -1(21\hat{i} - 21\hat{j} - 21\hat{k}) = -21\hat{i} + 21\hat{j} + 21\hat{k}$

EXAMPLE 5 :   *If $\vec{\alpha}, \vec{\beta}, \vec{\gamma}$ be unit vectors satisfying the condition $\vec{\alpha} + \vec{\beta} + \vec{\gamma} = \vec{0}$, show that*

$$\vec{\alpha} \cdot \vec{\beta} + \vec{\beta} \cdot \vec{\gamma} + \vec{\gamma} \cdot \vec{\alpha} = \frac{3}{2}. \qquad\qquad \textit{[NCERT]}$$

SOLUTION :   Since $\vec{\alpha} + \vec{\beta} + \vec{\gamma} = \vec{0}$

$\therefore \qquad \vec{\alpha} \cdot (\vec{\alpha} + \vec{\beta} + \vec{\gamma}) = \vec{\alpha} \cdot \vec{0} \quad$ or, $\quad \vec{\alpha} \cdot \vec{\alpha} + \vec{\alpha} \cdot \vec{\beta} + \vec{\alpha} \cdot \vec{\gamma} = 0$

or, $\qquad \vec{\alpha} \cdot \vec{\beta} + \vec{\gamma} \cdot \vec{\alpha} = -\vec{\alpha} \cdot \vec{\alpha} = -|\vec{\alpha}|^2 = -1 \qquad\qquad \text{...(1)}$

$$[\because \ \vec{\alpha} \cdot \vec{\gamma} = \vec{\gamma} \cdot \vec{\alpha} \ \text{and} \ |\vec{\alpha}| = 1]$$

Similarly, $\quad \vec{\beta} \cdot \vec{\gamma} + \vec{\alpha} \cdot \vec{\beta} = -1 \qquad\qquad\qquad\qquad \text{...(2)}$

and $\vec{\gamma} \cdot \vec{\alpha} + \vec{\beta} \cdot \vec{\gamma} = -1 \qquad\qquad\qquad\qquad\qquad \text{...(3)}$

Adding (1), (2) and (3) we get

$$2(\vec{\alpha} \cdot \vec{\beta} + \vec{\beta} \cdot \vec{\gamma} + \vec{\gamma} \cdot \vec{\alpha}) = -3$$

or, $\qquad \vec{\alpha} \cdot \vec{\beta} + \vec{\beta} \cdot \vec{\gamma} + \vec{\gamma} \cdot \vec{\alpha} = -\dfrac{3}{2}$

EXAMPLE 6 :   *If $\vec{a}, \vec{b}$ and $\vec{c}$ are three vectors such that $\vec{a} \neq \vec{0}$ and $\vec{a} \cdot \vec{b} = \vec{a} \cdot \vec{c}$, $\vec{a} \times \vec{b} = \vec{a} \times \vec{c}$, prove that $\vec{b} = \vec{c}$.*

SOLUTION :   We have, $\vec{a} \cdot \vec{b} = \vec{a} \cdot \vec{c}$ or, $\vec{a} \cdot (\vec{b} - \vec{c}) = 0 \qquad\qquad \text{...(1)}$

Again, $\vec{a} \times \vec{b} = \vec{a} \times \vec{c}$ or, $\vec{a} \times (\vec{b} - \vec{c}) = \vec{0} \qquad\qquad \text{...(2)}$

Since $\vec{a} \neq \vec{0}$, hence from (1) it follows that, either $\vec{b} - \vec{c} = \vec{0}$ *i.e.*, $\vec{b} = \vec{c}$

or, $\quad \vec{a}$ is perpendicular to $(\vec{b} - \vec{c})$ $\hfill ...(3)$

Again, from (2) it follows that,

either $\vec{b} - \vec{c} = \vec{0}$ *i.e.*, $\vec{b} = \vec{c}$

or, $\vec{a}$ and $(\vec{b} - \vec{c})$ are parallel. $\hfill ...(4)$

From (3) and (4) it readily follows that the conditions (1) and (2) hold simultaneously when $\vec{b} = \vec{c}$ (Proved).

EXAMPLE 7 :   *If $\vec{a} + \vec{b} + \vec{c} = \vec{0}$ and $|\vec{a}| = 3$, $|\vec{b}| = 5$ and $|\vec{c}| = 7$, find the angle between the vectors $\vec{a}$ and $\vec{b}$.*

SOLUTION :   Let θ be the required angle between the vectors $\vec{a}$ and $\vec{b}$. Then,

$$\cos\theta = \frac{\vec{a} \cdot \vec{b}}{|\vec{a}||\vec{b}|} \hspace{2cm} ...(1)$$

Now, $\vec{a} + \vec{b} + \vec{c} = \vec{0}$ or, $\vec{a} + \vec{b} = \vec{0} - \vec{c} = -\vec{c}$

or, $|\vec{a} + \vec{b}|^2 = |\vec{c}|^2$ or, $(\vec{a} + \vec{b}) \cdot (\vec{a} + \vec{b}) = |\vec{c}|^2$

or, $|\vec{a}|^2 + |\vec{b}|^2 + 2\vec{a} \cdot \vec{b} = |\vec{c}|^2$ $[\because \vec{b} \cdot \vec{a} = \vec{a} \cdot \vec{b}]$

or, $2(\vec{a} \cdot \vec{b}) = 7^2 - 3^2 = 15$ or, $\vec{a} \cdot \vec{b} = \frac{15}{2}$

Hence, from (1) we get,

$$\cos\theta = \frac{\dfrac{15}{2}}{3 \times 5} = \frac{1}{2} = \cos\frac{\pi}{3}$$

$$\therefore \;\; \theta = \frac{\pi}{3}$$

i.e., the angle between the vectors $\vec{a}$ and $\vec{b}$ is $\dfrac{\pi}{3}$.

EXAMPLE 8 :   *If $\vec{a} = 4\hat{i} - \hat{j} - 3\hat{k}$ and $\vec{b} = -2\hat{i} + \hat{j} + 2\hat{k}$ be two diagonals of a parallelogram, then find its area.*

SOLUTION :   We have,

$$|\vec{a} \times \vec{b}| = \text{modulus of} \begin{vmatrix} \hat{i} & \hat{j} & \hat{k} \\ 4 & -1 & -3 \\ -2 & 1 & 2 \end{vmatrix}$$

$$= |(-2+3)\hat{i} + (6-8)\hat{j} + (4-2)\hat{k}|$$

$$= |\hat{i} - 2\hat{j} + 2\hat{k}| = \sqrt{1^2 + (-2)^2 + 2^2}$$

$$= \sqrt{9} = 3$$

Therefore, the required area of the parallelgram

$$= \frac{1}{2}|\vec{a} \times \vec{b}| = \frac{1}{2} \times 3 = \frac{3}{2} \text{ square units}$$

EXAMPLE 9 :   *The dot products of a vector with the vectors $\hat{i} - 3\hat{k}$, $\hat{i} - 2\hat{k}$ and $\hat{i} + \hat{j} + 4\hat{k}$ are $0, 5, 8$ respectively. Find the vector.*

SOLUTION :   Let the required vector be $x\hat{i} + y\hat{j} + z\hat{k}$.

By question, $(x\hat{i} + y\hat{j} + z\hat{k}) \cdot (\hat{i} - 3\hat{k}) = 0$

or, $x - 3z = 0$ ...(1)

$$[\because \hat{i} \cdot \hat{i} = \hat{j} \cdot \hat{j} = \hat{k} \cdot \hat{k} = 1 \text{ and } \hat{i} \cdot \hat{j} = \hat{j} \cdot \hat{k} = \hat{k} \cdot \hat{i} = 0]$$

and $(x\hat{i} + y\hat{j} + z\hat{k}) \cdot (\hat{i} - 2\hat{k}) = 5$ or, $x - 2z = 5$ ...(2)

and $(x\hat{i} + y\hat{j} + z\hat{k}) \cdot (\hat{i} + \hat{j} + 4\hat{k}) = 8$ or, $x + y + 4z = 8$ ...(3)

Subtracting (1) from (2) we get,

     $z = 5$. Putting $z = 5$ in (1) we get, $x = 3z = 15$

Finally, putting $x = 15$ and $z = 5$ in (3) we get,

     $15 + y + 20 = 8$ or, $y = -27$

Therefore, the required vector is $x\hat{i} + y\hat{j} + z\hat{k} = 15\hat{i} - 27\hat{j} + 5\hat{k}$

EXAMPLE 10 :   *If $\vec{a} = \hat{i} + \hat{j} + \hat{k}$ and $\vec{b} = \hat{j} - \hat{k}$, find a vector $\vec{c}$ such that $\vec{a} \times \vec{c} = \vec{b}$ and $\vec{a} \cdot \vec{c} = 3.$*

SOLUTION :   Let $\vec{c} = x\hat{i} + y\hat{j} + z\hat{k}$; then

$$\vec{a} \times \vec{c} = \begin{vmatrix} \hat{i} & \hat{j} & \hat{k} \\ 1 & 1 & 1 \\ x & y & z \end{vmatrix} = (z-y)\hat{i} + (x-z)\hat{j} + (y-x)\hat{k}$$

By question, $\vec{a} \times \vec{c} = \vec{b}$

$\therefore \qquad (z-y)\hat{i} + (x-z)\hat{j} + (y-x)\hat{k} = \hat{j} - \hat{k}$

$\therefore \qquad z - y = 0$ or, $y = z$; $x - z = 1$

and $\qquad y - x = -1$ $\hfill ...(1)$

Again, $\vec{a} \cdot \vec{c} = 3 \qquad$ or, $(\hat{i} + \hat{j} + \hat{k}) \cdot (x\hat{i} + y\hat{j} + z\hat{k}) = 3$

or, $\qquad x + y + z = 3 \qquad$ or, $x + 2y = 3 \hfill [\because z = y]$

or, $\qquad y + 1 + 2y = 3 \hfill [\because \text{from}(1) \text{ we get, } x = y + 1]$

or, $\qquad 3y = 2 \qquad\qquad$ or, $y = \dfrac{2}{3} = z$ and $x = y + 1 = \dfrac{2}{3} + 1 = \dfrac{5}{3}$

Therefore, required $\vec{c} = x\hat{i} + y\hat{j} + z\hat{k} = \dfrac{5}{3}\hat{i} + \dfrac{2}{3}\hat{j} + \dfrac{2}{3}\hat{k}$

EXAMPLE 11 : *If $\vec{p}$ is a unit vector and $(\vec{x} - \vec{p}) \cdot (\vec{x} + \vec{p}) = 8$, then find $|\vec{x}|$.* *[NCERT]*

SOLUTION : We have, $(\vec{x} - \vec{p}) \cdot (\vec{x} + \vec{p}) = 8$

or, $\qquad \vec{x} \cdot \vec{x} + \vec{x} \cdot \vec{p} - \vec{p} \cdot \vec{x} - \vec{p} \cdot \vec{p} = 8$

or, $\qquad |\vec{x}|^2 - |\vec{p}|^2 = 8 \quad [\because \vec{x} \cdot \vec{p} = \vec{p} \cdot \vec{x}$ and $\vec{x} \cdot \vec{x} = |\vec{x}|^2]$

or, $\qquad |\vec{x}|^2 - 1^2 = 8 \quad [|\vec{p}| = 1 \text{ (given)}]$

or, $\qquad |\vec{x}|^2 = 9 = 3^2$

$\therefore \qquad |\vec{x}| = 3 \quad [\because |\vec{x}| \geq 0]$

EXAMPLE 12 : *If $\vec{a} = (\hat{i} - 2\hat{j} + 3\hat{k})$ and $\vec{b} = (2\hat{i} + 3\hat{j} - 5\hat{k})$ then find $(\vec{a} \times \vec{b})$ and verify that $(\vec{a} \times \vec{b})$ is perpendicular to each one of $\vec{a}$ and $\vec{b}$.*

SOLUTION : We have

$$(\vec{a} \times \vec{b}) = \begin{vmatrix} \hat{i} & \hat{j} & \hat{k} \\ 1 & -2 & 3 \\ 2 & 3 & -5 \end{vmatrix}$$

$$= (10 - 9)\hat{i} - (-5 - 6)\hat{j} + (3 + 4)\hat{k} = (\hat{i} + 11\hat{j} + 7\hat{k})$$

Now, $(\vec{a} \times \vec{b}) \cdot \vec{a} = (\hat{i} + 11\hat{j} + 7\hat{k}) \cdot (\hat{i} - 2\hat{j} + 3\hat{k})$

$\therefore \qquad (\vec{a} \times \vec{b}) \cdot \vec{a} = (1 - 22 + 21) = 0.$

$\therefore \qquad (\vec{a} \times \vec{b}) \perp \vec{a}$

And, $\quad (\vec{a} \times \vec{b}) \cdot \vec{b} = (\hat{i} + 11\hat{j} + 7\hat{k}) \cdot (2\hat{i} + 3\hat{j} - 5\hat{k})$

$$= (2 + 33 - 35) = 0$$

$\therefore \qquad (\vec{a} \times \vec{b}) \perp \vec{b}.$

EXAMPLE 13 : *If $\vec{a} = \hat{i} + \hat{j} + \hat{k}$ and $\vec{b} = \hat{j} - \hat{k}$, find a vector $\vec{c}$ such that $\vec{a} \times \vec{c} = \vec{b}$ and* $\vec{a} \cdot \vec{c} = 3.$ **[CBSE 2013]**

SOLUTION : Here $\vec{a} = \hat{i} + \hat{j} + \hat{k}$ and $\vec{b} = \hat{j} - \hat{k}$.

Let $\vec{c} = c_1\hat{i} + c_2\hat{j} + c_3\hat{k}$. Then,

$$\vec{a} \cdot \vec{c} = 3 \text{ and } \vec{a} \times \vec{c} = \vec{b}$$

$\Rightarrow \quad (\hat{i} + \hat{j} + \hat{k}) \cdot (c_1\hat{i} + c_2\hat{j} + c_3\hat{k}) = 3$

and $\quad (\hat{i} + \hat{j} + \hat{k}) \times (c_1\hat{i} + c_2\hat{j} + c_3\hat{k}) = (\hat{j} - \hat{k})$

$\Rightarrow \quad c_1 + c_2 + c_3 = 3 \qquad \qquad \qquad \text{...(1)}$

and $\quad \begin{vmatrix} \hat{i} & \hat{j} & \hat{k} \\ 1 & 1 & 1 \\ c_1 & c_2 & c_3 \end{vmatrix} = (\hat{j} - \hat{k}) \qquad \text{...(ii)}$

Now, (ii) gives: $(c_3 - c_2)\hat{i} - (c_3 - c_1)\hat{j} + (c_2 - c_1)\hat{k} = (\hat{j} - \hat{k})$

$\Rightarrow \quad c_3 - c_2 = 0, \; c_1 - c_3 = 1 \text{ and } c_2 - c_1 = -1$

$\Rightarrow \quad c_3 = c_2 \text{ and } c_1 - c_2 = 1.$

Putting $c_3 = c_2$ in (1), we get $c_1 + 2c_2 = 3.$

On solving $c_1 + 2c_2 = 3$ and $c_1 - c_2 = 1$, we get $c_2 = \dfrac{2}{3}$ and $c_1 = \dfrac{5}{3}$.

$\therefore \qquad c_1 = \dfrac{5}{3},\ c_2 = \dfrac{2}{3}$ and $c_3 = \dfrac{2}{3}$.

Hence, $\vec{c} = \dfrac{5}{3}\hat{i} + \dfrac{2}{3}\hat{j} + \dfrac{2}{3}\hat{k} \ \Rightarrow\ \vec{c} = \dfrac{1}{3}(5\hat{i} + 2\hat{j} + 2\hat{k}).$

EXAMPLE 14 : *Find the area of the triangle whose vertices are $P(-1, 2, -1)$, $Q(3, -1, 2)$ and $R(2, 3, -1)$.*

SOLUTION : Let $\vec{a}, \vec{b}$ and $\vec{c}$ be the position vectors of points P, Q and R, respectively.

Then, $\vec{a} = -\hat{i} + 2\hat{j} - \hat{k},\ \vec{b} = 3\hat{i} - \hat{j} + 2\hat{k}$ and $\vec{c} = 2\hat{i} + 3\hat{j} - \hat{k}$

Clearly, the area of $\Delta\, PQR = \dfrac{1}{2}\,|\overrightarrow{PQ} \times \overrightarrow{PR}|$

Now, $\overrightarrow{PQ}$ = Position vector of Q – Position vector of P

$\qquad = \vec{b} - \vec{a} = (3\hat{i} - \hat{j} + 2\hat{k}) - (-\hat{i} + 2\hat{j} - \hat{k})$

$\qquad = 4\hat{i} - 3\hat{j} + 3\hat{k}$

$\overrightarrow{PR}$ = Position vector of R – Position vector of P

$\qquad = \vec{c} - \vec{a} = (2\hat{i} + 3\hat{j} - \hat{k}) - (-\hat{i} + 2\hat{j} - \hat{k}) = 3\hat{i} + \hat{j}$

$\therefore \qquad \overrightarrow{PQ} \times \overrightarrow{PR} = \begin{vmatrix} \hat{i} & \hat{j} & \hat{k} \\ 4 & -3 & 3 \\ 3 & 1 & 0 \end{vmatrix} = (0-3)\hat{i} - (0-9)\hat{j} + (4+9)\hat{k}$

$\qquad\qquad = -3\hat{i} + 9\hat{j} + 13\hat{k}$

and $\quad |\overrightarrow{PQ} \times \overrightarrow{PR}| = \sqrt{(-3)^2 + (9)^2 + (13)^2}$

$\qquad\qquad = \sqrt{9 + 81 + 169} = \sqrt{259}$

So, area of $\Delta\, PQR = \dfrac{1}{2}\,|\overrightarrow{PQ} \times \overrightarrow{PR}|\, \dfrac{1}{2}\sqrt{259}$

EXAMPLE 15 : *If $\vec{a} = 2\hat{i} - 3\hat{j} + \hat{k},\ \vec{b} = -\hat{i} + \hat{k}$ and $\vec{c} = 2\hat{j} - \hat{k}$ are three vectors, then find* *the area of the parallelogram having diagonals $(\vec{a}+\vec{b})$ and $(\vec{b}+\vec{c})$.*

[Delhi 2014C]

SOLUTION : We have, $\vec{a}=2\hat{i}-3\hat{j}+\hat{k}$, $\vec{b}=-\hat{i}+\hat{k}$ and $\vec{c}=2\hat{j}-\hat{k}$

Now, $\vec{a}+\vec{b}=(2\hat{i}-3\hat{j}+\hat{k})+(-\hat{i}+\hat{k})=\hat{i}-3\hat{j}+2\hat{k}$

and $\vec{b}+\vec{c}=(-\hat{i}+\hat{k})+(2\hat{j}-\hat{k})=-\hat{i}+2\hat{j}$

$$\therefore \quad (\vec{a}+\vec{b})\times(\vec{b}+\vec{c})=\begin{vmatrix} \hat{i} & \hat{j} & \hat{k} \\ 1 & -3 & 2 \\ -1 & 2 & 0 \end{vmatrix}$$

$$=\hat{i}(0-4)-\hat{j}(0+2)+\hat{k}(2-3)$$

$$=-4\hat{i}-2\hat{j}-\hat{k}$$

Hence, the area of parallelogram having diagonals

$(\vec{a}+\vec{b})$ and $(\vec{b}+\vec{c})$

$$=\frac{|(\vec{a}+\vec{b})\times(\vec{b}+\vec{c})|}{2}=\frac{|4\hat{i}-2\hat{j}-\hat{k}|}{2}$$

$$=\frac{\sqrt{16+4+1}}{2}=\frac{\sqrt{21}}{2}=\frac{1}{2}\sqrt{21} \text{ sq units}$$

EXAMPLE 16 : *Let $\vec{a}=(\hat{i}+4\hat{j}+2\hat{k})$, $\vec{b}=(3\hat{i}-2\hat{j}+7\hat{k})$ and $\vec{c}=(2\hat{i}-\hat{j}+4\hat{k})$. Find a vector $\vec{d}$ which is perpendicular to both $\vec{a}$ and $\vec{b}$ such that $\vec{c}\cdot\vec{d}=18$.*

[CBSE 2010]

SOLUTION : Since $\vec{d}$ is perpendicular to both $\vec{a}$ and $\vec{b}$, it follows that $\vec{d}$ is parallel to $(\vec{a}\times\vec{b})$.

$$\text{Now, } (\vec{a}\times\vec{b})=\begin{vmatrix} \hat{i} & \hat{j} & \hat{k} \\ 1 & 4 & 2 \\ 3 & -2 & 7 \end{vmatrix}$$

$$=(28+4)\hat{i}-(7-6)\hat{j}+(-2-12)\hat{k}=(32\hat{i}-\hat{j}-14\hat{k})$$

Since $\vec{d}$ is parallel to $(\vec{a}\times\vec{b})$, we have $\vec{d}=\lambda(\vec{a}\times\vec{b})$ for some scalar λ.

$$\therefore \qquad \vec{d} = \lambda(32\hat{i} - \hat{j} - 14\hat{k}) = (32\hat{i} - \lambda\,\hat{j} - 14\lambda\,\hat{k}) \qquad \qquad \text{...(i)}$$

Since $\vec{c} \cdot \vec{d} = 18$, we have

$$(2\hat{i} - \hat{j} + 4\hat{k}) \cdot (32\lambda\,\hat{i} - \lambda\,\hat{j} - 14\lambda\,\hat{k}) = 18$$

$$\Rightarrow \qquad (64\lambda + \lambda - 56\lambda) = 18 \Rightarrow 9\lambda = 18 \Rightarrow \lambda = 2.$$

Hence, $\vec{d} = (64\hat{i} - 2\hat{j} - 28\hat{k})$ $\qquad\qquad$ [putting $\lambda = 2$ in (i)]

EXAMPLE 17 : *Find a vector of magnitude* **5** *units, perpendicular to each of the vectors* $(\vec{a} + \vec{b})$ *and* $(\vec{a} - \vec{b})$, *where* $\vec{a} = (\hat{i} + \hat{j} + \hat{k})$ *and* $\vec{b} = (\hat{i} + 2\hat{j} + 3\hat{k})$.

[CBSE 2008C]

SOLUTION : We have

$$(\vec{a} + \vec{b}) = (\hat{i} + \hat{j} + \hat{k}) + (\hat{i} + 2\hat{j} + 3\hat{k}) = (2\hat{i} + 3\hat{j} + 4\hat{k}) \text{ and}$$

$$(\vec{a} - \vec{b}) = (\hat{i} + \hat{j} + \hat{k}) - (\hat{i} + 2\hat{j} + 3\hat{k}) = (-\hat{j} - 2\hat{k})$$

$$\therefore \qquad (\vec{a} + \vec{b}) \times (\vec{a} - \vec{b}) = \begin{vmatrix} \hat{i} & \hat{j} & \hat{k} \\ 2 & 3 & 4 \\ 0 & -1 & -2 \end{vmatrix}$$

$$= (-6 + 4)\hat{i} - (-4 - 0)\hat{j} + (-2 - 0)\hat{k}$$

$$= (-2\hat{i} + 4\hat{j} - 2\hat{k})$$

$$\therefore \qquad |(\vec{a} + \vec{b}) \times (\vec{a} - \vec{b})| = \sqrt{(-2)^2 + 4^2 + (-2)^2} = \sqrt{24} = 2\sqrt{6}$$

So, the vectors of magnitude 5 units and perpendicular to each of the vectors $(\vec{a} + \vec{b})$ and $(\vec{a} - \vec{b})$ are:

$$\pm \frac{5\{(\vec{a} + \vec{b}) \times (\vec{a} - \vec{b})\}}{|(\vec{a} + \vec{b}) \times (\vec{a} - \vec{b})|} = \pm \frac{5(-2\hat{i} + 4\hat{j} - 2\hat{k})}{2\sqrt{6}} = \pm \frac{5(-\hat{i} + 2\hat{j} - \hat{k})}{\sqrt{6}}$$

EXAMPLE 18 : *If* $\vec{a} = 4\hat{i} + 3\hat{j} + 2\hat{k}$ *and* $\vec{b} = 3\hat{i} + 2\hat{k}$, *find* $|\vec{b} \times 2\vec{a}|$.

SOLUTION : We have

$$\vec{b} = (3\hat{i} + 2\hat{k}) \text{ and } 2\vec{a} = (8\hat{i} + 6\hat{j} + 4\hat{k})$$

$$\therefore \quad (\vec{b} \times 2\vec{a}) = \begin{vmatrix} \hat{i} & \hat{j} & \hat{k} \\ 3 & 0 & 2 \\ 8 & 6 & 4 \end{vmatrix}$$

$$= (0-12)\hat{i} + (16-12)\hat{j} + (18-0)\hat{k}$$

$$= (-12\hat{i} + 4\hat{j} + 18\hat{k})$$

$$\therefore \quad |\vec{b} \times 2\vec{a}| = |-12\hat{i} + 4\hat{j} + 18\hat{k}|$$

$$= \sqrt{(-12)^2 + 4^2 + (18)^2} = \sqrt{484} = 22$$

Hence, $|\vec{b} \times 2\vec{a}| = 22$

EXAMPLE 19 :   *If $|\vec{a}| = \sqrt{26}, |\vec{b}| = 7$ and $|\vec{a} \times \vec{b}| = 35$, find $\vec{a} \cdot \vec{b}$.*

SOLUTION :   Given that $|\vec{a}| = \sqrt{26}$ and $|\vec{b}| = 7$, and $|\vec{a} \times \vec{b}| = 35$

$$\therefore \quad |\vec{a} \times \vec{b}| = 35 \Rightarrow |\vec{a}||\vec{b}| \sin\theta = 35$$

$$\Rightarrow \sin\theta = \frac{35}{|\vec{a}||\vec{b}|} = \frac{35}{(\sqrt{26}) \times 7} = \frac{5}{\sqrt{26}}$$

Now, $\cos\theta = \sqrt{1 - \sin^2\theta} = \sqrt{1 - \dfrac{25}{26}} = \dfrac{1}{\sqrt{26}}$

$$\therefore \quad \vec{a} \cdot \vec{b} = |\vec{a}||\vec{b}| \cos\theta = \left(\sqrt{26} \times 7 \times \frac{1}{\sqrt{26}} \right) = 7$$

Hence, $\vec{a} \cdot \vec{b} = 7$.

EXAMPLE 20 :   *If $|\vec{a}| = 2, |\vec{b}| = 7$ and $(\vec{a} \times \vec{b}) = (3\hat{i} + 2\hat{j} + 6\hat{k})$, find the angle between $\vec{a}$ and $\vec{b}$.*

SOLUTION :   Let θ be the angle between $\vec{a}$ and $\vec{b}$. Then,

$$\vec{a} \times \vec{b} = 3\hat{i} + 2\hat{j} + 6\hat{k}$$

$$\Rightarrow \quad |\vec{a} \times \vec{b}| = \sqrt{3^2 + 2^2 + 6^2} = \sqrt{49} = 7$$

$$\Rightarrow \quad |\vec{a}||\vec{b}| \sin\theta = 7 \qquad\qquad [\because \ |\vec{a} \times \vec{b}| = |\vec{a}||\vec{b}| \sin\theta \ ]$$

$$\Rightarrow \quad \sin\theta = \frac{7}{|\vec{a}||\vec{b}|} = \frac{7}{(2\times 7)} = \frac{1}{2} \Rightarrow \theta = \frac{\pi}{6}$$

Hence, the required angle between $\vec{a}$ and $\vec{b}$ is $\frac{\pi}{6}$.

EXAMPLE 21 : *Find the sine of the angle between the vectors $\vec{a} = (2\hat{i} - \hat{j} + 3\hat{k})$ and $\vec{b} = (\hat{i} + 3\hat{j} + 2\hat{k})$.*

SOLUTION : We have

$$(\vec{a}\times\vec{b}) = \begin{vmatrix} \hat{i} & \hat{j} & \hat{k} \\ 2 & -1 & 3 \\ 1 & 3 & 2 \end{vmatrix}$$

$$= (-2 - 9)\hat{i} - (4 - 3)\hat{j} + (6 + 1)\hat{k}$$

$$= (-11\hat{i} - \hat{j} + 7\hat{k})$$

$$|\vec{a}\times\vec{b}| = \sqrt{(-11)^2 + (-1)^2 + 7^2} = \sqrt{171} = 3\sqrt{19}$$

$$|\vec{a}| = \sqrt{2^2 + (-1)^2 + 3^2} = \sqrt{14}$$

$$|\vec{b}| = \sqrt{1^2 + (3)^2 + 2^2} = \sqrt{14}$$

Let θ be the angle between $\vec{a}$ and $\vec{b}$. Then,

$$\sin\theta = \frac{|\vec{a}\times\vec{b}|}{|\vec{a}||\vec{b}|} = \frac{3\sqrt{19}}{(\sqrt{14})(\sqrt{14})} = \frac{3}{14}\sqrt{19}.$$

EXAMPLE 22 : *If the vectors $\vec{a}$ and $\vec{b}$ are such that $|\vec{a}| = 3, |\vec{b}| = \frac{2}{3}$ and $\vec{a}\times\vec{b}$ is a unit vector then write the angle between $\vec{a}$ and $\vec{b}$.* **[CBSE 2014]**

SOLUTION : Let θ be the angle between $\vec{a}$ and $\vec{b}$. Then,

$$|\vec{a}\times\vec{b}| = 1 \Rightarrow |\vec{a}||\vec{b}|\sin\theta = 1 \Rightarrow \left(3\times\frac{2}{3}\right)\sin\theta = 1$$

$$\Rightarrow \sin\theta = \frac{1}{2} \Rightarrow \theta = 30^0$$

Hence, the angle between $\vec{a}$ and $\vec{b}$ is 30^0

EXAMPLE 23 : *Find the area of the parallelogram whose adjacent sides are represented by the vectors $(3\hat{i} + \hat{j} - 2\hat{k})$ and $(\hat{i} - 3\hat{j} + 4\hat{k})$.*

SOLUTION : Let $\vec{a} = (3\hat{i} + \hat{j} - 2\hat{k})$ and $\vec{b} = (\hat{i} - 3\hat{j} + 4\hat{k})$

Then, vector area of the $||$gm is $(\vec{a} \times \vec{b})$.

$$\text{Now, } (\vec{a} \times \vec{b}) = \begin{vmatrix} \hat{i} & \hat{j} & \hat{k} \\ 3 & 1 & -2 \\ 1 & -3 & 4 \end{vmatrix}$$

$$= (4-6)\hat{i} - (12+2)\hat{j} + (-9-1)\hat{k}$$

$$= (-2\hat{i} - 14\hat{j} - 10\hat{k})$$

Required area $= |\vec{a} \times \vec{b}|$

$$= \sqrt{(-2)^2 + (-14)^2 + (-10)^2} \text{ sq untis}$$

$$= \sqrt{300} \text{ sq units}$$

$$= 10\sqrt{3} \text{ sq units}$$

EXAMPLE 24 : *Find the area of the parallelogram whose diagonals are represented by the vectors $\vec{d_1} = (2\hat{i} - \hat{j} + \hat{k})$ and $\vec{d_2} = (3\hat{i} + 4\hat{j} - \hat{k})$.*

SOLUTION : Given that $\vec{d_1} = (2\hat{i} - \hat{j} + \hat{k})$ and $\vec{d_2} = (3\hat{i} + 4\hat{j} - \hat{k})$

Vector area of the $||$gm is $\dfrac{1}{2}(\vec{d_1} \times \vec{d_2})$.

$$\text{Now, } (\vec{d_1} \times \vec{d_2}) = \begin{vmatrix} \hat{i} & \hat{j} & \hat{k} \\ 2 & -1 & 1 \\ 3 & 4 & -1 \end{vmatrix}$$

$$= (1-4)\hat{i} - (-2-3)\hat{j} + (8+3)\hat{k}$$

$$= (-3\hat{i} + 5\hat{j} + 11\hat{k})$$

Required area $= \dfrac{1}{2}|\vec{d_1} \times \vec{d_2}|$

$$= \dfrac{1}{2}\sqrt{(-3)^2 + 5^2 + (11)^2} \text{ sq units}$$

$$= \dfrac{1}{2}\sqrt{155} \text{ sq units.}$$

EXAMPLE 25 : *Using vectors find the area of $\triangle ABC$ whose vertics are $A(1,2,3)$, $B(2,-1,4)$ and $C(4,5,-1)$.* *[CBSE 2013]*

SOLUTION : We have

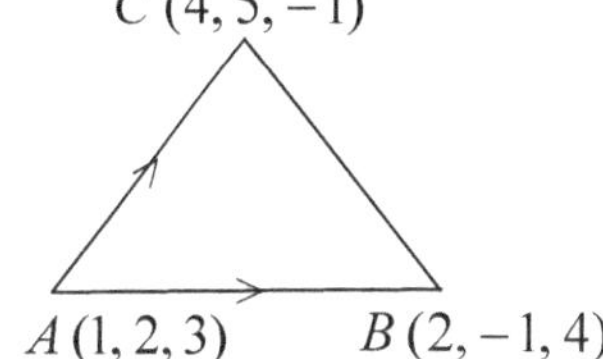

Position vector of $A = (\hat{i} + 2\hat{j} + 3\hat{k})$,

Position vector of $B = (2\hat{i} - \hat{j} + 4\hat{k})$ and

Position vector of $C = (4\hat{i} + 5\hat{j} - \hat{k})$

$\therefore \quad \overrightarrow{AB} = $ (Position vector of B) $-$ (Position vector of A)

$$= (2\hat{i} - \hat{j} + 4\hat{k}) - (\hat{i} + 2\hat{j} + 3\hat{k}) = (\hat{i} - 3\hat{j} + \hat{k})$$

$\overrightarrow{AC} = $ (Position vector of C) $-$ (Position vector of A)

$$= (4\hat{i} + 5\hat{j} - \hat{k}) - (\hat{i} + 2\hat{j} + 3\hat{k}) = (3\hat{i} + 3\hat{j} - 4\hat{k})$$

$\therefore \quad$ area of $\triangle ABC = \left|\dfrac{1}{2}(\overrightarrow{AB} \times \overrightarrow{AC})\right|$

Now, $\quad \overrightarrow{AB} \times \overrightarrow{AC} = \begin{vmatrix} \hat{i} & \hat{j} & \hat{k} \\ 1 & -3 & 1 \\ 3 & 3 & -4 \end{vmatrix}$

$$= (12 - 3)\hat{i} - (-4 - 3)\hat{j} + (3 + 9)\hat{k}$$

$$= (9\hat{i} + 7\hat{j} + 12\hat{k})$$

$\therefore \quad$ area of $\triangle ABC = \dfrac{1}{2}|\overrightarrow{AB} \times \overrightarrow{AC}|$

$$= \dfrac{1}{2}|(9\hat{i} + 7\hat{j} + 12\hat{k})|$$

$$= \frac{1}{2}\sqrt{(9)^2 + 7^2 + (12)^2}$$

$$= \frac{1}{2}\sqrt{(81 + 49 + 144)}$$

$$= \frac{1}{2}\sqrt{274} \text{ sq units.}$$

Hence, the area of $\triangle ABC$ is $\frac{1}{2}\sqrt{274}$ sq units.

EXAMPLE 26 : *Show that the points whose position vectors are* $(5\hat{i} + 6\hat{j} + 7\hat{k})$, $(7\hat{i} - 8\hat{j} + 9\hat{k})$ *and* $(3\hat{i} + 20\hat{j} + 5\hat{k})$ *are collinear.*

SOLUTION : Let the given points be A, B, and C respectively. Then,

$\overrightarrow{AB} = $ (Position vector of B) $-$ (Position vector of A)

$$= (7\hat{i} - 8\hat{j} + 9\hat{k}) - (5\hat{i} + 6\hat{j} + 7\hat{k})$$

$$= (2\hat{i} - 14\hat{j} + 2\hat{k})$$

And, $\overrightarrow{AC} = $ (Position vector of C) $-$ (Position vector of A)

$$= (3\hat{i} + 20\hat{j} + 5\hat{k}) - (5\hat{i} + 6\hat{j} + 7\hat{k})$$

$$= (-2\hat{i} + 14\hat{j} - 2\hat{k})$$

$$\therefore \quad (\overrightarrow{AB} \times \overrightarrow{AC}) = \begin{vmatrix} \hat{i} & \hat{j} & \hat{k} \\ 2 & -14 & 2 \\ -2 & 14 & -2 \end{vmatrix}$$

$$= 2 \times (-2)\begin{vmatrix} \hat{i} & \hat{j} & \hat{k} \\ 1 & -7 & 1 \\ 1 & -7 & 1 \end{vmatrix} = (-4) \times \vec{0} = \vec{0}$$

$$[\because R_2 \text{ and } R_3 \text{ are identical}]$$

So, $\overrightarrow{AB}$ and $\overrightarrow{AC}$ are parallel vectors, having a common end point, A. Hence, the given points A, B and C are collinear.

EXAMPLE 27 : *Prove that $(\vec{a} - \vec{b}) \times (\vec{a} + \vec{b}) = 2(\vec{a} \times \vec{b})$.*

SOLUTION : We have,

$$(\vec{a} - \vec{b}) \times (\vec{a} + \vec{b})$$

$$= \vec{a} \times \vec{a} + \vec{a} \times \vec{b} - \vec{b} \times \vec{a} - \vec{b} \times \vec{b} \qquad \text{[by the distributive law]}$$

$$= \vec{a} \times \vec{b} - \vec{b} \times \vec{a} \qquad [\because \ \vec{a} \times \vec{a} = \vec{0} \text{ and } \vec{b} \times \vec{b} = \vec{0}]$$

$$= (\vec{a} \times \vec{b}) + (\vec{a} \times \vec{b}) \qquad [\because \ -\vec{b} \times \vec{a} = (\vec{a} \times \vec{b})]$$

$$= 2(\vec{a} \times \vec{b}).$$

Hence, $(\vec{a} - \vec{b}) \times (\vec{a} + \vec{b}) = 2(\vec{a} \times \vec{b})$.

EXAMPLE 28 : *If $\vec{a} \times \vec{b} = \vec{c} \times \vec{d}$ and $\vec{a} \times \vec{c} = \vec{b} \times \vec{d}$, show that $(\vec{a} - \vec{d})$ is parallel to $(\vec{b} - \vec{c})$, it being given that $a \ne d$ and $b \ne c$.* *[CBSE 2009]*

SOLUTION : $\vec{a} \times \vec{b} = \vec{c} \times \vec{d}$, and $\vec{a} \times \vec{c} = \vec{b} \times \vec{d}$

$$\Rightarrow \quad \vec{a} \times \vec{b} - \vec{a} \times \vec{c} = \vec{c} \times \vec{d} - \vec{b} \times \vec{d}$$

$$\Rightarrow \quad \vec{a} \times \vec{b} - \vec{a} \times \vec{c} + \vec{b} \times \vec{d} - \vec{c} \times \vec{d} = \vec{0}$$

$$\Rightarrow \quad \vec{a} \times (\vec{b} - \vec{c}) + (\vec{b} - \vec{c}) \times \vec{d} = \vec{0}$$

$$\Rightarrow \quad \vec{a} \times (\vec{b} - \vec{c}) - \vec{d} \times (\vec{b} - \vec{c}) = \vec{0}$$

$$\Rightarrow \quad (\vec{a} - \vec{d}) \times (\vec{b} - \vec{c}) = \vec{0}$$

$$\Rightarrow \quad (\vec{a} - \vec{d}) || (\vec{b} - \vec{c}).$$

Hence, $(\vec{a} - \vec{d})$ is parallel to $(\vec{b} - \vec{c})$.

EXAMPLE 29 : *If $\vec{a} + \vec{b} + \vec{c} = \vec{0}$, prove that $(\vec{a} \times \vec{b}) = (\vec{b} \times \vec{c}) = (\vec{c} \times \vec{a})$.* *[CBSE 2001, '04C]*

SOLUTION : $\vec{a} + \vec{b} + \vec{c} = \vec{0}$

$$\Rightarrow \quad \vec{a} + \vec{b} = -\vec{c}$$

$$\Rightarrow \quad (\vec{a} + \vec{b}) \times \vec{b} = (-\vec{c}) \times \vec{b}$$

$$\Rightarrow \quad (\vec{a} \times \vec{b}) + (\vec{b} \times \vec{b}) = (-\vec{c}) \times \vec{b} \qquad \text{[by the distributive law]}$$

$$\Rightarrow \quad (\vec{a} \times \vec{b}) + \vec{0} = (\vec{b} \times \vec{c})$$

$$[\because \vec{b} \times \vec{b} = \vec{0} \text{ and } (-\vec{c}) \times \vec{b} = \vec{b} \times \vec{c}]$$

$$\Rightarrow \quad \vec{a} \times \vec{b} = \vec{b} \times \vec{c} \qquad \qquad \dots(i)$$

Also, $\qquad \vec{a} + \vec{b} + \vec{c} = \vec{0}$

$$\Rightarrow \quad \vec{b} + \vec{c} = -\vec{a}$$

$$\Rightarrow \quad (\vec{b} + \vec{c}) \times \vec{c} = (-\vec{a}) \times \vec{c}$$

$$\Rightarrow \quad (\vec{b} \times \vec{c}) + (\vec{c} \times \vec{c}) = (-\vec{a}) \times \vec{c} \qquad \text{[by the distributive law]}$$

$$\Rightarrow \quad (\vec{b} \times \vec{c}) + \vec{0} = \vec{c} \times \vec{a} \qquad [\because \vec{c} \times \vec{c} = \vec{0} \text{ and } (-\vec{a}) \times \vec{c} = \vec{c} \times \vec{a}]$$

$$\Rightarrow \quad \vec{b} \times \vec{c} = \vec{c} \times \vec{a} \qquad \qquad \dots(ii)$$

From (i) and (ii), we get $\vec{a} \times \vec{b} = \vec{b} \times \vec{c} = \vec{c} \times \vec{a}$.

(vi) EXERCISE

1. If θ is the angle between two vectors $\hat{i} - 2\hat{j} + 3\hat{k}$ and $3\hat{i} - 2\hat{j} + \hat{k}$, find θ. *[CBSE 2018]*

Ans: $\dfrac{2\sqrt{6}}{7}$

2. Find λ and μ, if $(2\hat{i} + 6\hat{j} + 27\hat{k}) \times (\hat{i} + \lambda\,\hat{j} + \mu\,\hat{k}) = \vec{0}$. *[NCERT]*

Ans: $\lambda = 3$ *and* $\mu = \dfrac{27}{2}$

3. Find λ and μ, if $(\hat{i} + 3\hat{j} + 9\hat{k}) \times (3\hat{i} - \lambda\,\hat{j} + \mu\,\hat{k}) = \vec{0}$. *[All India 2016]*

Ans: $\lambda = -9$, $\mu = 27$

4. If $|\vec{a}| = 8$, $|\vec{b}| = 3$ and $|\vec{a} \times \vec{b}| = 12$, then find the angle between $\vec{a}$ and $\vec{b}$. *[All India 2014C]*

Ans: $\dfrac{\pi}{6}$

5. Find the angle between two vectors $\vec{a}$ and $\vec{b}$ having the same length $\sqrt{2}$ and their vector product is $-\hat{i} - \hat{j} + \hat{k}$. *[All India 2016C]*

Ans: $\dfrac{\pi}{3}$

6. Evaluate $(2\vec{a} + 3\vec{b}) \times (5\vec{a} + 7\vec{b})$.

Ans: $-(\vec{a} \times \vec{b})$

7. Find λ if $(2\hat{i} + 6\hat{j} + 14\hat{k}) \times (\hat{i} - \lambda\,\hat{j} + 7\hat{k}) = \vec{0}$.　　　　*[CBSE 2010]*

Ans: $\lambda = -3$

8. If $\vec{a} = (-3\hat{i} + 4\hat{j} - 7\hat{k})$ and $\vec{b} = (6\hat{i} + 2\hat{j} - 3\hat{k})$, find $(\vec{a} \times \vec{b})$.

Ans: $(2\hat{i} - 51\hat{j} - 30\hat{k})$

9. Find the value of:

   (i) $(\hat{i} \times \hat{j}) + \hat{i} \cdot \hat{j}$　　　*(ii) $(\hat{k} \times \hat{j}) \cdot \hat{i} + \hat{j} \cdot \hat{k}$*　　　*[CBSE 2012]*

   (iii) $\hat{i} \times (\hat{j} + \hat{k}) + \hat{j} \times (\hat{k} + \hat{i}) + \hat{k} \times (\hat{i} + \hat{j})$　　　*[CBSE 2014]*

Ans: (i) 1　　　　*(ii)* -1　　　*(iii)* 0

10. Find the vunit vectors perpendicular to both $\vec{a}$ and $\vec{b}$ when

   (i) $\vec{a} = 3\hat{i} + \hat{j} - 2\hat{k}$ and $\vec{b} = 2\hat{i} + 3\hat{j} - \hat{k}$

   (ii) $\vec{a} = \hat{i} - 2\hat{j} + 3\hat{k}$ and $\vec{b} = \hat{i} + 2\hat{j} - \hat{k}$

Ans: (i) $\pm\dfrac{1}{5\sqrt{3}}(5\hat{i} - \hat{j} + 7\hat{k})$　　　*(ii)* $\pm\dfrac{1}{\sqrt{3}}(-\hat{i} + \hat{j} + \hat{k})$

11. Find the unit vectors perpendicular to the plane of the vectors $\vec{a} = 2\hat{i} - 6\hat{j} - 3\hat{k}$ and $\vec{b} = 4\hat{i} + 3\hat{j} - \hat{k}$.

Ans: $\pm\dfrac{1}{7}(3\hat{i} - 2\hat{j} + 6\hat{k})$

12. Find a vector of magnitude 6 which is perpendicular to both the vectors $\vec{a} = 4\hat{i} - \hat{j} + 3\hat{k}$ and $\vec{b} = -2\hat{i} + \hat{j} - 2\hat{k}$.

Ans: $\pm 2(-\hat{i} + 2\hat{j} + 2\hat{k})$

13. Find a vector of magnitude 5 units, perpendicular to both the vectors $(\vec{a} + \vec{b})$ and $(\vec{a} - \vec{b})$, where $\vec{a} = (\hat{i} + \hat{j} + \hat{k})$ and $\vec{b} = (\hat{i} + 2\hat{j} + 3\hat{k})$.

Ans: $\pm\dfrac{5(-\hat{i} + 2\hat{j} - \hat{k})}{\sqrt{6}}$

14. Find the angle between two vectors $\vec{a}$ and $\vec{b}$ with magnitudes 1 and 2 respectively and $|\vec{a} \times \vec{b}| = \sqrt{3}$.　　　*[CBSE 2009]*

Ans: $\dfrac{\pi}{3}$

15. *If* $\vec{a} = (\hat{i} - \hat{j})$, $\vec{b} = (3\hat{j} - \hat{k})$ *and* $\vec{c} = (7\hat{i} - \hat{k})$, *find a vector* $\vec{d}$ *which is perpendicular to both* $\vec{a}$ *and* $\vec{b}$ *and for which* $\vec{c} \cdot \vec{d} = 1$. *[CBSE 2010]*

Ans: $\dfrac{1}{4}(\hat{i} + \hat{j} + 3\hat{k})$

16. *If* $\vec{a} = (4\hat{i} + 5\hat{j} - \hat{k})$, $\vec{b} = (\hat{i} - 4\hat{j} + 5\hat{k})$, *and* $\vec{c} = (3\hat{i} + \hat{j} - \hat{k})$, *find a vector* $\vec{d}$ *which is perpendicular to both* $\vec{a}$ *and* $\vec{b}$ *and for which* $\vec{c} \cdot \vec{d} = 21$.

Ans: $7(\hat{i} - \hat{j} - \hat{k})$

17. *Prove that* $|\vec{a} \times \vec{b}| = (\vec{a} \cdot \vec{b}) \tan \theta$, *where* θ *is the angle between* $\vec{a}$ *and* $\vec{b}$.

Ans:

18. *Write the value of* p *for which* $\vec{a} = (3\hat{i} + 2\hat{j} + 9\hat{k})$ *and* $\vec{b} = (\hat{i} + p\hat{j} + 3\hat{k})$ *are parallel vectors.* *[CBSE 2009]*

Ans: $\dfrac{2}{3}$

19. *Verify that* $\vec{a} \times (\vec{b} + \vec{c}) = (\vec{a} \times \vec{b}) + (\vec{a} \times \vec{c})$, *when*

   (i) $\vec{a} = \hat{i} - \hat{j} - 3\hat{k}$, $\vec{b} = 4\hat{i} - 3\hat{j} + \hat{k}$ *and* $\vec{c} = 2\hat{i} - \hat{j} + 2\hat{k}$

   (ii) $\vec{a} = 4\hat{i} - \hat{j} + \hat{k}$, $\vec{b} = \hat{i} + \hat{j} + \hat{k}$ *and* $\vec{c} = \hat{i} - \hat{j} + \hat{k}$.

20. *Prove that,*

   (i) $(\vec{a} - \vec{b}) \times (\vec{a} + \vec{b}) = 2(\vec{a} \times \vec{b})$

   (ii) $(\vec{a} \times \vec{b})^2 + (\vec{a} \cdot \vec{b})^2 = |\vec{a}|^2 |\vec{b}|^2$

   (iii) $\vec{a} \times (\vec{b} + \vec{c}) + \vec{b} \times (\vec{c} + \vec{a}) + \vec{c} \times (\vec{a} + \vec{b}) = \vec{0}$

21. *Find a unit vector perpendicular to each of the vectors* $\vec{a} + \vec{b}$ *and* $\vec{a} - \vec{b}$, *where* $\vec{a} = \hat{i} + \hat{j} + \hat{k}$ *and* $\vec{b} = \hat{i} + 2\hat{j} + 3\hat{k}$. *[NCERT]*

Ans: $-\dfrac{1}{\sqrt{6}}\hat{i} + \dfrac{2}{\sqrt{6}}\hat{j} - \dfrac{1}{\sqrt{6}}\hat{k}$

22. *If* $\vec{a} = \hat{i} + 2\hat{j} + \hat{k}$, $\vec{b} = 2\hat{i} + \hat{j}$ *and* $\vec{c} = 3\hat{i} - 4\hat{j} - 5\hat{k}$, *then find a unit vector perpendicular to both of the vectors* $(\vec{a} - \vec{b})$ *and* $(\vec{c} - \vec{b})$. *[All India 2015]*

Ans: $\dfrac{-\hat{j}}{\sqrt{2}} + \dfrac{\hat{k}}{\sqrt{2}}$

23. Find the area of the parallelogram whose diagonals are represented by the vectors.

(i) $\vec{d_1} = 3\hat{i} + \hat{j} - 2\hat{k}$ *and* $\vec{d_2} = \hat{i} - 3\hat{j} + 4\hat{k}$ **[CBSE 2004]**

(ii) $\vec{d_1} = 2\hat{i} - \hat{j} + \hat{k}$ *and* $\vec{d_2} = 3\hat{i} + 4\hat{j} - \hat{k}$

Ans: (i) $5\sqrt{3}$ *sq. units* (ii) $\dfrac{1}{2}\sqrt{155}$ *sq. units*

24. Find the area of the triangle whose two adjacent sides are determined by the vectors

(i) $\vec{a} = -2\hat{i} - 5\hat{k}$ *and* $\vec{b} = \hat{i} - 2\hat{j} - \hat{k}$

(ii) $\vec{a} = 3\hat{i} + 4\hat{j}$ *and* $\vec{b} = -5\hat{i} + 7\hat{j}$

Ans: (i) $\dfrac{1}{2}\sqrt{165}$ *sq. units* (ii) $\dfrac{41}{2}$ *sq. units*

25. Using vectors, find the area of $\triangle ABC$ whose vertices are

(i) $A(1, 1, 2)$, $B(2, 3, 5)$ *and* $C(4, 5, -1)$ **[CBSE 2011]**

(ii) $A(1, 2, 3)$, $B(2, -1, 4)$ *and* $C(4, 5, -1)$ **[CBSE 2013]**

(iii) $A(3, -1, 2)$, $B(1, -1, -3)$ *and* $C(4, -3, 1)$

Ans: (i) $\dfrac{\sqrt{61}}{2}$ (ii) $\dfrac{\sqrt{274}}{2}$

26. If the vectors $\vec{a}, \vec{b}$ *and* $\vec{c}$ are given as $a_1\hat{i} + a_2\hat{j} + a_3\hat{k}$, $b_1\hat{i} + b_2\hat{j} + b_3\hat{k}$ *and* $c_1\hat{i} + c_2\hat{j} + c_3\hat{k}$.

Then, show that $\vec{a} \times (\vec{b} + \vec{c}) = (\vec{a} \times \vec{b}) + (\vec{a} \times \vec{c})$. **[NCERT Exemplar]**

27. For any three vectors $\vec{a}, \vec{b}$ *and* $\vec{c}$, evaluate $\vec{a} \times (\vec{b} + \vec{c}) + \vec{b}(\vec{c} + \vec{a}) + \vec{c} \times (\vec{a} + \vec{b})$.

Ans: 0

28. If $\vec{a} \times \vec{b} = \vec{c} \times \vec{d}$ *and* $\vec{a} \times \vec{c} = \vec{b} \times \vec{d}$, then show that $\vec{a} - \vec{d}$ *is parallel to* $\vec{b} - \vec{c}$.

29. Using vectors, find the area of the $\triangle ABC$, whose vertices are $A(1, 2, 3)$, $B(2, -1, 4)$ *and* $C(4, 5, -1)$. **[Delhi 2017; All India 2013]**

Ans: $\dfrac{1}{2}\sqrt{274}$ *sq. units*

30. Using vectors, find the area of triangle with vertices $A(1, 1, 2)$, $B(2, 3, 5)$ *and* $C(1, 5, 6)$. **[All India 2011]**

Ans: $2\sqrt{3}$ *sq. units*

31. **Show that** $(\vec{a} \times \vec{b})^2 = \begin{vmatrix} \vec{a} \cdot \vec{a} & \vec{a} \cdot \vec{b} \\ \vec{a} \cdot \vec{b} & \vec{b} \cdot \vec{b} \end{vmatrix}$

32. **If** $\vec{a}, \vec{b}$ **and** $\vec{c}$ **are three vectors such that** $\vec{a} + \vec{b} + \vec{c} = \vec{0}$, **then prove that** $\vec{a} \times \vec{b} = \vec{b} \times \vec{c} = \vec{c} \times \vec{a}$.

33. **If** $\vec{r} = x\hat{i} + y\hat{j} + z\hat{k}$, **then find** $(\vec{r} \times \hat{i}) \cdot (\vec{r} \times \hat{j}) + xy$.   *[Delhi 2015]*

Ans: 0

34. **If** $\vec{a} = \hat{i} + \hat{j} + \hat{k}$ **and** $\vec{b} = \hat{j} - \hat{k}$, **then find a vector** $\vec{c}$ **such that** $\vec{a} \times \vec{c} = \vec{b}$ **and** $\vec{a} \cdot \vec{c} = 3$.

[Delhi 2013]

Ans: $\dfrac{5}{3}\hat{i} + \dfrac{2}{3}\hat{j} + \dfrac{2}{3}\hat{k}$

35. **Let** $\vec{a} = 4\hat{i} + 5\hat{j} - \hat{k}$, $\vec{b} = \hat{i} - 4\hat{j} + 5\hat{k}$ **and** $\vec{c} = 3\hat{i} + \hat{j} - \hat{k}$. **Find a vector** $\vec{d}$ **which is perpendicular to both** $\vec{a}$ **and** $\vec{b}$ **and satisfying** $\vec{d} \cdot \vec{c} = 21$. *[Delhi 2016C]*

Ans: $7\hat{i} - 7\hat{j} - 7\hat{k}$

36. **Using vector method, show that the given points** A, B, C **are collinear:**

   (i) $A(3, -5, 1)$, $B(-1, 0, 8)$ **and** $C(7, -10, -6)$

   (ii) $A(6, -7, -1)$, $B(2, -3, 1)$ **and** $C(4, -5, 0)$

37. **Show that the points** A, B, C **with position vectors** $(3\hat{i} - 2\hat{j} + 4\hat{k}), (\hat{i} + \hat{j} + \hat{k})$ **and** $(-\hat{i} + 4\hat{j} - 2\hat{k})$ **respectively are collinear.**

38. **Show that the points having position vectors** $\vec{a}, \vec{b}$, $(\vec{c} = 3\vec{a} - 2\vec{b})$ **are collinear, whatever be** $\vec{a}, \vec{b}, \vec{c}$.

39. **Show that the points having position vectors** $(-2\vec{a} + 3\vec{b} + 5\vec{c}), (\vec{a} + 2\vec{b} + 3\vec{c})$ **and** $(7\vec{a} - \vec{c})$ **are collinear, whatever be** $\vec{a}, \vec{b}, \vec{c}$.

SCALAR TRIPLE PRODUCT:

The scalar triple product is defined as the dot product of one of the vectors with the cross product of the other two vectors. Suppose $\vec{a}$, $\vec{b}$ and $\vec{c}$ are three vectors. Then, scalar product of $\vec{a}$ and $(\vec{b} \times \vec{c})$, i.e. $\vec{a} \cdot (\vec{b} \times \vec{c})$ is called the scalar triple product of $\vec{a}$, $\vec{b}$ and $\vec{c}$ and it is denoted by $[\vec{a} \ \vec{b} \ \vec{c}]$ or $[\vec{a}, \vec{b}, \vec{c}]$. Thus, $[\vec{a} \ \vec{b} \ \vec{c}] = \vec{a} \cdot (\vec{b} \times \vec{c})$.

(i) SCALAR TRIPLE PRODUCT IN COMPONENT FORM:

Suppose three vectors $\vec{a}$, $\vec{b}$ and $\vec{c}$ are given in componentn form, say $\vec{a} = a_1\hat{i} + a_2\hat{j} + a_3\hat{k}$, $\vec{b} = b_1\hat{i} + b_2\hat{j} + b_3\hat{k}$ and $\vec{c} = c_1\hat{i} + c_2\hat{j} + c_3\hat{k}$.

Then, $(\vec{b} \times \vec{c}) = \begin{vmatrix} \hat{i} & \hat{j} & \hat{k} \\ b_1 & b_2 & b_3 \\ c_1 & c_2 & c_3 \end{vmatrix}$

$$= (b_2c_3 - b_3c_2)\hat{i} + (b_3c_1 - b_1c_3)\hat{j} + (b_1c_2 - b_2c_1)\hat{k}$$

$$\therefore \ \vec{a} \cdot (\vec{b} \times \vec{c}) = (a_1\hat{i} + a_2\hat{j} + a_3\hat{k})[(b_2c_3 - b_3c_2)\hat{i} + (b_3c_1 - b_1c_3)\hat{j} + (b_1c_2 - b_2c_1)\hat{k}]$$

$$= a_1(b_2c_3 - b_3c_2) + a_2(b_3c_1 - b_1c_3) + a_3(b_1c_2 - b_2c_1)$$

Hence, $\vec{a} \cdot (\vec{b} \times \vec{c}) = \begin{vmatrix} a_1 & a_2 & a_3 \\ b_1 & b_2 & b_3 \\ c_1 & c_2 & c_3 \end{vmatrix}$

EXAMPLE : *If $\vec{a} = \hat{i} + 4\hat{j} + 4\hat{k}$, $\vec{b} = 2\hat{i} - 3\hat{j} + 2\hat{k}$ and $\vec{c} = -2\hat{i} + \hat{j} + 3\hat{k}$, then find $[\vec{a} \ \vec{b} \ \vec{c}]$.*

SOLUTION : Given, $\vec{a} = \hat{i} + 4\hat{j} + 4\hat{k}$

$$\vec{b} = 2\hat{i} - 3\hat{j} + 2\hat{k}$$

and $\vec{c} = -2\hat{i} + \hat{j} + 3\hat{k}$

We know that,

$$[\vec{a} \ \vec{b} \ \vec{c}] = \begin{vmatrix} 1 & 4 & 5 \\ 2 & -3 & 2 \\ -2 & 1 & 3 \end{vmatrix}$$

$$= 1(-9 - 2) - 4(6 + 4) + 5(2 - 6)$$

$$= -11 - 40 - 20$$

$$= -71$$

EXAMPLE : *Find the scalar triple product of vectors* $\vec{a} = \{1, 2, 3\}$; $\vec{b} = \{1, 1, 1\}$; $\vec{c} = \{1, 2, 1\}$.

SOLUTION :

$$[\vec{a}\ \vec{b}\ \vec{c}] = \begin{vmatrix} 1 & 2 & 3 \\ 1 & 1 & 1 \\ 1 & 2 & 1 \end{vmatrix}$$

$$= 1(1-2) - 2(1-1) + 3(2-1)$$

$$= -1 - 0 + 3$$

$$= 2$$

(ii) GEOMETRICAL INTERPRETATION:

(*a*) Module of scalar triple product of vectors $\vec{a}, \vec{b}$ and $\vec{c}$ is equal to the volume of the parallelopiped formed by these vectors:

$$\text{Vparallelopiped} = |\vec{a} \cdot [\vec{b} \times \vec{c}]|$$

(*b*) The volume of the pyramid formed by three vectors $\vec{a}, \vec{b}$ and $\vec{c}$ is equal to one sixth of the modulas of the scalar triple product of this vectors:

$$\text{Vpyramid} = \frac{1}{6} |\vec{a} \cdot [\vec{b} \times \vec{c}]|$$

(iii) SOME IMPORTANT RESULTS ON SCALAR TRIPLE PRODUCT:

(*a*) We know that cross product of two vectors $\vec{b}$ and $\vec{c}$ i.e. $\vec{b} \times \vec{c}$ is a vector and $\vec{b} \cdot \vec{c}$ is a scalar quantity, therefore, $\vec{a} \cdot (\vec{b} \times \vec{c})$, i.e. $[\vec{a}\ \vec{b}\ \vec{c}]$ is a scalar quantity.

(*b*) If cyclic order of three vectors is unchnged, then scalar triple product remains unchanged.

i.e. $(\vec{a} \times \vec{b}) \cdot \vec{c} = (\vec{b} \times \vec{c}) \cdot \vec{a} = (\vec{c} \times \vec{a}) \cdot \vec{b}$

(*c*) If cyclic order of three vectors is changed, then scalar triple product changes in sign but not in magnitude.

i.e. $[\vec{a}\ \vec{b}\ \vec{c}] = -[\vec{b}\ \vec{a}\ \vec{c}] = -[\vec{c}\ \vec{b}\ \vec{a}] = -[\vec{a}\ \vec{c}\ \vec{b}]$

(*d*) In scalar triple product the dot and cross between $\vec{a}, \vec{b}$ and $\vec{c}$ can be interchanged in same alphabetical order or cyclic order, *i.e.* $(\vec{a} \times \vec{b}) \cdot \vec{c} = \vec{a} \cdot (\vec{b} \times \vec{c}) = \vec{b} \cdot (\vec{c} \times \vec{a}) = \vec{c} \cdot (\vec{a} \times \vec{b})$

(*e*) The scalar triple product of three vectors is zero, if any two of them are same.

i.e. $[\vec{a}\ \vec{a}\ \vec{b}] = [\vec{b}\ \vec{b}\ \vec{c}] = [\vec{c}\ \vec{c}\ \vec{a}] = 0$

(*f*) If $\vec{a}$, $\vec{b}$ and $\vec{c}$ are any three vectors and is a scalar quantity, then

$$[k\vec{a}\ \vec{b}\ \vec{c}] = k[\vec{a}\ \vec{b}\ \vec{c}]$$

(iv) COPLANARITY OF THREE VECTORS:

Three non-zero, non-collinear vector $\vec{a}$, $\vec{b}$ and $\vec{c}$ are colanar if and only if $[\vec{a}\ \vec{b}\ \vec{c}] = 0$, *i.e.* $\vec{a} \cdot (\vec{b} \times \vec{c}) = 0$.

Again, four points are coplanar, if the three vectors $\overrightarrow{AB}$, $\overrightarrow{AC}$ and $\overrightarrow{AD}$ are coplanar.

(v) SOLVED EXAMPLES

EXAMPLE 1 : *If $\vec{a} = 5\hat{i} - \hat{j} + 4\hat{k}$, $\vec{b} = 2\hat{i} + 3\hat{j} + 5\hat{k}$ and $\vec{c} = 5\hat{i} - 2\hat{j} + 6\hat{k}$, then find $\vec{b} \cdot (\vec{c} \times \vec{a})$.*

SOLUTION : We have,

$$\vec{c} \times \vec{a} = \begin{vmatrix} \hat{i} & \hat{j} & \hat{k} \\ 5 & -2 & 6 \\ 5 & -1 & 4 \end{vmatrix}$$

$$= (-8 + 6)\hat{i} + (30 - 20)\hat{j} + (-5 + 10)\hat{k}$$

$$= -2\hat{i} + 10\hat{j} + 5\hat{k}$$

$$\therefore \quad \vec{b} \cdot (\vec{c} \times \vec{a}) = (2\hat{i} + 3\hat{j} + 5\hat{k}) \cdot (-2\hat{i} + 10\hat{j} + 5\hat{k})$$

$$= -4 + 30 + 25 = 51$$

Alternative Method

We have,

$$\vec{b} \cdot (\vec{c} \times \vec{a}) = \begin{vmatrix} 2 & 3 & 5 \\ 5 & -2 & 6 \\ 5 & -1 & 4 \end{vmatrix}$$

$$= 2(-8+6) + 3(30-20) + 5(-5+10)$$

$$= -4 + 30 + 25 = 51$$

EXAMPLE 2 : *Find the volume of the parallelopiped whose sides are the vectors* $-12\hat{i} + 3\hat{k},\ 3\hat{j} - \hat{k}$ *and* $2\hat{i} + \hat{j} - 15\hat{k}$.

SOLUTION : Required volume of the parallelopiped

= scalar triple products of the given vectors

$$= |(-12\hat{i} + 3\hat{k}) \cdot \{(3\hat{j} - \hat{k}) \times (2\hat{i} + \hat{j} - 15\hat{k}\}|$$

$$= \text{modules of} \begin{vmatrix} -12 & 0 & 3 \\ 0 & 3 & -1 \\ 2 & 1 & -15 \end{vmatrix}$$

$$= |-12(-45+1) + 3(0-6)|$$

$$= |(-12) \times (-44) - 18| = |528 - 18| = 510 \text{ cubic unit}$$

EXAMPLE 3 : *If vectors* $\hat{i} + 2\hat{j} - 3\hat{k},\ p\hat{i} - \hat{j} + \hat{k}$ *and* $3\hat{i} - 4\hat{j} + 5\hat{k}$ *are coplanar then find* P.

SOLUTION : Let $\vec{a} = \hat{i} + 2\hat{j} - 3\hat{k},\ \vec{b} = p\hat{i} - \hat{j} + \hat{k}$

and $\vec{c} = 3\hat{i} - 4\hat{j} + 5\hat{k}$

Since the vectors $\vec{a}, \vec{b}, \vec{c}$ are coplanar, hence

$$[\vec{a}\ \vec{b}\ \vec{c}] = 0$$

or, $\quad \vec{a} \cdot (\vec{b} \times \vec{c}) = 0 \begin{vmatrix} 1 & 2 & -3 \\ p & -1 & 1 \\ 3 & -4 & 5 \end{vmatrix} = 0$

or, $\quad 1(-5+4) + 2(3-5p) - 3(-4p+3) = 0$

or, $\quad -1 + 6 - 10p + 12p - 9 = 0$

or, $\quad 2p = 4 \text{ or, } p = 2$

Therefore, required $p = 2$

EXAMPLE 4 : *The position vectors of the points* A, B, C *and* D *are* $6\hat{i} - 7\hat{j}$, $16\hat{i} - 19\hat{j} - 4\hat{k}$, $3\hat{j} - 6\hat{k}$ *and* $2\hat{i} - 5\hat{j} + 10\hat{k}$ *respectively. Show that the points* A, B, C *and* D *are coplanar.*

SOLUTION : Clearly,

$$\overrightarrow{AB} = (\text{Position vector of } B) - (\text{Position vector of } A)$$

$$= (16\hat{i} - 19\hat{j} - 4\hat{k}) - (6\hat{i} - 7\hat{j}) = 10\hat{i} - 12\hat{j} - 4\hat{k}$$

Similarly, $\overrightarrow{AC} = (3\hat{j} - 6\hat{k}) - (6\hat{i} - 7\hat{j}) = -6\hat{i} + 10\hat{j} - 6\hat{k}$

and $\quad \overrightarrow{AD} = (2\hat{i} - 5\hat{j} + 10\hat{k}) - (6\hat{i} - 7\hat{j}) = -4\hat{i} + 2\hat{j} + 10\hat{k}$

$\therefore \quad [\overrightarrow{AB}\ \overrightarrow{AC}\ \overrightarrow{AD}]$

$$= \overrightarrow{AB} \cdot (\overrightarrow{AC} \times \overrightarrow{AD}) = \begin{vmatrix} 10 & -12 & -4 \\ -6 & 10 & -6 \\ -4 & 2 & 10 \end{vmatrix}$$

$$= 8 \begin{vmatrix} 5 & -6 & -2 \\ -3 & 5 & -3 \\ -2 & 1 & 5 \end{vmatrix}$$

$$= 8[5(25+3) + 6(-15-6) - 2(-3+10)]$$

$$= 8[140 - 126 - 14] = 8(140 - 140) = 0$$

Since $[\overrightarrow{AB}\ \overrightarrow{AC}\ \overrightarrow{AD}] = 0$ hence the vectors $\overrightarrow{AB}, \overrightarrow{AC}$ and $\overrightarrow{AD}$ are coplanar.

i.e., the points A, B, C and D are coplanar.

EXAMPLE 5 : *Show that the vectors* $2\hat{i} - \hat{j} - \hat{k}, 7\hat{j} + 3\hat{k}$ *and* $\hat{i} + 3\hat{j} + \hat{k}$ *are coplanar.*

SOLUTION : Let $\vec{a} = 2\hat{i} - \hat{j} - \hat{k},\ \vec{b} = 7\hat{j} + 3\hat{k}$

and $\vec{c} = \hat{i} + 3\hat{j}z + \hat{k}$. Then,

$$\vec{a} \cdot (\vec{b} \times \vec{c}) = \begin{vmatrix} 2 & -1 & -1 \\ 0 & 7 & 3 \\ 1 & 3 & 1 \end{vmatrix}$$

$$= 2(7-9) + 1(-3+7)$$

$$= -4 + 4 = 0$$

Since, $\vec{a} \cdot (\vec{b} \times \vec{c}) = 0$, hence the vectors $\vec{a}$, $\vec{b}$, $\vec{c}$ are coplanar.

EXAMPLE 6 : *Prove that for any three vectors $\vec{a}, \vec{b}$ and $\vec{c}$, $[\vec{a}+\vec{b} \ \ \vec{b}+\vec{c} \ \ \vec{c}+\vec{a}] = 2[\vec{a} \ \vec{b} \ \vec{c}]$.*

[NCERT; Delhi 2014]

SOLUTION :

$$LHS = [\vec{a}+\vec{b} \ \ \vec{b}+\vec{c} \ \ \vec{c}+\vec{a}]$$

$$= (\vec{a}+\vec{b}) \cdot [(\vec{b}+\vec{c}) \times (\vec{c}+\vec{a})]$$

$$= (\vec{a}+\vec{b}) \cdot [\vec{b} \times \vec{c} + \vec{b} \times \vec{a} + \vec{c} \times \vec{c} + \vec{c} \times \vec{a}] \qquad \text{[by distributive law]}$$

$$= (\vec{a}+\vec{b}) \cdot [\vec{b} \times \vec{c} + \vec{b} \times \vec{a} + \vec{c} \times \vec{a}] \qquad [\because \ \vec{c} \times \vec{c} = \vec{0}]$$

$$= \vec{a} \cdot (\vec{b} \times \vec{c}) + \vec{a} \cdot (\vec{b} \times \vec{a}) + \vec{a} \cdot (\vec{c} \times \vec{a}) + \vec{b} \cdot (\vec{b} \times \vec{c}) + \vec{b} \cdot (\vec{b} \times \vec{a}) + \vec{b} \cdot (\vec{c} \times \vec{a})$$

$$\text{[by distributive law]}$$

$$= [\vec{a} \ \vec{b} \ \vec{c}] + [\vec{a} \ \vec{b} \ \vec{a}] + [\vec{a} \ \vec{c} \ \vec{a}] + [\vec{b} \ \vec{b} \ \vec{c}] + [\vec{b} \ \vec{b} \ \vec{a}] + [\vec{b} \ \vec{c} \ \vec{a}]$$

$$= [\vec{a} \ \vec{b} \ \vec{c}] + [\vec{b} \ \vec{c} \ \vec{a}]$$

$$[\because [\vec{a} \ \vec{b} \ \vec{a}] = [\vec{a} \ \vec{c} \ \vec{a}] = [\vec{b} \ \vec{b} \ \vec{c}] = [\vec{b} \ \vec{b} \ \vec{a}] = 0]$$

$$= [\vec{a} \ \vec{b} \ \vec{c}] + [\vec{a} \ \vec{b} \ \vec{c}] \qquad [\because [\vec{b} \ \vec{c} \ \vec{a}] = [\vec{a} \ \vec{b} \ \vec{c}]]$$

$$= 2[\vec{a} \ \vec{b} \ \vec{c}] = RHS$$

EXAMPLE 7 : *Find the volume of the parallelepiped whose coterminous edges are represented by the vectors*

$$\vec{a} = 2\hat{i} - 3\hat{j} + \hat{k}, \ \vec{b} = \hat{i} - \hat{j} + 2\hat{k} \ \text{and} \ \vec{c} = 2\hat{i} + \hat{j} - \hat{k}. \qquad \textit{[CBSE 2000C]}$$

SOLUTION : We have

$$[\vec{a} \ \vec{b} \ \vec{c}] = \begin{vmatrix} 2 & -3 & 1 \\ 1 & -1 & 2 \\ 2 & 1 & -1 \end{vmatrix} = \begin{vmatrix} 0 & -1 & -3 \\ 1 & -1 & 2 \\ 0 & 3 & -5 \end{vmatrix}$$

$$[R_1 \to R_1 - 2R_2, \ \text{and} \ R_3 \to R_3 - 2R_2]$$

$$= (-1) \cdot (5 + 9) = -14.$$

$\therefore \qquad$ volume of the parallelepiped

$$= |[\vec{a} \ \vec{b} \ \vec{c}]| = |-14| = 14 \ \text{cubic units}$$

EXAMPLE 8 : *Show that the vectors $\hat{i} - 3\hat{j} + 4\hat{k}$, $2\hat{i} - \hat{j} + 2\hat{k}$ and $4\hat{i} - 7\hat{j} + 10\hat{k}$ are co-planar.*

SOLUTION : Let $\vec{a} = \hat{i} + \hat{j} + \hat{k}$, $\vec{b} = 2\hat{i} - \hat{j} + 2\hat{k}$ and $\vec{c} = 4\hat{i} - 7\hat{j} + 10\hat{k}$.

$$\therefore \quad [\vec{a}\ \vec{b}\ \vec{c}] = \begin{vmatrix} 1 & -3 & 4 \\ 2 & -1 & 2 \\ 4 & -7 & 10 \end{vmatrix} = \begin{vmatrix} 1 & -3 & 4 \\ 0 & 5 & -6 \\ 4 & 5 & -6 \end{vmatrix} \begin{matrix} R_2 \to R_2 - 2R_1 \\ R_3 \to R_3 - 4R_1 \end{matrix}$$

$$= (-30 + 30) = 0$$

Hence, the given vectors are coplanar.

EXAMPLE 9 : *Find the value of so that the vectors $\vec{a} = 2\hat{i} - 3\hat{j} + \hat{k}$, $\vec{b} = \hat{i} + 2\hat{j} - 3\hat{k}$ and $\vec{c} = \hat{j} + \lambda\hat{k}$ are coplanar.*

SOLUTION : The given vectors will be coplanar if $[\vec{a}\ \vec{b}\ \vec{c}] = 0$.

$$\text{Now, } [\vec{a}\ \vec{b}\ \vec{c}] = 0 \Leftrightarrow \begin{vmatrix} 1 & -3 & 4 \\ 2 & -1 & 2 \\ 4 & -7 & 10 \end{vmatrix} = 0 \Leftrightarrow \begin{vmatrix} 1 & -3 & 4 \\ 0 & 5 & -6 \\ 4 & 5 & -6 \end{vmatrix} = 0$$

$$[R_1 \to R_1 - 2R_2]$$

$$\Leftrightarrow (-1)(-7\lambda - 7) = 0 \Leftrightarrow 7\lambda + 7 = 0 \Leftrightarrow \lambda = -1.$$

Hence, the given vectors are coplanar when $\lambda = -1$.

EXAMPLE 10 : *Show that the four points with position vectors $(4\hat{i} + 5\hat{j} + \hat{k})$, $(-\hat{j} - \hat{k})$, $(3\hat{i} + 9\hat{j} + 4\hat{k})$ and $4(-\hat{i} + \hat{j} + \hat{k})$ are coplanar. [CBSE 2014]*

SOLUTION : Let the given points be A, B, C, D respectively.

Points A, B, C, D are coplanar $\Leftrightarrow \overrightarrow{AB}, \overrightarrow{AC}$ and $\overrightarrow{AD}$ are coplanar

$$\Leftrightarrow [\overrightarrow{AB}\ \overrightarrow{AC}\ \overrightarrow{AD}] = 0$$

Now, $\overrightarrow{AB} = (\text{p.v. of } B) - (\text{p.v. of } A)$

$$= (-\hat{j} - \hat{k}) - (4\hat{i} + 5\hat{j} + \hat{k}) = (-4\hat{i} - 6\hat{j} - 2\hat{k})$$

$$\overrightarrow{AC} = (\text{p.v. of } C) - (\text{p.v. of } A)$$

$$= (3\hat{i} + 9\hat{j} + 4\hat{k}) - (4\hat{i} + 5\hat{j} + \hat{k}) = (-\hat{i} + 4\hat{j} + 3\hat{k})$$

$$\overrightarrow{AD} = (\text{p.v. of } D) - (\text{p.v. of } A)$$

$$= (-4\hat{i} + 4\hat{j} + 4\hat{k}) - (4\hat{i} + 5\hat{j} + \hat{k}) = (-8\hat{i} - \hat{j} + 3\hat{k})$$

$$\therefore \quad [\overrightarrow{AB}\ \overrightarrow{AC}\ \overrightarrow{AD}] = \begin{vmatrix} -4 & -6 & -2 \\ -1 & 4 & 3 \\ -8 & -1 & 3 \end{vmatrix}$$

$$= \begin{vmatrix} 0 & -22 & -14 \\ -1 & 4 & 3 \\ 0 & -21 & -33 \end{vmatrix} \begin{Bmatrix} R_1 \rightarrow R_1 - 4R_2 \\ R_3 \rightarrow R_3 - 8R_2 \end{Bmatrix}$$

$$= -(-1)[462 - 462] = 0.$$

$\therefore \overrightarrow{AB},\ \overrightarrow{AC}$ and $\overrightarrow{AD}$ are coplanar.

Hence, the points A, B, C, D are coplanar.

EXAMPLE 11 : *Find the value of λ so that the four points with position vectors $(-6\hat{i} + 3\hat{j} + 2\hat{k}), (3\hat{i} + \lambda\hat{j} + 4\hat{k}), (5\hat{i} + 7\hat{j} + 3\hat{k})$ and $(-13\hat{i} + 17\hat{j} - 2\hat{k})$ are coplanar. [CBSE 2000]*

SOLUTION : Let the given points be A, B, C, D respectively. Then,

$$\overrightarrow{AB} = (\text{p.v. of } B) - (\text{p.v. of } A)$$

$$= (3\hat{i} + \lambda\hat{j} + 4\hat{k}) - (-6\hat{i} + 3\hat{j} + 2\hat{k})$$

$$= 9\hat{i} + (\lambda - 3)\hat{j} + 2\hat{k}$$

$$\overrightarrow{AC} = (\text{p.v. of } C) - (\text{p.v. of } A)$$

$$= (5\hat{i} + 7\hat{j} + 3\hat{k}) - (-6\hat{i} + 3\hat{j} + 2\hat{k})$$

$$= (11\hat{i} + 4\hat{j} + \hat{k})$$

$$\overrightarrow{AD} = (\text{p.v. of } D) - (\text{p.v. of } A)$$

$$= (-13\hat{i} + 17\hat{j} - \hat{k}) - (-6\hat{i} + 3\hat{j} + 2\hat{k})$$

$$= (-7\hat{i} + 14\hat{j} - 3\hat{k})$$

Now, A, B, C, D are coplanar

$$\Leftrightarrow [\overrightarrow{AB}\ \overrightarrow{AC}\ \overrightarrow{AD}] = 0 \Leftrightarrow \begin{vmatrix} 9 & \lambda-3 & 2 \\ 11 & 4 & 1 \\ -7 & 14 & -3 \end{vmatrix} = 0$$

$$\Leftrightarrow 9(-12-14) - (\lambda-3)(-33+7) + 2(154+28) = 0$$

$$\Leftrightarrow -234 + 26\lambda - 78 + 364 = 0 \Leftrightarrow 26\lambda = -52 \Leftrightarrow \lambda = -2$$

Hence, the required value of is -2.

EXAMPLE 12 : *Show that the vectors $\vec{a} = -2\hat{i} - 2\hat{j} + 4\hat{k}$, $\vec{b} = -2\hat{i} + 4\hat{j} - 2\hat{k}$ and $\vec{c} = 4\hat{i} - 2\hat{j} - 2\hat{k}$ are coplanar.*

SOLUTION : We know that three vectors $\vec{a}$, $\vec{b}$ and $\vec{c}$ are coplanar, if their scalar triple product is zero, *i.e.* $[\vec{a}\ \vec{b}\ \vec{c}] = 0$.

We have,
$$[\vec{a}\ \vec{b}\ \vec{c}] = \begin{vmatrix} -2 & -2 & 4 \\ -2 & 4 & -2 \\ 4 & -2 & -2 \end{vmatrix}$$

$$= -2(-8-4) + 2(4+8) + 4(4-16)$$
$$= (-2)\times(-12) + 2\times12 + 4\times(-12)$$
$$= 24 + 24 - 48 = 0$$

Hence, the given vectors are coplanar.

EXAMPLE 13 : *Show that the four points A, B, C and D with position vectors $4\hat{i} + 5\hat{j} + \hat{k}$, $-(\hat{j} + \hat{k}), 3\hat{i} + 9\hat{j} + 4\hat{k}$ and $4(-\hat{i} + \hat{j} + \hat{k})$, respectively are coplanar.*

[All India 2014]

SOLUTION : We know that the four points A, B, C and D are coplanar, if three vectors $\overrightarrow{AB}$, $\overrightarrow{AC}$ and $\overrightarrow{AD}$ are coplanar.

i.e. if $[\overrightarrow{AB}\ \overrightarrow{AC}\ \overrightarrow{AD}] = 0$

Here, $\overrightarrow{AB}$ = Position vector of B − Position vector of A

$$= -(\hat{j} + \hat{k}) - (4\hat{i} + 5\hat{j} + \hat{k})$$

$$= -4\hat{i} - 6\hat{j} - 2\hat{k}$$

$$\overrightarrow{AC} = \text{Position vector of } B - \text{Position vector of } A$$

$$= (3\hat{i} + 9\hat{j} + 4\hat{k}) - (4\hat{i} + 5\hat{j} + \hat{k})$$

$$= -\hat{i} + 4\hat{j} + 3\hat{k}$$

$$\overrightarrow{AD} = \text{Position vector of } D - \text{Position vector of } A$$

$$= 4(-\hat{i} + \hat{j} + \hat{k}) - (4\hat{i} + 5\hat{j} + \hat{k})$$

$$= -8\hat{i} - \hat{j} + 3\hat{k}$$

$$\therefore \quad [\overrightarrow{AB}\ \overrightarrow{AC}\ \overrightarrow{AD}] = \begin{vmatrix} -4 & -6 & -2 \\ -1 & 4 & 3 \\ -8 & -1 & 3 \end{vmatrix}$$

$$= -4(12+3) + 6(-3+24) - 2(1+32)$$

$$= -60 + 126 - 66 = 0$$

Hence, the points A, B, C and D are coplanar.

(vi) EXERCISE

1. **Find $\vec{a} \cdot (\vec{b} \times \vec{c})$, if $\vec{a} = 2\hat{i} + \hat{j} + 3\hat{k}$, $\vec{b} = -\hat{i} + 2\hat{j} + \hat{k}$ and $\vec{c} = 3\hat{i} + \hat{j} + 2\hat{k}$.**

[NCERT; All India 2014]

 Ans: -10

2. **Find $[\vec{a}\ \vec{b}\ \vec{c}]$, if $\vec{a} = \hat{i} - 2\hat{j} + 3\hat{k}$, $\vec{b} = 2\hat{i} - 3\hat{j} + \hat{k}$ and $\vec{c} = 3\hat{i} + \hat{j} - 2\hat{k}$.** *[NCERT]*

 Ans: 24

3. **Evaluate $[\hat{i}\ \hat{k}\ \hat{j}] + [\hat{i}\ \hat{j}\ \hat{k}]$.**

 Ans: 0

4. **Find the value of $\hat{i} \cdot (\hat{j} \times \hat{k}) + \hat{j} \cdot (\hat{k} \times \hat{i}) + \hat{k} \cdot (\hat{i} \times \hat{j})$.** *[NCERT]*

 Ans: 3

5. **Find the volume of a parallelopiped whose sides are given by $-3\hat{i} + 7\hat{j} + 7\hat{k}$, $-5\hat{i} + 7\hat{j} - 3\hat{k}$ and $7\hat{i} - 5\hat{j} - 3\hat{k}$.**

 Ans: 264 *cu units*

6. Show that the vectors $\vec{a} = \hat{i} - 2\hat{j} + 3\hat{k}$, $\vec{b} = -2\hat{i} + 3\hat{j} - 4\hat{k}$ and $\vec{c} = \hat{i} - 3\hat{j} + 5\hat{k}$ are coplanar.

[NCERT]

7. Find the value of λ, if the vectors $\vec{a} = 2\hat{i} - \hat{j} + \hat{k}$, $\vec{b} = \hat{i} + 2\hat{j} - 3\hat{k}$ and $\vec{c} = 3\hat{i} + \lambda\hat{j} + 5\hat{k}$ are coplanar.

Ans: -4

8. If the vectors $\hat{i} - \hat{j} + \hat{k}$, $3\hat{i} + \hat{j} + 2\hat{k}$ and $\hat{i} + \lambda\hat{j} - 3\hat{k}$ are coplanar, then find the value of λ.

[All India 2017C]

Ans: 15

9. Prove that $[\vec{a}\ \vec{b}\ \vec{c} + \vec{d}] = [\vec{a}\ \vec{b}\ \vec{c}] + [\vec{a}\ \vec{b}\ \vec{d}]$.

[NCERT]

10. Show that the vectors $\vec{a}, \vec{b}, \vec{c}$ are coplanar, when

(i) $\vec{a} = \hat{i} - 2\hat{j} + 3\hat{k}$, $\vec{b} = -2\hat{i} + 3\hat{j} - 4\hat{k}$ and $\vec{c} = \hat{i} - 3\hat{j} + 5\hat{k}$

(ii) $\vec{a} = \hat{i} + 3\hat{j} + \hat{k}$, $\vec{b} = 2\hat{i} - \hat{j} - \hat{k}$ and $\vec{c} = 7\hat{j} + 3\hat{k}$

11. Find the value of λ for which the vectors $\vec{a}, \vec{b}, \vec{c}$ are coplanar, where

(i) $\vec{a} = (2\hat{i} - \hat{j} + \hat{k})$, $\vec{b} = (\hat{i} + 2\hat{j} + 3\hat{k})$ and $\vec{c} = (3\hat{i} + \lambda\hat{j} + 5\hat{k})$ *[CBSE 2004]*

(ii) $\vec{a} = \lambda\hat{i} - 10\hat{j} - 5\hat{k}$, $\vec{b} = -7\hat{i} - 5\hat{j}$ and $\vec{c} = \hat{i} - 4\hat{j} - 3\hat{k}$

(iii) $\vec{a} = \hat{i} - \hat{j} + \hat{k}$, $\vec{b} = 2\hat{i} + \hat{j} - \hat{k}$ and $\vec{c} = \lambda\hat{i} - \hat{j} + \lambda\hat{k}$ *[CBSE 2004C]*

Ans: (i) -4 *(ii)* -3 *(iii)* 1

12. If $\vec{a} = (2\hat{i} - \hat{j} + \hat{k})$, $\vec{b} = (\hat{i} - 3\hat{j} - 5\hat{k})$ and $\vec{c} = (3\hat{i} - 4\hat{j} - \hat{k})$, find $[\vec{a}, \vec{b}, \vec{c}]$ and interpret the result.

Ans: 0, *the given vectors are coplaner.*

13. The volume of the prallelepiped whose edges are $(-12\hat{i} + \lambda\hat{k})$, $(3\hat{j} - \hat{k})$ and $(2\hat{i} + \hat{j} - 15\hat{k})$ is 546 cubic units. Find the value of λ. *[CBSE 2004]*

Ans: -3

14. Show that the vectors $\vec{a} = (\hat{i} + 3\hat{j} + \hat{k})$, $\vec{b} = (2\hat{i} - \hat{j} - \hat{k})$ and $\vec{c} = (7\hat{j} + 3\hat{k})$ are parallel to the same plane. {HINT: Show that $[\vec{a}\ \vec{b}\ \vec{c}] = 0$ }

15. If the vectors $(a\hat{i} + a\hat{j} + c\hat{k})$, $(\hat{i} + \hat{k})$ and $(c\hat{i} + c\hat{j} + b\hat{k})$ be coplanar, show that $c^2 = ab$.

[CBSE 2005]

16. Show that the four points with position vectors $(4\hat{i} + 8\hat{j} + 12\hat{k})$, $(2\hat{i} + 4\hat{j} + 6\hat{k})$, $(3\hat{i} + 5\hat{j} + 4\hat{k})$ and $(5\hat{i} + 8\hat{j} + 5\hat{k})$ are coplanar.

17. *If the vectors $\vec{a} = 2\hat{i} - \lambda\hat{j} + 3\hat{k}$, $\vec{b} = 3\hat{i} + 2\hat{j} - \mu\hat{k}$ and $\vec{c} = \hat{i} + \hat{j} + \hat{k}$ are coplanar, find μ in terms of λ.*

Ans: $\mu = \dfrac{3\lambda + 7}{\lambda + 2}$

18. *Prove that*

(i) $(\vec{a} + \vec{b}) \cdot \{(\vec{b} + \vec{c}) \times (\vec{c} + \vec{a})\} = 2\vec{a} \cdot (\vec{b} + \vec{c})$ *[NCERT]*

(ii) $\vec{a} \cdot \{\vec{b} \times (\vec{c} + \vec{d})\} = \vec{a} \cdot (\vec{b} \times \vec{c}) + \vec{a} \cdot (\vec{b} \times \vec{d})$

19. *$\vec{\alpha} = \lambda\hat{i} + \hat{j} + 3\hat{k}$, $\vec{\beta} = -\hat{i} + 2\hat{j} + \hat{k}$, $\vec{\gamma} = 3\hat{i} + \hat{j} + 2\hat{k}$ and $[\vec{\alpha}\,\vec{\beta}\,\vec{\gamma}] = -10$, then find the value of λ.*

Ans: $\lambda = 2$

20. *If the vectors $a\hat{j} + c\hat{k}$, $\hat{i} + \hat{k}$ and $c\hat{i} + c\hat{j} + b\hat{k}$ be coplanar, show that $c^2 = ab$.*

21. *Let $\vec{a} = \hat{i} + \hat{j} + \hat{k}$, $\vec{b} = \hat{i}$ and $\vec{c} = c_1\hat{i} + c_2\hat{j} + c_3\hat{k}$ then, if $c_1 = 1$ and $c_2 = 2$, find c_3 which makes $\vec{a}$, $\vec{b}$ and $\vec{c}$ coplanar.* *[NCERT]*

Ans: 2

22. *Find x such that the four points $A(3, 2, 1)$, $B(4, x, 5)$, $C(4, 2, -2)$ and $D(6, 5, -1)$ are coplanar.* *[NCERT]*

Ans: $x = 5$

23. *Show that the four points with position vectors $(6\hat{i} - 7\hat{j})$, $(16\hat{i} - 19\hat{j} - 4\hat{k})$, $(3\hat{j} - 6\hat{k})$ and $(2\hat{i} - 5\hat{j} + 10\hat{k})$ are coplanar.* *[CBSE 2004, '05]*

24. *Find the value of λ for which the four points with position vectors $(\hat{i} + 2\hat{j} + 3\hat{k})$, $(3\hat{i} - \hat{j} + 2\hat{k})$, $(-2\hat{i} + \lambda\hat{j} + \hat{k})$ and $(6\hat{i} - 4\hat{j} + 2\hat{k})$ are coplanar.* *[CBSE 2000]*

Ans: 3

25. *Find the value of λ for which the four points with position vectors $(-\hat{j} + \hat{k})$, $(2\hat{i} - \hat{j} - \hat{k})$, $(\hat{i} + \lambda\hat{j} + \hat{k})$ and $(3\hat{j} + 3\hat{k})$ are coplanar.* *[CBSE 2000]*

Ans: 1

26. *Using vector method, show that the points $A(4, 5, 1)$, $B(0, -1, -1)$, $C(3, 9, 4)$ and $D(-4, 4, 4)$ are coplanar.*

27. *Find the value of λ for which the points $A(3, 2, 1)$, $B(4, \lambda, 5)$, $C(4, 2, -2)$ and $D(6, 5, -1)$ are coplanar.* *[CBSE 2004C]*

Ans: $\lambda = 5$

28. *For any three vectors $\vec{a}, \vec{b}$ and $\vec{c}$, show that $\vec{a} - \vec{b}, \vec{b} - \vec{c}, \vec{c} - \vec{a}$ are coplanar.*

29. *Show that the vectors* $\vec{a}, \vec{b}$ *and* $\vec{c}$ *are coplanar if and only if* $\vec{a}+\vec{b}, \vec{b}+\vec{c}$ *and* $\vec{c}+\vec{a}$ *are coplanar.* **[NCERT; Delhi 2016; Foreign 2014]**

30. *Let* $\vec{a} = \hat{i} + \hat{j} + \hat{k}$, $\vec{b} = \hat{i}$ *and* $\vec{c} = c_1\hat{i} + c_2\hat{j} + c_3\hat{k}$.

(i) *If* $c_1 = 1$ *and* $c_2 = 2$, *then find* c_3 *which makes* $\vec{a}, \vec{b}$ *and* $\vec{c}$ *coplanar.*

Ans: 2

(ii) *If* $c_2 = -1$ *and* $c_3 = 1$, *then show that no value of* c_1 *can make,* $\vec{a}, \vec{b}$ *and* $\vec{c}$ *coplanar.*

[Delhi 2017]

31. *Find the value of for which the four points with position vectors* $3\hat{i} - 2\hat{j} - \hat{k}$, $2\hat{i} + 3\hat{j} - 4\hat{k}$, $-\hat{i} + \hat{j} + 2\hat{k}$ *and* $4\hat{i} + 5\hat{j} + \lambda\hat{k}$ *are coplanar.*

Ans: $\dfrac{-146}{17}$

32. *If four points* A, B, C *and* D *with position vectors* $4\hat{i} + 3\hat{j} + 3\hat{k}$, $5\hat{i} + x\hat{j} + 7\hat{k}$, $5\hat{i} + 3\hat{j}$ *and* $7\hat{i} + 6\hat{j} + \hat{k}$ *respectively are coplanar, then find the value of* x. **[Delhi 2017C]**

Ans: 6

<u>NCERT SOLUTION</u>

(i) EXERCISE : 10.1

1. *Represent graphically a displacement of 40 km, 30^0 east of north.*

SOLUTION : Displacement 40 km, 30^0, East of North.

$\Rightarrow$ Displacement vector $\overrightarrow{OA}$ (say)

such that $|\overrightarrow{OA}| = 40$ (given) and vector

$\overrightarrow{OA}$ makes an angle 30^0 with North in East-North quadrant.

NOTE : α^0 South of West $\Rightarrow A$ vector in South-West quadrant making an angle of α^0 with West.

2. *Check the following measures as scalars and vectors:*

    (i) *10 kg*   (ii) *2 meters north-west*   (iii) *40^0*

    (iv) *40 Watt*   (v) *10^{-19} coulomb*   (vi) *20 m/sec².*

SOLUTION :   (*i*) 10 kg is a measure of mass and therefore a scalar.

(∵ 10 kg has no direction, it is magnitude only).

(*ii*) 2 meters North-West is a measure of velocity (*i.e.*, has magnitude and direction both) and hence is a vector.

(*iii*) 40^0 is a measure of angle *i.e.*, is magnitude only and, therefore, a scalar.

(*iv*) 40 Watt is a measure of power (*i.e.*, 40 watt has no direction) and, therefore, a scalar.

(*v*) 10^{-19} coulomb is a measure of electric charge (*i.e.*, is magnitude only) and, therefore, a scalar.

(*vi*) 20 m/sec^2 is a measure of acceleration *i.e.*, is a measure of rate of change of velocity and hence is a vector.

3. Classify the following as scalar and vector quantities :

    (*i*) *time period*   (*ii*) *distance*   (*iii*) *force*

    (*iv*) *velocity*   (*v*) *work done*

SOLUTION :   (*i*) Time-scalar   (*ii*) Distance-scalar   (*iii*) force

    (*iv*) Velocity-vector   (*v*) Work done-scalar.

4. In the adjoining figure, (a square), identify the following vectors :

    (*i*) *Coinitial*   (*ii*) *Equal*   (*iii*) *Collinear but not equal.*

SOLUTION :   (*i*) $\vec{a}$ and $\vec{d}$ have same initial point and, therefore, coinitial vectors.

(*ii*) $\vec{b}$ and $\vec{d}$ have same direction and same magnitude. Therefore, and are equal vectors.

(*iii*) $\vec{a}$ and $\vec{c}$ have parallel supports, so that they are collinear. Since they have opposite directions, they are not equal.

Hence $\vec{a}$ and $\vec{c}$ are collinear but not equal.

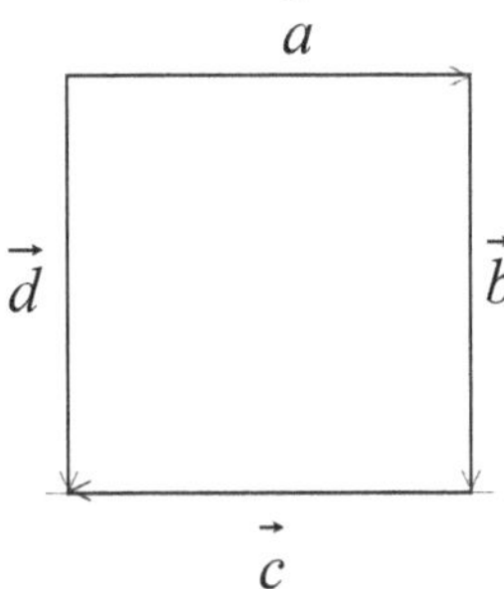

5. Answer the following as true or false :

(*i*) *and are collinear.*

(*ii*) *Two collinear vectors are always equal in magnitude.*

(*iii*) *Two vectors having same magnitude are collinear.*

(*iv*) *Two collinear vectors having the same magnitude are equal.*

SOLUTION :   (i) True.

(ii) False. ($\because \vec{a}$ and $2\vec{a}$ are collinear vectors but $|2\vec{a}| = 2|\vec{a}|$)

(iii) False.

($\because |\hat{i}| = |\hat{j}| = 1$ but $\hat{i}$ and $\hat{j}$ are vectors along x-axis (OX) and y-axis (OY) respectively.)

(iv) False.

($\because$ Vectors $\vec{a}$ and $-\vec{a}\ (= (-1)\vec{a} = m\vec{a})$ are collinear vectors and $|\vec{a}| = |-\vec{a}|$ but we know that $\vec{a} \neq -\vec{a}$ because their directions are opposite).

NOTE :   **Two vectors $\vec{a}$ and $\vec{b}$ are said to be equal if**

(i) $|\vec{a}| = |\vec{b}|$ (ii) $\vec{a}$ and $\vec{b}$ have same (like) direction.

NCERT SOLUTION

(ii) EXERCISE : 10.2

1. Compute the magnitude of the following vectors:

$$\vec{a} = \hat{i} + \hat{j} + \hat{k}, \quad \vec{b} = 2\hat{i} - 7\hat{j} - 3\hat{k},$$

$$\vec{c} = \frac{1}{\sqrt{3}}\hat{i} + \frac{1}{\sqrt{3}}\hat{j} - \frac{1}{\sqrt{3}}\hat{k}.$$

SOLUTION :   **Given :** $\vec{a} = \hat{i} + \hat{j} + \hat{k}$

Therefore, $|\vec{a}| = \sqrt{x^2 + y^2 + z^2} = \sqrt{1+1+1} = \sqrt{3}$

$$\vec{b} = 2\hat{i} - 7\hat{j} - 3\hat{k}$$

Therefore, $|\vec{b}| = \sqrt{4+49+9} = \sqrt{62}$

$$\vec{c} = \frac{1}{\sqrt{3}}\hat{i} + \frac{1}{\sqrt{3}}\hat{j} - \frac{1}{\sqrt{3}}\hat{k}$$

Therefore, $|\vec{c}| = \sqrt{\left(\frac{1}{\sqrt{3}}\right)^2 + \left(\frac{1}{\sqrt{3}}\right)^2 + \left(\frac{-1}{\sqrt{3}}\right)^2}$

$$= \sqrt{\frac{1}{3}+\frac{1}{3}+\frac{1}{3}} = \sqrt{\frac{3}{3}} = \sqrt{1} = 1$$

2. Write two different vectors having same magnitude.

SOLUTION :   Let $\vec{a} = \hat{i} + \hat{j} + \hat{k}$ and $\vec{b} = \hat{i} + \hat{j} - \hat{k}$.

Clearly, $\vec{a} \neq \vec{b}$ ($\because$ Coefficients of $\hat{i}$ and $\hat{j}$ are same in vectors $\vec{a}$ and $\vec{b}$ but coefficients of $\hat{k}$ in $\vec{a}$ and $\vec{b}$ are unequal as $1 \neq -1$).

But $|\vec{a}| = \sqrt{x^2 + y^2 + z^2} = \sqrt{1+1+1} = \sqrt{3}$

and $|\vec{b}| = \sqrt{1+1+1} = \sqrt{3}$ $\therefore \; |\vec{a}| = |\vec{b}|$

REMARK :   In this way, we can construct an infinite number of possible answers.

3. Write two different vectors having same direction.

SOLUTION :   Let $\vec{a} = \hat{i} + 2\hat{j} + 3\hat{k}$

and $\vec{b} = 2(\hat{i} + 2\hat{j} + 3\hat{k})$

$= 2\vec{a}$

$\therefore \;\; \vec{b} = m\vec{a}$ where $m = 2 > 0$

$\therefore$ Vectors $\vec{a}$ and $\vec{b}$ have the same direction.

But $\vec{b} \neq \vec{a} \, [\because \; \vec{b} = 2\vec{a} \Rightarrow |\vec{b}| = |2| \, |\vec{a}| = 2|\vec{a}| \neq |\vec{a}|]$

REMARK :   In this way, we can construct an infinite number of possible answers.

4. Find the values of x and y so that the vectors $2\hat{i} + 3\hat{j}$ and $x\hat{i} + y\hat{j}$ are equal.

SOLUTION :   **Given :** $2\hat{i} + 3\hat{j} = x\hat{i} + y\hat{j}$

Comparing coefficients of $\hat{i}$ and $\hat{j}$ on both sides,

we have $x = 2$ and $y = 3$.

5. Find the scalar and vector components of the vector with initial point (2, 1) and terminal point (–5, 7).

SOLUTION :   Let $\overrightarrow{AB}$ be the vector with initial point $A\,(2, 1)$ and terminal point $B\,(-5, 7)$.

$\Rightarrow$ $P.V.$ (Position Vector) of point A is $(2, 1) = 2\hat{i} + \hat{j}$ and $P.V.$ of point B is $(-5, 7) = -5\hat{i} + 7\hat{j}$.

$\therefore$ $\overrightarrow{AB} = P.V.$ of point $B - P.V.$ of point A

$$= (-5\hat{i} + 7\hat{j})) - (2\hat{i} + \hat{j}) = -5\hat{i} + 7\hat{j} - 2\hat{i} - \hat{j}$$

$$\Rightarrow \overrightarrow{AB} = -7\hat{i} + 6\hat{j}.$$

$\therefore$ By definition, scalar components of the vectors $\overrightarrow{AB}$ are coefficients of $\hat{i}$ and $\hat{j}$ in $\overrightarrow{AB}$ i.e., -7 and 6 and vector components of the vector $\overrightarrow{AB}$ are $-7\hat{i}$ and $6\hat{j}$.

6. Find the sum of the vectors :

$$\vec{a} = \hat{i} - 2\hat{j} + \hat{k}, \ \vec{b} = -2\hat{i} + 4\hat{j} + 5\hat{k}$$

and $\quad \vec{c} = \hat{i} - 6\hat{j} - 7\hat{k}.$

SOLUTION :   **Given :** $\vec{a} = \hat{i} + \hat{j} + \hat{k}, \ \vec{b} = -2\hat{i} + 4\hat{j} + 5\hat{k}$

and $\vec{c} = \hat{i} - 6\hat{j} - 7\hat{k}$

Adding $\vec{a} + \vec{b} + \vec{c} = 0\hat{i} - 4\hat{j} - \hat{k} = -4\hat{j} - \hat{k}.$

7. Find the unit vector in the direction of the vector $\vec{a} = \hat{i} + \hat{j} + 2\hat{k}$.

SOLUTION :   We know that a unit vector in the direction of the vector

$$\vec{a} = \hat{i} + \hat{j} + 2\hat{k} \text{ is } \hat{a} = \frac{\vec{a}}{|\vec{a}|} = \frac{\hat{i} + \hat{j} + 2\hat{k}}{\sqrt{1+1+4}}$$

$$\Rightarrow \hat{a} = \frac{\hat{i} + \hat{j} + 2\hat{k}}{\sqrt{6}} = \frac{1}{\sqrt{6}}\hat{i} + \frac{1}{\sqrt{6}}\hat{j} + \frac{2}{\sqrt{6}}\hat{k}.$$

8. Find the unit vector in the direction of the vector $\overrightarrow{PQ}$ where P and Q are the points (1, 2, 3) and (4, 5, 6) respectively.

SOLUTION :   Because points P and Q are $P(1, 2, 3)$ and $Q(4, 5, 6)$ (given), therefore, position vector of point $P = \overrightarrow{OP} = 1\hat{i} + 2\hat{j} + 3\hat{k}$

and position vector of point $Q = \overrightarrow{OQ} = 4\hat{i} + 5\hat{j} + 6\hat{k}$

where O is the origin.

$\therefore \qquad \overrightarrow{PQ} = $ Position vector of point $Q -$ Position vector of point P

$$= \overrightarrow{OQ} - \overrightarrow{OP} = 3\hat{i} + 3\hat{j} + 3\hat{k}$$

Therefore, a unit vector in the direction of vector $\overrightarrow{PQ}$

$$= \frac{\overrightarrow{PQ}}{|\overrightarrow{PQ}|} = \frac{3\hat{i} + 3\hat{j} + 3\hat{k}}{\sqrt{9+9+9} = \sqrt{27} = \sqrt{9 \times 3}}$$

$$= \frac{3(\hat{i} + \hat{j} + \hat{k})}{3\sqrt{3}} = \frac{(\hat{i} + \hat{j} + \hat{k})}{3\sqrt{3}} = \frac{1}{\sqrt{3}}\hat{i} + \frac{1}{\sqrt{3}}\hat{j} + \frac{1}{\sqrt{3}}\hat{k}.$$

9. For given vectors $\vec{a} = 2\hat{i} - \hat{j} + 2\hat{k}$ and $\vec{b} = -\hat{i} + \hat{j} - \hat{k}$; find the unit vector in the direction of $\vec{a} + \vec{b}$.

SOLUTION :   **Given:** Vectors $\vec{a} = 2\hat{i} - \hat{j} + 2\hat{k}$ and $\vec{b} = -\hat{i} + \hat{j} - \hat{k}$

$\therefore \qquad \vec{a} + \vec{b} = 2\hat{i} - \hat{j} + 2\hat{k} - \hat{i} + \hat{j} - \hat{k} = \hat{i} + 0\hat{j} + \hat{k}$

$\therefore \qquad |\vec{a} + \vec{b}| = \sqrt{(1)^2 + (0)^2 + (1)^2} = \sqrt{2}$

$\therefore \qquad$ A unit vector in the direction of $\vec{a} + \vec{b}$ is

$$\frac{\vec{a} + \vec{b}}{|\vec{a} + \vec{b}|} = \frac{\hat{i} + 0\hat{j} + \hat{k}}{\sqrt{2}} = \frac{\hat{i} + \hat{k}}{\sqrt{2}} = \frac{1}{\sqrt{2}}\hat{i} + \frac{1}{\sqrt{2}}\hat{k}.$$

10. Find a vector in the direction of vector $5\hat{i} - \hat{j} + 2\hat{k}$ which has magnitude 8 units.

SOLUTION :   Let $\vec{a} = 5\hat{i} - \hat{j} + 2\hat{k}$

$\therefore$ A vector in the direction fo vector $\vec{a}$ which has magnitude 8 units.

$$= 8\hat{a} = 8 \cdot \frac{\vec{a}}{|\vec{a}|} = \frac{8(5\hat{i} - \hat{j} + 2\hat{k})}{\sqrt{25 + 1 + 4}}$$

$$= \frac{8}{\sqrt{30}}(5\hat{i} - \hat{j} + 2\hat{k}) = \frac{40}{\sqrt{30}}\hat{i} - \frac{8}{\sqrt{30}}\hat{j} + \frac{16}{\sqrt{30}}\hat{k}.$$

11. Show that the vectors $2\hat{i} - 3\hat{j} + 4\hat{k}$ and $-4\hat{i} + 6\hat{j} - 8\hat{k}$ are collinear.

SOLUTION :   Let $\vec{a} = 2\hat{i} - 3\hat{j} + 4\hat{k}$ ... (i)

and $\vec{b} = -4\hat{i} + 6\hat{j} - 8\hat{k}$

$$= -2(2\hat{i} - 3\hat{j} + 4\hat{k}) = -2\vec{a} \qquad \text{[By (i)]}$$

$$\Rightarrow \vec{b} = -2\vec{a} = m\vec{a} \text{ where } m = -2 < 0$$

$\therefore$ Vectors $\vec{a}$ and $\vec{b}$ are collinear (unlike because $m = -2 < 0$).

12. Find the direction cosines of the vector $\hat{i} + 2\hat{j} + 3\hat{k}$.

SOLUTION :   The given vector is $(\vec{a}) = \hat{i} + 2\hat{j} + 3\hat{k}$

$$= \frac{\hat{i} + 2\hat{j} + 3\hat{k}}{\sqrt{14}} = \frac{1}{\sqrt{14}}\hat{i} + \frac{2}{\sqrt{14}}\hat{j} + \frac{3}{\sqrt{14}}\hat{k}$$

We know that direction cosines of a vector $\vec{a}$ are coefficients of $\hat{i}, \hat{j}, \hat{k}$ in

$\hat{a}$ i.e., $\dfrac{1}{\sqrt{14}}, \dfrac{2}{\sqrt{14}}, \dfrac{3}{\sqrt{14}}$.

13. Find the direction cosines of the vector joining the points A(1, 2, –3) and B(–1, –2, 1) directed from A to B.

SOLUTION :   Given: Points $A(1, 2, -3)$ and $B(-1, -2, 1)$

A —————→———— B
(1, 2, −3)   (−1, −2, 1)

$= P.V.$ (Position Vector, $\overrightarrow{OA}$) of point A is $A(1, 2, -3) = \hat{i} + 2\hat{j} - 3\hat{k}$ and

$P.V$ of point B is $B(-1, -2, 1) = -\hat{i} - 2\hat{j} + \hat{k}$.

$\therefore$ Vector $\overrightarrow{AB}$ (directed from A to B)

$= P.V.$ of point $B - P.V.$ of point A

$$= -\hat{i} - 2\hat{j} + \hat{k} - (\hat{i} + 2\hat{j} - 3\hat{k})$$

$$= -\hat{i} - 2\hat{j} + \hat{k} - \hat{i} - 2\hat{j} + 3\hat{k} = -2\hat{i} - 4\hat{j} + 4\hat{k}$$

$\therefore \qquad AB = |\overrightarrow{AB}| = \sqrt{(-2)^2 + (-4)^2 + 4^2} = \sqrt{4 + 16 + 16} = 6$

$$\therefore \text{ A unit vector along } \overrightarrow{AB} = \frac{\overrightarrow{AB}}{|\overrightarrow{AB}|}$$

$$= \frac{-2\hat{i} - 4\hat{j} + 4\hat{k}}{6} = -\frac{2}{6}\hat{i} - \frac{4}{6}\hat{j} + \frac{4}{6}\hat{k} = \frac{-1}{3}\hat{i} - \frac{2}{3}\hat{j} + \frac{2}{3}\hat{k}.$$

We know that Direction Cosines of the vector $\overrightarrow{AB}$ are the coefficients of $\hat{i}, \hat{j}, \hat{k}$

in a unit vector along $\overrightarrow{AB}$ i.e., $\frac{-1}{3}, \frac{-2}{3}, \frac{2}{3}.$

14. Show that the vector $\hat{i} + \hat{j} + \hat{k}$ is equally inclined to the axes OX, OY and OZ.

SOLUTION :   Let $\vec{a} = \hat{i} + \hat{j} + \hat{k}$.

Let us find angle θ_1 (say) between vector $\vec{a}$ and $OX\,(\Rightarrow \hat{i}\,)$

($\because \hat{i}$ represents OX in vector form)

$$\therefore \qquad \theta_1 = \frac{\vec{a}.\hat{i}}{|\vec{a}||\hat{i}|}$$

$$\Rightarrow \cos\theta_1 = \frac{(\hat{i} + \hat{j} + \hat{k}).(\hat{i} + 0\hat{j} + 0\hat{k})}{|\hat{i} + \hat{j} + \hat{k}||\hat{i} + \hat{j} + \hat{k}|}$$

$$\Rightarrow \cos\theta_1 = \frac{1(1) + 1(0) + 1(0)}{\sqrt{1+1+1}\sqrt{1+0+0}} = \frac{1}{\sqrt{3}} \Rightarrow \theta_1 = \cos^{-1}\frac{1}{\sqrt{3}}$$

Similarly, angle θ_2 between vectors $\vec{a}$ and $\hat{j}\,(OY)$ is $\cos^{-1}\frac{1}{\sqrt{3}}$

and angle θ_3 between vectors $\vec{a}$ and $\hat{k}\,(OZ)$ is also $\cos^{-1}\frac{1}{\sqrt{3}}$

$$\therefore \quad \theta_1 = \theta_2 = \theta_3$$

$\therefore$ Vectors $\vec{a} = \hat{i} + \hat{j} + \hat{k}$ is equally inclined to OX, OY and $OZ.$

15. Find the position vector of a point R which divides the line joining two points P and Q whose position vectors are $\hat{i} + 2\hat{j} - \hat{k}$ and $-\hat{i} + \hat{j} + \hat{k}$ respectively, in the ratio 2 : 1 (i) internally

(ii) externally.

SOLUTION : $P.V.$ of point P is $\vec{a} = \hat{i} + 2\hat{j} - \hat{k}$

and $P.V.$ of point Q is $\vec{b} = -\hat{i} + \hat{j} + \hat{k}$

(*i*) Therefore $P.V.$ of point R dividing PQ internally (*i.e.*, R lies within the segment PQ) in the ratio $2:1 = (m:n)$ $(= PR:QR)$ is

$$\frac{m\,\vec{b} + n\,\vec{a}}{m + n}$$

$$= \frac{2(-\hat{i} + \hat{j} + \hat{k}) + \hat{i} + 2\hat{j} - \hat{k}}{2 + 1}$$

$$= \frac{-2\hat{i} + 2\hat{j} + 2\hat{k} + \hat{i} + 2\hat{j} - \hat{k}}{3}$$

$$= \frac{-\hat{i} + 4\hat{j} + \hat{k}}{3} = \frac{-1}{3}\hat{i} + \frac{4}{3}\hat{j} + \frac{1}{3}\hat{k}$$

(*ii*) $P.V.$ of point R dividing PQ externally (*i.e.*, R lies outside PQ and to the right of point Q because ratio $2:1 = \dfrac{2}{1} > 1$ as PR is

2 times PQ *i.e.*, $\left. \dfrac{PR}{QR} = \dfrac{2}{1} \right)$ is $\dfrac{m\,\vec{b} - n\,\vec{a}}{m - n}$

$$= \frac{2(-\hat{i} + \hat{j} + \hat{k}) - (\hat{i} + 2\hat{j} - \hat{k})}{2 - 1}$$

$$= -2\hat{i} + 2\hat{j} + 2\hat{k} - \hat{i} - 2\hat{j} + \hat{k} = -3\hat{i} + \hat{k}$$

Remark : In the above question 15(*ii*), had R been dividing PQ externally in the ration $1:2$; then R will lie to the left of point P and $\dfrac{PR}{QR} = \dfrac{1}{2}$.

16. Find the position vector of the mid-point of the vector joining the points P(2, 3, 4) and Q(4, 1, − 2).

SOLUTION : **Given:** Point P is $(2, 3, 4)$ and Q is $(4, 1, -2)$.

$\Rightarrow$ $P.V.$ of point $P\,(2, 3, 4)$ is $\vec{a} = 2\hat{i} + 3\hat{j} + 4\hat{k}$

and $P.V.$ of point $Q\,(4,1,-2)$ is $\vec{b} = 4\hat{i} + \hat{j} - 2\hat{k}$

$\therefore$ $P.V.$ of mid-point R of PQ is $\dfrac{\vec{a} + \vec{b}}{2}$

[By Formula of Internal division]

$$= \frac{2\hat{i} + 3\hat{j} + 4\hat{k} + 4\hat{i} + \hat{j} - 2\hat{k}}{2}$$

$$= \frac{6\hat{i} + 4\hat{j} + 2\hat{k}}{2} = 3\hat{i} + 2\hat{j} + \hat{k}$$

17. Show that the points A, B and C with position vectors $\vec{a} = 3\hat{i} - 4\hat{j} - 4\hat{k}$, $\vec{b} = 2\hat{i} - \hat{j} + \hat{k}$ and $\vec{c} = \hat{i} - 3\hat{j} - 5\hat{k}$, respectively form the vertices of a right-angled triangle.

SOLUTION :   **Given :** $P.V.$ of points A, B, C respectively are $\vec{a}\,(=\overrightarrow{OA}) = 3\hat{i} - 4\hat{j} - 4\hat{k}$,

$\vec{b}\,(=\overrightarrow{OB}) = 2\hat{i} - \hat{j} + \hat{k}$ and $\vec{c}\,(=\overrightarrow{OC}) = \hat{i} - 3\hat{j} - 5\hat{k}$, where O is the origin.

Step I. $\therefore$ $\overrightarrow{AB} = P.V.$ of point $B - P.V.$ of point A

$$= 2\hat{i} - \hat{j} + \hat{k} - (3\hat{i} - 4\hat{j} - 4\hat{k})$$

$$= 2\hat{i} - \hat{j} + \hat{k} - 3\hat{i} + 4\hat{j} + 4\hat{k}$$

or $\qquad \overrightarrow{AB} = -\hat{i} + 3\hat{j} + 5\hat{k}$ $\hspace{3cm}$ ... (i)

$\overrightarrow{BC} = P.V.$ of point $C - P.V.$ of point B

$$= (\hat{i} - 3\hat{j} - 5\hat{k}) - (2\hat{i} - \hat{j} + \hat{k})$$

$$= \hat{i} - 3\hat{j} - 5\hat{k} - 2\hat{i} + \hat{j} - \hat{k}$$

$$= -\hat{i} - 2\hat{j} - 6\hat{k} \hspace{3cm} ...\,(ii)$$

$\overrightarrow{AC} = P.V.$ of point $C - P.V.$ of point A

$$= \hat{i} - 3\hat{j} - 5\hat{k} - (3\hat{i} - 4\hat{j} - 4\hat{k})$$

$$= \hat{i} - 3\hat{j} - 5\hat{k} - 3\hat{i} + 4\hat{j} + 4\hat{k}$$

$$= -2\hat{i} + \hat{j} - \hat{k} \hspace{3cm} ...\,(iii)$$

Adding (i) and (ii),

$$\overrightarrow{AB} + \overrightarrow{BC} = -\hat{i} + 3\hat{j} + 5\hat{k} - \hat{i} - 2\hat{j} - 6\hat{k}$$

$$-2\hat{i} + \hat{j} - \hat{k} = \overrightarrow{AC} \qquad\qquad\qquad\qquad [\text{By } (iii)]$$

$\therefore$ By Triangle Law of addition of Vectors, Points A, B, C are the Vertices of a triangle or points A, B, C are collinear.

Step II.

From (i) $AB = |\overrightarrow{AB}| = \sqrt{1+9+25} = \sqrt{35}$

From (ii), $BC = |\overrightarrow{BC}| = \sqrt{1+4+36} = \sqrt{41}$

From (iii), $AC = |\overrightarrow{AC}| = \sqrt{4+1+1} = \sqrt{6}$

We can observe that $(\text{Longest side } BC)^2 = (\sqrt{41})^2 = 41 = 35 + 6$

$$= AB^2 + AC^2$$

$\therefore$ Points A, B, C are the vertices of a right-angled triangle.

18. In triangle ABC (Fig. below), which of the following is not true:

(A) $\overrightarrow{AB} + \overrightarrow{BC} + \overrightarrow{CA} = \vec{0}$

(B) $\overrightarrow{AB} + \overrightarrow{BC} - \overrightarrow{AC} = \vec{0}$

(C) $\overrightarrow{AB} + \overrightarrow{BC} - \overrightarrow{CA} = \vec{0}$

(D) $\overrightarrow{AB} - \overrightarrow{CB} + \overrightarrow{CA} = \vec{0}$

SOLUTION: Option (C) is not true.

Because we know by Triangle Law of Addition of vectors that

$$\overrightarrow{AB} + \overrightarrow{BC} = \overrightarrow{AC}, \text{ i.e.,} \qquad \boxed{\overrightarrow{AB} + \overrightarrow{BC} = -\overrightarrow{CA}}$$

$$\Rightarrow \quad \overrightarrow{AB} + \overrightarrow{BC} - \overrightarrow{AC} = \overrightarrow{0} \quad \boxed{\Rightarrow \quad \overrightarrow{AB} + \overrightarrow{BC} + \overrightarrow{CA} = \overrightarrow{0}}$$

But for option (C), $\overrightarrow{AB} + \overrightarrow{BC} - \overrightarrow{CA} = \overrightarrow{AC} + \overrightarrow{AC} = 2\overrightarrow{AC} \neq \overrightarrow{0}$

Option (D) is same as option (A).

19. If $\vec{a}$ and $\vec{b}$ are two collinear vectors, then which of the following are incorrect :

(A) $\vec{b} = \lambda \vec{a}$, for some scalar λ.

(B) $\vec{a} = \pm\vec{b}$

(C) the respective components of $\vec{a}$ and $\vec{b}$ are proportional

(D) both the vectors $\vec{a}$ and $\vec{b}$ have same direction, but different magnitudes.

SOLUTION : Option (D) is not true because two collinear vectors can have **different** directions and also different magnitudes.

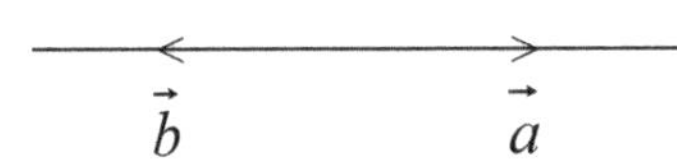

The options (A) and (C) are true by definition of collinear vectors. Option (B) is a particular case of option (A) (taking $\lambda = \pm 1$).

<u>NCERT SOLUTION</u>

(iii) EXERCISE : 10.3

1. Find the angle between two vectors $\vec{a}$ and $\vec{b}$ with magnitude $\sqrt{3}$ and, respectively having $\vec{a}.\vec{b} = \sqrt{6}$.

SOLUTION : **Given:** $|\vec{a}| = \sqrt{3}$, $|\vec{b}| = 2$ and $\vec{a}.\vec{b} = \sqrt{6}$

Let θ be the angle between the vectors $\vec{a}$ and $\vec{b}$. We know that

$$\cos\theta = \frac{\vec{a}.\vec{b}}{|\vec{a}||\vec{b}|}$$

Putting values, $\cos\theta = \dfrac{\sqrt{6}}{\sqrt{3}(2)}$

$$= \frac{\sqrt{6}}{\sqrt{3}\sqrt{4}} = \frac{\sqrt{6}}{\sqrt{12}} = \frac{\sqrt{1}}{\sqrt{2}} = \frac{1}{\sqrt{2}} = \cos\frac{\pi}{4} \qquad \therefore \quad \theta = \frac{\pi}{4}$$

2. Find the angle between the vectors $\hat{i} - 2\hat{j} + 3\hat{k}$ and $3\hat{i} - 2\hat{j} + \hat{k}$.

SOLUTION :   **Given:** Let $\vec{a} = \hat{i} - 2\hat{j} + 3\hat{k}$ and $\vec{b} = 3\hat{i} - 2\hat{j} + \hat{k}$.

$$\therefore \quad |\vec{a}| = \sqrt{1+4+9} = \sqrt{14} \quad |\because |x\hat{i} + y\hat{j} + z\hat{k}| = \sqrt{x^2 + y^2 + z^2}$$

and $\quad |\vec{b}| = \sqrt{9+4+1} = \sqrt{14}$

Also, $\vec{a} \cdot \vec{b}$ = Product of coefficients of $\hat{i}$ + Product of coefficient of $\hat{j}$

+ Product of coefficients of $\hat{k}$

$$= 1(3) + (-2)(-2) + 3(1) = 3 + 4 + 3 = 10$$

Let θ be the angle between the vectors $\vec{a}$ and $\vec{b}$.

We know that $\cos\theta = \dfrac{\vec{a}\cdot\vec{b}}{|\vec{a}||\vec{b}|} = \dfrac{10}{\sqrt{14}\sqrt{14}} = \dfrac{10}{14} = \dfrac{5}{7}$

$$\therefore \quad \theta = \cos^{-1}\dfrac{5}{7}.$$

3. Find the projection of the vector $\hat{i} - \hat{j}$ on the vector $\hat{i} + \hat{j}$.

SOLUTION :   Let $\vec{a} = \hat{i} - \hat{j} = \hat{i} - \hat{j} + 0\hat{k}$

and $\vec{b} = \hat{i} + \hat{j} = \hat{i} + \hat{j} + 0\hat{k}$

Projection of vector $\vec{a}$ and $\vec{b}$

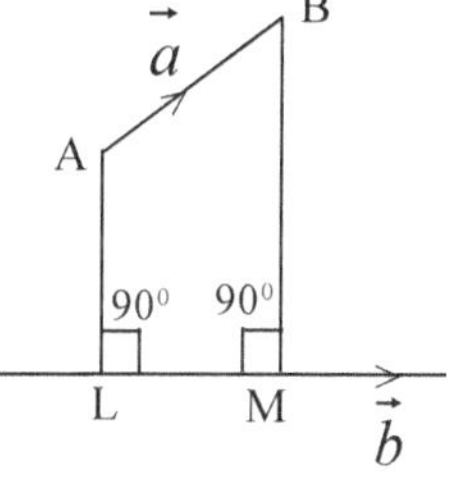

$$= \text{Length LM} = \dfrac{\vec{a}\cdot\vec{b}}{|\vec{b}|}$$

$$= \dfrac{(1)(1) + (-1)(1) + 0(0)}{\sqrt{(1)^2 + (1)^2 + 0^2}} = \dfrac{1-1+0}{\sqrt{0}} = \dfrac{0}{\sqrt{2}} = 0.$$

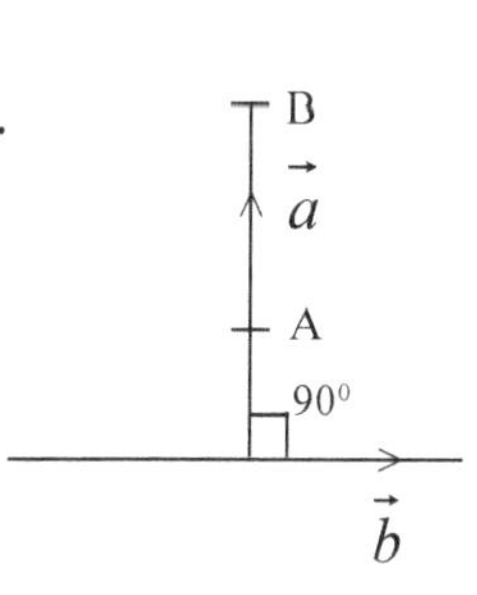

Remark : If projection of vector $\vec{a}$ on $\vec{b}$ is zero, then vector $\vec{a}$ is perpendicular to vector $\vec{b}$.

4. Find the projection of the vector $\hat{i} + 3\hat{j} + 7\hat{k}$ on the vector $7\hat{i} - \hat{j} + 8\hat{k}$.

SOLUTION :   Let $\vec{a} = \hat{i} + 3\hat{j} + 7\hat{k}$ and $\vec{b} = 7\hat{i} - \hat{j} + 8\hat{k}$

We know that projection of vector $\vec{a}$ on vector $\vec{b} = \dfrac{\vec{a}.\vec{b}}{|\vec{b}|}$

$$= \frac{1(7)+3(-1)+7(8)}{\sqrt{(7)^2+(-1)^2+(8)^2}} = \frac{7-3+56}{\sqrt{49+1+64}} = \frac{60}{\sqrt{114}}$$

5. Show that each of the given three vectors is a unit vector : $\dfrac{1}{7}(2\hat{i}+3\hat{j}+6\hat{k})$, $\dfrac{1}{7}(3\hat{i}+6\hat{j}+2\hat{k})$, $\dfrac{1}{7}(6\hat{i}+2\hat{j}-3\hat{k})$.

Also show that they are mutually perpendicular to each other.

SOLUTION : Let $\vec{a} = \dfrac{1}{7}(2\hat{i}+3\hat{j}+6\hat{k}) = \dfrac{2}{7}\hat{i}+\dfrac{3}{7}\hat{j}+\dfrac{6}{7}\hat{k}$ ...(i)

$$\vec{b} = \frac{1}{7}(3\hat{i}-6\hat{j}+2\hat{k}) = \frac{3}{7}\hat{i}-\frac{6}{7}\hat{j}+\frac{2}{7}\hat{k} \qquad ...(ii)$$

$$\vec{c} = \frac{1}{7}(6\hat{i}+2\hat{j}-3\hat{k}) = \frac{6}{7}\hat{i}+\frac{2}{7}\hat{j}-\frac{3}{7}\hat{k} \qquad ...(iii)$$

$$\therefore \quad |\vec{a}| = \sqrt{\left(\frac{2}{7}\right)^2+\left(\frac{3}{7}\right)^2+\left(\frac{6}{7}\right)^2} = \sqrt{\frac{4}{49}+\frac{9}{49}+\frac{36}{49}}$$

$$= \sqrt{\frac{4}{49}} = \sqrt{1} = 1$$

$$|\vec{b}| = \sqrt{\left(\frac{3}{7}\right)^2+\left(\frac{-6}{7}\right)^2+\left(\frac{2}{7}\right)^2} = \sqrt{\frac{9}{49}+\frac{36}{49}+\frac{4}{49}} = \sqrt{\frac{49}{49}}$$

$$= \sqrt{1} = 1$$

$$|\vec{c}| = \sqrt{\left(\frac{6}{7}\right)^2+\left(\frac{2}{7}\right)^2+\left(\frac{-3}{7}\right)^2} = \sqrt{\frac{36}{49}+\frac{4}{49}+\frac{9}{49}}$$

$$= \sqrt{\frac{49}{49}} = \sqrt{1} = 1$$

$\therefore$ Each of the three given vectors $\vec{a}$, $\vec{b}$, $\vec{c}$ is a unit vector. From (i) and (ii), and are perpendicular to each other. From (i) and (ii).

$$\vec{a}.\vec{b} = \left(\frac{2}{7}\right).\left(\frac{2}{7}\right) + \left(\frac{3}{7}\right)\left(\frac{-6}{7}\right) + \left(\frac{6}{7}\right)\left(\frac{2}{7}\right)$$

$$[\vec{a}.\vec{b} = a_1 b_1 + a_2 b_2 + a_3 b_3]$$

$$= \frac{6}{49} - \frac{18}{49} + \frac{12}{49} = \frac{6-18+12}{49} = \frac{0}{49} = 0$$

$\therefore \ \vec{a}$ and $\vec{b}$ are perpendicular to each other.

From (ii) and (iii),

$$\vec{b}.\vec{c} = \left(\frac{3}{7}\right)\left(\frac{6}{7}\right) + \left(\frac{-6}{7}\right)\left(\frac{2}{7}\right) + \frac{2}{7}\left(\frac{-3}{7}\right)$$

$$= \frac{18}{49} - \frac{12}{49} - \frac{6}{49} = \frac{18-12-6}{49} = \frac{0}{49} = 0$$

$\therefore \ \vec{b}$ and $\vec{c}$ are perpendicular to each other.

From (i) and (iii),

$$\vec{a}.\vec{c} = \frac{2}{7}\left(\frac{6}{7}\right) + \frac{3}{7}\left(\frac{2}{7}\right) + \left(\frac{6}{7}\right)\left(\frac{-3}{7}\right)$$

$$= \frac{12}{49} + \frac{6}{49} - \frac{18}{49} = \frac{12+6-18}{49} = \frac{0}{49} = 0$$

$\therefore \ \vec{a}$ and $\vec{c}$ are perpendicular to each other.

Hence, $\vec{a}, \vec{b}, \vec{c}$ are mutually perpenducular vectors.

6. Find $|\vec{a}|$ and $|\vec{b}|$, if $(\vec{a}+\vec{b}).(\vec{a}-\vec{b}) = 8$ and $|\vec{a}| = 8|\vec{b}|$.

SOLUTION :   **Given:** $(\vec{a}+\vec{b}).(\vec{a}-\vec{b}) = 8$ and $|\vec{a}| = 8|\vec{b}|$ ...(i)

$$\Rightarrow \quad \vec{a}.\vec{a} - \vec{a}.\vec{b} + \vec{b}.\vec{a} - \vec{b}.\vec{b} = 8$$

$$\Rightarrow \quad |\vec{a}|^2 - \vec{a}.\vec{b} + \vec{a}.\vec{b} - |\vec{b}|^2 = 8$$

$[\because$ We know that $\vec{a}.\vec{a} = |\vec{a}|^2$ and $\vec{b}.\vec{b} = |\vec{b}|^2$ and $\vec{b}.\vec{a} = \vec{a}.\vec{b}]$

$$\Rightarrow \quad |\vec{a}|^2 - |\vec{b}|^2 = 8 \qquad ...(ii)$$

Putting $|\vec{a}| = 8|\vec{b}|$ from (i) in (ii), $64|\vec{b}|^2 - |\vec{b}|^2 = 8$

or $(64-1)|\vec{b}|^2 = 8$ $\Rightarrow$ $63|\vec{b}|^2 = 8$

$\Rightarrow$ $|\vec{b}|^2 = \dfrac{8}{63}$ $\Rightarrow$ $|\vec{b}| = \sqrt{\dfrac{8}{63}} = \sqrt{\dfrac{4 \times 2}{9 \times 7}}$

($\because$ Length *i.e.*, modulus of a vector is never negative.)

$\Rightarrow$ $|\vec{b}| = \dfrac{2}{3}\sqrt{\dfrac{2}{7}}$

Putting this value of $|\vec{b}|$ in (i),

$$|\vec{a}| = 8\left(\dfrac{2}{3}\sqrt{\dfrac{2}{7}}\right) = \dfrac{16}{3}\sqrt{\dfrac{2}{7}}$$

7. Evaluate the product $(3\vec{a} - 5\vec{b}) \cdot (2\vec{a} + 7\vec{b})$.

SOLUTION : The given expression $= (3\vec{a} - 5\vec{b}) \cdot (2\vec{a} + 7\vec{b})$

$$= (3\vec{a}) \cdot (2\vec{a}) + (3\vec{a}) \cdot (7\vec{b}) - (5\vec{b}) \cdot (2\vec{a}) - (5\vec{b}) \cdot (7\vec{b})$$

$$= 6\vec{a} \cdot \vec{a} + 21\vec{a} \cdot \vec{b} - 10\vec{b} \cdot \vec{a} - 35\vec{b} \cdot \vec{b}$$

$$= 6|\vec{a}|^2 + 21\vec{a} \cdot \vec{b} - 10\vec{a} \cdot \vec{b} - 35|\vec{b}|^2$$

$$[\because \vec{a} \cdot \vec{a} = |\vec{a}|^2 \text{ and } \vec{b} \cdot \vec{b} = |\vec{b}|^2 \text{ and } \vec{b} \cdot \vec{a} = \vec{a} \cdot \vec{b}]$$

$$= 6|\vec{a}|^2 + 11\vec{a} \cdot \vec{b} - 35|\vec{b}|^2$$

8. Find the magnitude of two vectors $\vec{a}$ and $\vec{b}$, having the same magnitude such that the angle between them is and their scalar product is $\dfrac{1}{2}$.

SOLUTION : **Given :** $|\vec{a}| = |\vec{b}|$ and angle θ (say) between $\vec{a}$ and $\vec{b}$ is 60^0 and their

scalar (*i.e.*, dot) product $= \dfrac{1}{2}$

i.e., $\quad \vec{a}.\vec{b} = \dfrac{1}{2}$

$$\Rightarrow |\vec{a}||\vec{b}| \cos\theta = \dfrac{1}{2} \qquad [\because \ \vec{a}.\vec{b} = |\vec{a}||\vec{b}| \cos\theta \ ]$$

Putting $|\vec{b}| = |\vec{a}|$ (given) and $\theta = 60^0$ (given), we have

$$|\vec{a}||\vec{a}| \cos 60^0 = \dfrac{1}{2} \qquad\qquad \Rightarrow |\vec{a}|^2 \left(\dfrac{1}{2}\right) = \dfrac{1}{2}$$

Multiplying by 2, $\quad |\vec{a}|^2 = 1 \qquad\qquad \Rightarrow |\vec{a}| = 1 \qquad\qquad ...(i)$

$$(\because \ \text{Length of a vector is never negative})$$

$\therefore \ \ |\vec{b}||\vec{a}| = 1 \qquad\qquad\qquad\qquad\qquad\qquad\qquad\qquad [\text{By } (i)]$

$\therefore \ \ |\vec{a}| = 1 \ \text{ and } \ |\vec{b}| = 1.$

9. Find $|\vec{x}|$, if for a unit vector $\vec{a}, (\vec{x} - \vec{a}).(\vec{x} + \vec{a}) = 12$.

SOLUTION : $\qquad$ **Given:** $\vec{a}$ is a unit vector $\Rightarrow |\vec{a}| = 1 \qquad\qquad\qquad ...(i)$

Also given $\qquad (\vec{x} - \vec{a}).(\vec{x} + \vec{a}) = 12$

$$\Rightarrow \vec{x}.\vec{x} + \vec{x}.\vec{a} - \vec{a}.\vec{x} - \vec{a}.\vec{a} = 12$$

$$\Rightarrow |\vec{x}|^2 + \vec{a}.\vec{x} - \vec{a}.\vec{x} - |\vec{a}|^2 = 12$$

$$\Rightarrow |\vec{x}|^2 - |\vec{a}|^2 = 12$$

Putting $|\vec{a}| = 1$ from (i), $|\vec{x}|^2 - 1 = 12$

$$\Rightarrow |\vec{x}|^2 = 13 \qquad\qquad \Rightarrow |\vec{x}| = \sqrt{13}$$

$$(\because \ \text{Length of a vector is never negative.})$$

10. If $\vec{a} = 2\hat{i} + 2\hat{j} + 3\hat{k}, \ \vec{b} = -\hat{i} + 2\hat{j} + \hat{k}$ and $\vec{c} = 3\hat{i} + \hat{j}$ are such that $\vec{a} + \lambda\vec{b}$ is perpendicular to $\vec{c}$, then find the value λ.

SOLUTION : $\qquad$ **Given:** $\vec{a} = 2\hat{i} + 2\hat{j} + 3\hat{k}, \ \vec{b} = -\hat{i} + 2\hat{j} + \hat{k}$

and $\qquad \vec{c} = 3\hat{i} + \hat{j}$

Now, $\quad \vec{a} + \lambda \vec{b} = 2\hat{i} + 2\hat{j} + 3\hat{k} + \lambda(-\hat{i} + 2\hat{j} + \hat{k})$

$$= 2\hat{i} + 2\hat{j} + 3\hat{k} - \lambda\hat{i} + 2\lambda\hat{j} + \lambda\hat{k}$$

$$\Rightarrow \vec{a} + \lambda \vec{b} = (2 - \lambda)\hat{j} + (2 + 2\lambda)\hat{j} + (3 + \lambda)\hat{k}$$

Again given $\vec{c} = 3\hat{i} + \hat{j} = 3\hat{i} + \hat{j} + 0\hat{k}$

Because vector $\vec{a} + \lambda \vec{a}$ is perpendicular to $\vec{c}$, therefore,

$$(\vec{a} + \lambda \vec{b}) \cdot \vec{c} = 0$$

i.e., Product of coefficients of $\quad \hat{i} + \ldots\ldots\ldots = 0$

$$\Rightarrow \quad (2 - \lambda)3 + (2 + 2\lambda)1 + (3 + \lambda)0 = 0$$

$$\Rightarrow \quad 6 - 3\lambda + 2 + 2\lambda = 0$$

$$\Rightarrow \quad -\lambda + 8 = 0$$

$$\Rightarrow \quad -\lambda = -8$$

$$\Rightarrow \quad \lambda = 8.$$

11. Show that $|\vec{a}|\vec{b} + |\vec{b}|\vec{a}$ is perpendicular to $|\vec{a}|\vec{b} - |\vec{b}|\vec{a}$, for any two non-zero vectors $\vec{a}$ and $\vec{b}$.

SOLUTION : $\quad$ Let $\vec{c} = |\vec{a}|\vec{b} + |\vec{b}|\vec{a} = l\vec{b} + m\vec{a}$

Where $l = |\vec{a}|$ and $m = |\vec{b}|$

Let $\quad \vec{d} = |\vec{a}|\vec{b} - |\vec{b}|\vec{a} = l\vec{b} - m\vec{a}$

Now, $\quad \vec{c} \cdot \vec{d} = (l\vec{b} + m\vec{a}) \cdot (l\vec{b} - m\vec{a})$

$$= l^2 \vec{b} \cdot \vec{b} - l\,m\,\vec{b} \cdot \vec{a} + l\,m\,\vec{a} \cdot \vec{b} - m^2 \vec{a}\,\vec{a}$$

$$= l^2 |\vec{b}|^2 - l\,m\,\vec{a} \cdot \vec{b} + l\,m\,\vec{a} \cdot \vec{b} - m^2 |\vec{a}|^2 = l^2 |\vec{b}|^2 - m^2 |\vec{a}|$$

Putting $l = |\vec{a}|$ and $m = |\vec{b}|$,

$$= |\vec{a}|^2 |\vec{b}|^2 - |\vec{b}|^2 |\vec{a}|^2 = 0$$

i.e., $\quad \vec{c} \cdot \vec{d} = 0$

Vectors $\vec{c}$ and $\vec{d}$ are perpendicular to each other.

12. If $\vec{a}\cdot\vec{a}=0$ and $\vec{a}\cdot\vec{b}=0$, then what can be concluded about the vector $\vec{b}$?

SOLUTION :   **Given:** $\vec{a}\cdot\vec{a}=0 \Rightarrow |\vec{a}|^2=0 \Rightarrow |\vec{a}|=0$ ...(i)

$(\Rightarrow \vec{a}$ is a zero vector by definition of zero vector.)

Again given $\vec{a}\cdot\vec{b}=0$ $\Rightarrow |\vec{a}||\vec{b}|\cos\theta=0$

Putting $|\vec{a}|=0$ from (i), we have $0|\vec{b}|=\cos\theta=0$

i.e., $0=0$ for all (any) vectors $\vec{b}$. $\therefore \vec{b}$ can be any vector.

Note : $(\vec{a}+\vec{b}+\vec{c})^2 = (\vec{a}+(\vec{b}+\vec{c}))^2$

$$= \vec{a}^2 + (\vec{b}+\vec{c})^2 + 2\vec{a}\cdot(\vec{b}+\vec{c})$$

$$[\because \ (\vec{A}+\vec{B})^2 = \vec{A}^2 + \vec{B}^2 + 2\vec{A}\cdot\vec{B}]$$

$$= \vec{a}^2 + \vec{b}^2 + \vec{c}^2 + 2\vec{b}\cdot\vec{c} + 2\vec{a}\cdot\vec{b} + 2\vec{a}\cdot\vec{c}$$

Using $\vec{a}\cdot\vec{c} = \vec{c}\cdot\vec{a}$

or $(\vec{a}+\vec{b}+\vec{c})^2 = \vec{a}^2 + \vec{b}^2 + \vec{c}^2 + 2(\vec{a}\cdot\vec{b} + \vec{b}\cdot\vec{c} + \vec{c}\cdot\vec{a})$

13. If $\vec{a},\vec{b},\vec{c}$ are unit vectors such that $\vec{a}+\vec{b}+\vec{c}=\vec{0}$, find the value of $\vec{a}\cdot\vec{b}+\vec{b}\cdot\vec{c}+\vec{c}\cdot\vec{a}$.

SOLUTION :   Because $\vec{a},\ \vec{b},\ \vec{c}$ are unit vectors, therefore,

$$|\vec{a}|=1, |\vec{b}|=1 \text{ and } |\vec{c}|=1 \qquad ...(i)$$

Again given $\vec{a}+\vec{b}+\vec{c}=\vec{0}$

Squaring both sides $(\vec{a}+\vec{b}+\vec{c})^2 = 0$

Using formula of **Note** above

$$\Rightarrow \vec{a}^2+\vec{b}^2+\vec{c}^2+2(\vec{a}\cdot\vec{b}+\vec{b}\cdot\vec{c}+\vec{c}\cdot\vec{a})=0$$

or $|\vec{a}|^2 + |\vec{b}|^2 + |\vec{c}|^2 + 2(\vec{a}\cdot\vec{b}+\vec{b}\cdot\vec{c}+\vec{c}\cdot\vec{a})=0$

Putting $|\vec{a}|=1, |\vec{b}|=1, |\vec{c}|=1$ from (i),

$$1+1+1+2(\vec{a}\cdot\vec{b}+\vec{b}\cdot\vec{c}+\vec{c}\cdot\vec{a})=0$$

$$\Rightarrow \ 2(\vec{a}\cdot\vec{b}+\vec{b}\cdot\vec{c}+\vec{c}\cdot\vec{a}) = -3$$

Dividing both sides by 2, $\vec{a}\cdot\vec{b}+\vec{b}\cdot\vec{c}+\vec{c}\cdot\vec{a} = \dfrac{-3}{2}$.

14. If either vector $\vec{a} = \vec{0}$ or $\vec{b} = \vec{0}$, then $\vec{a}\cdot\vec{b} = 0$. But the converse need not be true. Justify your answer with an example.

SOLUTION :   **Case I.** Vector $\vec{a} = \vec{0}$. Therefore, by definition of zero vector,

$$|\vec{a}| = 0 \qquad\qquad\qquad\qquad ...(i)$$

$$\therefore \quad \vec{a}\cdot\vec{b} = |\vec{a}||\vec{b}|\cos\theta = 0(|\vec{b}|\cos\theta) \qquad\qquad [\text{By } (i)]$$

$$= 0$$

Case II. Vector $\vec{b} = \vec{0}$. Proceeding as above we can prove that $\vec{a}\cdot\vec{b} = 0$

But the converse is not true.

Let us justify it with an example.

Let $\vec{a} = \hat{i} + \hat{j} + \hat{k}$. Therefore, $|\vec{a}| = \sqrt{1^2 + 1^2 + 1^2} = \sqrt{3} \neq 0$.

Therefore $\vec{a} \neq \vec{0}$ (By definition of Zero Vector)

Let $\quad \vec{b} = \hat{i} + \hat{j} - 2\hat{k}$

Therefore, $|\vec{b}| = \sqrt{(1)^2 + (1)^2 + (-2)^2} = \sqrt{6} \neq 0$

Therefore, $\vec{b} \neq \vec{0}$.

But $\quad \vec{a}\cdot\vec{b} = 1(1) + 1(1) + 1(-2) = 1 + 1 - 2 = 0$

So here $\vec{a}\cdot\vec{b} = 0$ but neither $\vec{a} = \vec{0}$ nor $\vec{b} = \vec{0}$.

15. If the vertices A, B, C of a triangle ABC are (1, 2, 3), (–1, 0, 0) and (0, 1, 2), respectively, then find $\angle ABC$.

SOLUTION :   **Given :** Vertices A, B, C of a triangle are $A(1, 2, 3)$, $B(-1, 0, 0)$ and $C(0, 1, 2)$ respectively.

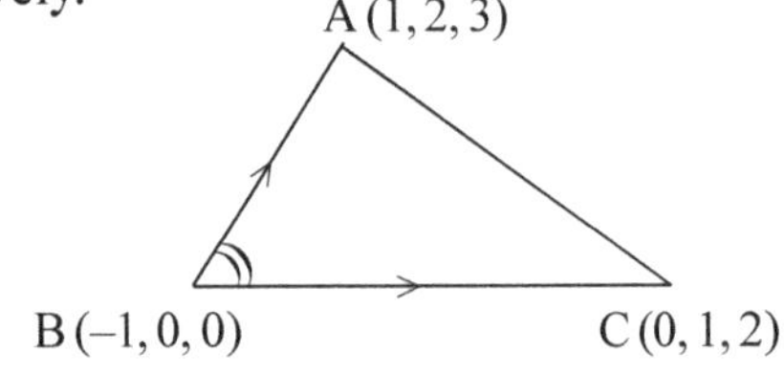

$\therefore$ Position vector $(P.V.)$ of point $A\,(= s\,\overrightarrow{OA}) = (1,\,2,\,3)$

$$= \hat{i} + 2\hat{j} + 3\hat{k}$$

Position vector $(P.V.)$ of point $B\,(=\overrightarrow{OB}) = (-1,\,0,\,0)$

$$= -\hat{i} + 0\hat{j} + 0\hat{k}$$

and psition vector $(P.V.)$ of point $C\,(-\overrightarrow{OC}) = (0,\,1,\,2)$

$$= 0\hat{i} + \hat{j} + 2\hat{k}$$

We can see from the above figure that $\angle ABC$ is the angle between the vectors $\overrightarrow{BA}$ and $\overrightarrow{BC}$

Now $\overrightarrow{BA} = P.V.$ of terminal point $A - P.V.$ of initial point B

$$= \hat{i} + 2\hat{j} + 3\hat{k} - (-\hat{i} + 0\hat{j} + 0\hat{k})$$

$$= \hat{i} + 2\hat{j} + 3\hat{k} + \hat{i} - 0\hat{j} - 0\hat{k} = 2\hat{i} + 2\hat{j} + 3\hat{k} \qquad \ldots (i)$$

and $\overrightarrow{BC} = P.V.$ of point $C - P.V.$ of point B

$$= 0\hat{i} + \hat{j} + 2\hat{k} - (-\hat{i} + 0\hat{j} + 0\hat{k})$$

$$= 0\hat{i} + \hat{j} + 2\hat{k} + \hat{i} - 0\hat{j} - 0\hat{k} = \hat{i} + \hat{j} + 2\hat{k} \qquad \ldots (ii)$$

We know that $\cos \angle ABC = \dfrac{\overrightarrow{BA} \cdot \overrightarrow{BC}}{|\overrightarrow{BA}|\,|\overrightarrow{BC}|}$ $\qquad\qquad \cos\theta = \dfrac{\vec{a}\cdot\vec{b}}{|\vec{a}|\,|\vec{b}|}$

Using (i) and (ii)

$$= \frac{2(1) + 2(1) + 3(2)}{\sqrt{4+4+9}\,\sqrt{1+1+4}}$$

$$= \frac{10}{\sqrt{17}\sqrt{6}} = \frac{10}{\sqrt{102}}$$

$$\therefore \qquad \angle ABC = \cos^{-1}\frac{10}{\sqrt{102}}.$$

16. Show that the points A(1, 2, 7), B(2, 6, 3) and C(3, 10, −1) are collinear.

SOLUTION :   Given points are $A\,(1,\,2,\,7)$, $B\,(2,\,6,\,3)$ and $C\,(3,\,10,\,-1)$.

$\Rightarrow P.V.$'s $\overrightarrow{OA},\ \overrightarrow{OB},\ \overrightarrow{OC}$ of points $A,\,B,\,C$ are

$$\overrightarrow{OA} = (1,\, 2,\, 7) = \hat{i} + 2\hat{j} + 7\hat{k}$$

$$\overrightarrow{OB} = (2,\, 6,\, 3) = 2\hat{i} + 6\hat{j} + 3\hat{k}$$

and $\overrightarrow{OC} = (3,\, 10,\, -1) = 3\hat{i} + 10\hat{j} - \hat{k}$

$\therefore\ \overrightarrow{AB} = P.V.$ of terminal point $B - P.V.$ of initial point A

$$= 2\hat{i} + 6\hat{j} + 3\hat{k} - (\hat{i} + 2\hat{j} + 7\hat{k})$$

$$= 2\hat{i} + 6\hat{j} + 3\hat{k} - \hat{i} - 2\hat{j} - 7\hat{k} = \hat{i} + 4\hat{j} - 4\hat{k} \qquad \dots (i)$$

and $\overrightarrow{AC} = P.V.$ of point $C - P.V.$ of point A

$$= 3\hat{i} + 10\hat{j} - \hat{k} - (\hat{i} + 2\hat{j} + 7\hat{k})$$

$$= 3\hat{i} + 10\hat{j} - \hat{k} - \hat{i} - 2\hat{j} - 7\hat{k}$$

$$= 2\hat{i} + 8\hat{j} - 8\hat{k} = 2(\hat{i} + 4\hat{j} - 4\hat{k})$$

$$\Rightarrow \overrightarrow{AC} = 2\,\overrightarrow{AB} \qquad\qquad [\text{By }(i)]$$

$\Rightarrow$ Vectors $\overrightarrow{AB}$ and $\overrightarrow{AC}$ are collinear or parallel. $\qquad |\because\ \vec{a} = m\vec{b}$

$\Rightarrow$ Points are collinear.

($\because$ Vectors $\overrightarrow{AB}$ and $\overrightarrow{AC}$ have a common point A and hence can't be parallel.)

Remark : When we come to exercise 10.4 and learn that Exercise, we have a second solution for proving points $A,\ B,\ C$ to be collinear.

Prove that $\overrightarrow{AB} \times \overrightarrow{AC} = \vec{o}$

17. Show that the vectors $2\hat{i} - \hat{j} + \hat{k},\ \hat{i} - 3\hat{j} - 5\hat{k}$ and $3\hat{i} - 4\hat{j} - 4\hat{k}$ form the vertices of a right angled triangle.

SOLUTION : Let the given (position) vectors be $P.V.$'s of the points $A,\ B,\ C$ respectively.

$P.V.$ of point A is $2\hat{i} - \hat{j} + \hat{k}$ and

$P.V.$ of point B is $\hat{i} - 3\hat{j} - 5\hat{k}$ and

$P.V.$ of point C is $3\hat{i} - 4\hat{j} - 4\hat{k}$.

$\therefore\ \overrightarrow{AB} = P.V.$ of point $B - P.V.$ of point A

$$= \hat{i} - 3\hat{j} - 5\hat{k} - (2\hat{i} - \hat{j} + \hat{k}) = \hat{i} - 3\hat{j} - 5\hat{k} - 2\hat{i} + \hat{j} - \hat{k}$$

$$= -\hat{i} - 2\hat{j} - 6\hat{k} \qquad \qquad \text{...}(i)$$

and $\overrightarrow{BC} = P.V.$ of point $C - P.V.$ of point B

$$= 3\hat{i} - 4\hat{j} - 4\hat{k} - (\hat{i} - 3\hat{j} - 5\hat{k}) = 3\hat{i} - 4\hat{j} - 4\hat{k} - \hat{i} + 3\hat{j} + 5\hat{k}$$

$$= 2\hat{i} - \hat{j} + \hat{k} \qquad \qquad \text{...}(ii)$$

and $\overrightarrow{AC} = P.V.$ of point $C - P.V.$ of point A

$$= 3\hat{i} - 4\hat{j} - 4\hat{k} - (2\hat{i} - \hat{j} + \hat{k}) = 3\hat{i} - 4\hat{j} - 4\hat{k} - 2\hat{i} + \hat{j} - \hat{k}$$

$$= \hat{i} - 3\hat{j} - 5\hat{k} \qquad \qquad \text{...}(iii)$$

Adding (i) and (ii), we have

$$\overrightarrow{AB} + \overrightarrow{BC} = -\hat{i} - 2\hat{j} - 6\hat{k} + 2\hat{i} - \hat{j} + \hat{k}$$

$$= \hat{i} - 3\hat{j} - 5\hat{k} = \overrightarrow{AC} \qquad \qquad [\text{By } (iii)]$$

$\therefore$ By Triangle Law of addition of vectors, points A, B, C are the vertices of a triangle ABC or points A, B, C are collinear.

Now from (i) and (ii), $\quad \overrightarrow{AB} \cdot \overrightarrow{BC} = (-1)(2) + (-2)(-1) + (-6)(1)$

$$= -2 + 2 - 6 = -6 \neq 0$$

From (ii) and (iii), $\qquad \overrightarrow{BC} \cdot \overrightarrow{AC} = 2(1) + (-1)(-3) + 1(-5)$

$$= 2 + 3 - 5 = 0$$

$\Rightarrow \overrightarrow{BC}$ is perpendicular to $\overrightarrow{AC}$

Angle C is 90^0 $\qquad\qquad \therefore \triangle ABC$ right angled at point C.

Points, A, B, C are the vertices of a right angled triangle.

18. If $\vec{a}$ is a non-zero vector of magnitude 'a' and λ is a non-zero scalar, then $\lambda \vec{a}$ is a unit vector if

(A) $\lambda = 1$ (B) $\lambda = -1$ (C) $a = |\lambda|$ (D) $a = \dfrac{1}{|\lambda|}$

SOLUTION : **Given :** $\vec{a}$ is a non-zero vector of magnitude a

$$\Rightarrow |\vec{a}| = 1$$

Also given : $\lambda \neq 0$ and $\lambda \vec{a}$ is a unti vector.

$$\Rightarrow |\lambda \vec{a}| = 1$$

$$\Rightarrow |\lambda||\vec{a}| = 1$$

$$\Rightarrow |\lambda| a = 1$$

$$\Rightarrow a = \frac{1}{|\lambda|}$$

Option (D) is the correct answer.

NCERT SOLUTION

(iv) EXERCISE : 10.4

1. Find $|\vec{a} \times \vec{b}|$, $\vec{a} = \hat{i} - 7\hat{j} + 7\hat{k}$ and $\vec{b} = 3\hat{i} - 2\hat{j} + 2\hat{k}$.

SOLUTION :   **Given :** $\vec{a} = \hat{i} - 7\hat{j} + 7\hat{k}$ and $\vec{b} = 3\hat{i} - 2\hat{j} + 2\hat{k}$

Therefore, $\vec{a} \times \vec{b} = \begin{vmatrix} \hat{i} & \hat{j} & \hat{k} \\ 1 & -7 & 7 \\ 3 & -2 & 2 \end{vmatrix}$

$[\because$ if $\vec{a} = a_1\hat{i} + a_2\hat{j} + a_3\hat{k}$ and $\vec{b} = b_1\hat{i} + b_2\hat{j} + b_3\hat{k};$

then $\vec{a} \times \vec{b} = \begin{vmatrix} \hat{i} & \hat{j} & \hat{k} \\ a_1 & a_2 & a_3 \\ b_1 & b_2 & b_3 \end{vmatrix}]$

Expanding along first row,

$$\vec{a} \times \vec{b} = \hat{i}\begin{vmatrix} -7 & 7 \\ -2 & 2 \end{vmatrix} - \hat{j}\begin{vmatrix} 1 & 7 \\ 3 & 2 \end{vmatrix} + \hat{k}\begin{vmatrix} 1 & -7 \\ 3 & -2 \end{vmatrix}$$

$$\Rightarrow \vec{a} \times \vec{b} = \hat{i}(-14+14) - \hat{j}(2-21) + \hat{k}(-2+21)$$

$$= 0\hat{i} + 19\hat{j} + 19\hat{k}$$

$$\therefore |\vec{a} \times \vec{b}| = \sqrt{0^2 + (19)^2 + (19)^2}$$

$$= \sqrt{2(19)^2} = \sqrt{2}(19) = 19\sqrt{2}.$$

Result : We know that $\vec{n} = \vec{a} \times \vec{b}$ is a vector perpendicular to both the vectors $\vec{a}$ and $\vec{b}$.

Therefore, a unit vector perpendicular to both the vectors $\vec{a}$ and $\vec{b}$ is

$$\hat{n} = \pm \frac{\vec{a} \times \vec{b}}{|\vec{a} \times \vec{b}|} \qquad \left[\because \hat{A} = \frac{\vec{A}}{|\vec{A}|} \right]$$

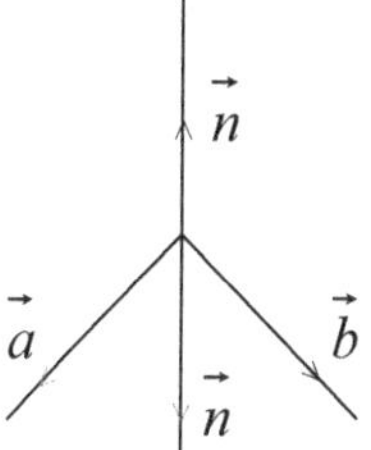

2. Find a unit vector perpendicular to each of the vectors $\vec{a} + \vec{b}$ and $\vec{a} - \vec{b}$ where $\vec{a} = 3\hat{i} + 2\hat{j} + 2\hat{k}$ and $\vec{b} = \hat{i} + 2\hat{j} - 2\hat{k}$.

SOLUTION :   **Given:** $\vec{a} = 3\hat{i} + 2\hat{j} + 2\hat{k}$ and $\vec{b} = \hat{i} + 2\hat{j} - 2\hat{k}$

Adding, $\vec{c} = \vec{a} + \vec{b} = 4\hat{i} + 4\hat{j} + 0\hat{k}$

Subtracting $\vec{d} = \vec{a} - \vec{b} = 2\hat{i} + 0\hat{j} + 4\hat{k}$

Therefore, $\vec{n} = \vec{c} \times \vec{d} = \begin{vmatrix} \hat{i} & \hat{j} & \hat{k} \\ 4 & 4 & 0 \\ 2 & 0 & 4 \end{vmatrix}$

Expanding along first row $= \hat{i}(16 - 0) - \hat{j}(16 - 0) + \hat{k}(0 - 8)$

$$\Rightarrow \quad \vec{n} = 16\hat{i} - 16\hat{j} - 8\hat{k}$$

$$\therefore \quad |\vec{n}| = \sqrt{(16)^2 + (-16)^2 + (-8)^2}$$

$$= \sqrt{256 + 256 + 64} = \sqrt{576} = 24$$

Therefore, a unit vector perpendicular to both $\vec{a}$ and $\vec{b}$ is

$$\hat{n} = \pm \frac{\vec{n}}{|\vec{n}|} = \pm \frac{(16\hat{i} - 16\hat{j} - 8\hat{k})}{24}$$

$$= \pm \left(\frac{16}{24}\hat{i} - \frac{16}{24}\hat{j} - \frac{8}{24}\hat{k} \right)$$

$$= \pm \left(\frac{2}{3}\,\hat{i} - \frac{2}{3}\,\hat{j} - \frac{1}{3}\,\hat{k} \right)$$

3. If a unit vector $\hat{a}$ makes an angle $\dfrac{\pi}{3}$ with $\hat{i}$, $\dfrac{\pi}{4}$ with $\hat{j}$ and an acute angle θ with $\hat{k}$, then find θ and hence, the components of $\hat{a}$.

SOLUTION :   Let $\vec{a} = x\hat{i} + y\hat{j} + z\hat{k}$ be a unit vector   ... (i)

$$\Rightarrow \ |\vec{a}| = 1 \ \Rightarrow \sqrt{x^2 + y^2 + z^2} = 1$$

Squaring both sides, $x^2 + y^2 + z^2 = 1$ ... (ii)

Given : Angle between vectors $\hat{a}$ and $\hat{i} = \hat{i} + 0\hat{j} + 0\hat{k}$ is $\dfrac{\pi}{3}$.

$$\therefore \ \cos\frac{\pi}{3} = \frac{\hat{a}\cdot\hat{i}}{|\hat{a}||\hat{i}|} \qquad\qquad \left[\because \ \cos\theta = \frac{\vec{a}\cdot\vec{b}}{|\vec{a}||\vec{b}|} \right]$$

$$\Rightarrow \ \frac{1}{2} = \frac{x(1) + y(0) + z(0)}{(1)(1)} \quad \text{or} \quad \frac{1}{2} = x \qquad\qquad ... (iii)$$

Again, **Given :** Angle between vectors $\hat{a}$ and $\hat{j} = 0\hat{i} + \hat{j} + 0\hat{k}$ is $\dfrac{\pi}{4}$.

$$\therefore \ \cos\frac{\pi}{4} = \frac{\hat{a}\cdot\hat{j}}{|\hat{a}||\hat{j}|} \qquad \Rightarrow \ \frac{1}{\sqrt{2}} = \frac{x(0) + y(1) + z(0)}{(1)(1)}$$

$$\Rightarrow \ \frac{1}{\sqrt{2}} = y \qquad\qquad ... (iv)$$

Again, **Given :** Angle between vectors $\hat{a}$ and $\hat{k} = 0\hat{i} + 0\hat{j} + \hat{k}$ is θ where θ is acute.

$$\therefore \ \cos\theta = \frac{\hat{a}\cdot\hat{k}}{|\hat{a}||\hat{k}|} = \frac{x(0) + y(0) + z(1)}{(1)(1)} = z \qquad\qquad ... (v)$$

Putting values of x, y, and z from (iii), (iv) and (v) in (ii),

$$\frac{1}{4} + \frac{1}{2} + \cos^2\theta = 1$$

$$\Rightarrow \ \cos^2\theta = 1 - \frac{1}{4} - \frac{1}{2}$$

$$= \frac{4-1-2}{4} = \frac{1}{4}$$

$$\Rightarrow \quad cos\,\theta = \pm\frac{1}{2}$$

But θ is acute angle (given)

$$\Rightarrow \quad cos\,\theta \text{ is positive and hence } = \frac{1}{2} = cos\frac{\pi}{3} \;\Rightarrow\; \theta = \frac{\pi}{3}$$

From (v), $\quad z = cos\,\theta = \frac{1}{2}$

Putting values of $x,\ y,\ z$ in (i), $\quad \hat{a} = \frac{1}{2}\,\hat{i} + \frac{1}{\sqrt{2}}\,\hat{j} + \frac{1}{2}\,\hat{k}$

$\therefore$ Components of $\hat{a}$ are coefficients of $\hat{i},\ \hat{j},\ \hat{k}$ in $\hat{a}$

i.e., $\frac{1}{2},\ \frac{1}{\sqrt{2}},\ \frac{1}{2}$ and acute angle. $\theta = \frac{\pi}{3}$.

4. Show that $(\vec{a} - \vec{b}) \times (\vec{a} + \vec{b}) = 2\,\vec{a} \times \vec{b}$.

SOLUTION : $\qquad$ L.H.S. $= (\vec{a} - \vec{b}) \times (\vec{a} + \vec{b})$

$$= \vec{a} \times \vec{a} + \vec{a} \times \vec{b} - \vec{b} \times \vec{a} - \vec{b} \times \vec{b}$$

$$= \vec{0} + \vec{a} \times \vec{b} + \vec{a} \times \vec{b} - \vec{0}$$

$$[\because\ \vec{a} \times \vec{a} = \vec{0},\ \vec{b} \times \vec{b} = \vec{0} \text{ and } \vec{b} \times \vec{a} = -\,\vec{a} \times \vec{b}]$$

$$= 2\,\vec{a} \times \vec{b} = R.H.S.$$

5. Find λ and μ if $(2\hat{i} + 6\hat{j} + 27\hat{k}) \times (\hat{i} + \lambda\hat{j} + \mu\hat{k}) = \vec{0}$.

SOLUTION : $\qquad$ **Given :** $(2\hat{i} + 6\hat{j} + 27\hat{k}) \times (\hat{i} + \lambda\hat{j} + \mu\hat{k}) = \vec{0}$

$$\Rightarrow \quad \begin{vmatrix} \hat{i} & \hat{j} & \hat{k} \\ 2 & 6 & 27 \\ 1 & \lambda & \mu \end{vmatrix} = \vec{0}$$

Expanding along first row,

$$\hat{i}(6\mu - 27\lambda) - \hat{j}(2\mu - 27) + \hat{k}(2\lambda - 6) = \vec{0} = 0\hat{i} + 0\hat{j} + 0\hat{k}$$

Comparing coefficients of $\hat{i}$, $\hat{j}$, $\hat{k}$ on both sides, we have

$$6\mu - 27\lambda = 0 \qquad \qquad \qquad \text{... } (i)$$

$$2\mu - 27 = 0 \qquad \qquad \qquad \text{... } (ii)$$

and $\qquad 2\lambda - 6 = 0 \qquad \qquad \qquad \text{... } (iii)$

From (ii), $\qquad 2\mu = 27 \qquad \Rightarrow \mu = \dfrac{27}{2}$

From (iii), $\qquad 2\lambda = 6 \qquad \Rightarrow \lambda = \dfrac{6}{2} = 3$

Putting $\lambda = 3$ and $\mu = \dfrac{27}{2}$ in (i), $\quad 6\left(\dfrac{27}{2}\right) - 27(3) = 0$

or $81 - 81 = 0$ or $0 = 0$ which is true. $\therefore$ $\lambda = 3$ and $\mu = \dfrac{27}{2}$.

6. Given that $\vec{a}\cdot\vec{b} = 0$ and $\vec{a}\times\vec{b} = \vec{0}$. What can you conclude about the vectors $\vec{a}$ and $\vec{b}$?

SOLUTION : **Given :** $\vec{a}\cdot\vec{b} = 0 \Rightarrow |\vec{a}|\,|\vec{b}|\cos\theta = 0$

$\Rightarrow \qquad$ Either $|\vec{a}| = 0$

or $|\vec{b}| = 0$ or $\cos\theta = 0$ $(\Rightarrow \theta = 90^{0})$

$\Rightarrow \qquad$ Either $\vec{a} = \vec{0}$ or $\vec{b} = \vec{0}$

or vector $\vec{a}$ is perpendicular to $\vec{b}$. $\qquad \qquad \text{... } (i)$

($\because$ By definition, vector $\vec{a}$ is zero vector if and only if $|\vec{a}| = 0$)

Again given $\vec{a}\times\vec{b} = \vec{0}$ $\quad \Rightarrow |\vec{a}\times\vec{b}| = 0$

$\Rightarrow \quad |\vec{a}|\,|\vec{b}|\sin\theta = 0$

$[\because \;\; |\vec{a}\times\vec{b}| = |\vec{a}|\,|\vec{b}|\sin\theta]$

$\Rightarrow \quad$ Either $|\vec{a}| = 0$ or $|\vec{b}| = 0$ or $\sin\theta = 0$ $(\Rightarrow \theta = 0)$

$\Rightarrow \quad$ Either $\vec{a} = \vec{0}$ or $\vec{b} = \vec{0}$ or vectors $\vec{a}$ and $\vec{b}$ are collinear (or parallel) vectors. $\qquad \qquad \text{... } (ii)$

We know from common sense that vectors $\vec{a}$ and $\vec{b}$ are perpendicular to each other as well as are parallel (or collinear) is impossible. $\qquad \text{... } (iii)$

$\therefore$ From (i), (ii) and (iii), either $\vec{a} = \vec{0}$ or $\vec{b} = \vec{0}$

$\therefore$ $\vec{a} \cdot \vec{b} = 0$ and $\vec{a} \times \vec{b} = \vec{0}$

$\Rightarrow$ Either $\vec{a} = \vec{0}$ or $\vec{b} = \vec{0}$.

7. Let the vectors $\vec{a}, \vec{b}, \vec{c}$ be given as $a_1\hat{i} + a_2\hat{j} + a_3\hat{k}$, $b_1\hat{i} + b_2\hat{j} + b_3\hat{k}$, $c_1\hat{i} + c_2\hat{j} + c_3\hat{k}$.

Then show that $\vec{a} \times (\vec{b} + \vec{c}) = \vec{a} \times \vec{b} + \vec{a} \times \vec{c}$.

SOLUTION :   **Given :** Vectors $\vec{a} = a_1\hat{i} + a_2\hat{j} + a_3\hat{k}$, $\vec{b} = b_1\hat{i} + b_2\hat{j} + b_3\hat{k}$,

$$\vec{c} = c_1\hat{i} + c_2\hat{j} + c_3\hat{k}$$

$\therefore$ $\vec{b} + \vec{c} = (b_1 + c_1)\hat{i} + (b_1 + c_1)\hat{j} + (b_3 + c_3)\hat{k}$

$$\text{L.H.S.} = \vec{a} \times (\vec{b} + \vec{c}) = \begin{vmatrix} \hat{i} & \hat{j} & \hat{k} \\ a_1 & a_2 & a_3 \\ b_1 + c_1 & b_2 + c_2 & b_3 + c_3 \end{vmatrix}$$

$$= \begin{vmatrix} \hat{i} & \hat{j} & \hat{k} \\ a_1 & a_2 & a_3 \\ b_1 & b_2 & b_3 \end{vmatrix} + \begin{vmatrix} \hat{i} & \hat{j} & \hat{k} \\ a_1 & a_2 & a_3 \\ c_1 & c_2 & c_3 \end{vmatrix}$$

[By Property of Determinants]

$= \vec{a} \times \vec{b} + \vec{a} \times \vec{c}$ = R.H.S.

8. If either $\vec{a} = \vec{0}$ or $\vec{b} = \vec{0}$, then $\vec{a} \times \vec{b} = \vec{0}$. Is the converse true? Justify your answer with an example.

SOLUTION :   **Given :** Either $\vec{a} = \vec{0}$ or $\vec{b} = \vec{0}$

$\therefore$ $|\vec{a}| = |\vec{0}| = 0$ or $|\vec{b}| = |\vec{0}| = 0$ ... (i)

$\therefore$ $|\vec{a} \times \vec{b}| = |\vec{a}||\vec{b}| \sin\theta = 0(\sin\theta) = 0$ [By (i)]

$\therefore$ $\vec{a} \times \vec{b} = \vec{0}$ (By definition of zero vector)

But the converse is not true.

Let $\vec{a} = \hat{i} + \hat{j} + \hat{k}$ $\therefore$ $|\vec{a}| = \sqrt{1+1+1} = \sqrt{3} \neq 0$.

$\therefore$ $\vec{a}$ is a non-zero vector.

Let $|\vec{b}| = 2(\hat{i} + \hat{j} + \hat{k}) = 2\hat{i} + 2\hat{j} + 2\hat{k}$

$\therefore \quad |\vec{b}| = \sqrt{4+4+4}$ or $|\vec{b}| = \sqrt{12} = \sqrt{4 \times 3} = 2\sqrt{3} \neq 0$

$$\therefore \quad \vec{b} \text{ is a non-zero vector.}$$

But $\vec{a} \times \vec{b} = \begin{vmatrix} \hat{i} & \hat{j} & \hat{k} \\ 1 & 1 & 1 \\ 2 & 2 & 2 \end{vmatrix}$

Taking 2 common from R_3 $= \begin{vmatrix} \hat{i} & \hat{j} & \hat{k} \\ 1 & 1 & 1 \\ 1 & 1 & 1 \end{vmatrix} = \vec{0}$

$$(\because R_2 \text{ and } R_3 \text{ are identical})$$

9. Find the area of the triangle with vertices $A(1, 1, 2)$, $B(2, 3, 5)$ and $C(1, 5, 5)$.

SOLUTION : Vertices of $\triangle ABC$ are $A(1, 1, 2)$, $B(2, 3, 5)$ and $C(1, 5, 5)$.

$\therefore$ Position Vector $(P.V)$ of point A is $(1, 1, 2) = \hat{i} + \hat{j} + 2\hat{k}$

$P.V$ of point B is $(2, 3, 5) = 2\hat{i} + 3\hat{j} + 5\hat{k}$

$P.V$ of point C is $(1, 5, 5) = \hat{i} + 5\hat{j} + 5\hat{k}$

$\therefore \overrightarrow{AB} = P.V.$ of point $B - P.V.$ of point A

$= 2\hat{i} + 3\hat{j} + 5\hat{k} - (\hat{i} + \hat{j} + 2\hat{k})$

$= 2\hat{i} + 3\hat{j} + 5\hat{k} - \hat{i} - \hat{j} - 2\hat{k}$

$= \hat{i} + 2\hat{j} + 3\hat{k}$

and $\overrightarrow{AC} = P.V.$ of point $C - P.V.$ of point A

$= \hat{i} + 5\hat{j} + 5\hat{k} - (\hat{i} + \hat{j} + 2\hat{k})$

$= \hat{i} + 5\hat{j} + 5\hat{k} - \hat{i} - \hat{j} - 2\hat{k}$

$= 0\hat{i} + 4\hat{j} + 3\hat{k}$

$\therefore \overrightarrow{AB} \times \overrightarrow{AC} = \begin{vmatrix} \hat{i} & \hat{j} & \hat{k} \\ 1 & 2 & 3 \\ 0 & 4 & 3 \end{vmatrix}$

$$= \hat{i}(6-12) - \hat{j}(3-0) + \hat{k}(4-0) = -6\hat{i} - 3\hat{j} + 4\hat{k}$$

We know that area of triangle ABC

$$= \frac{1}{2}|\overrightarrow{AB} \times \overrightarrow{AC}| = \frac{1}{2}\sqrt{36+9+16} \mid \sqrt{x^2+y^2+z^2}$$

$$= \frac{1}{2}\sqrt{61} \text{ sq. units.}$$

10. Find the area of the parallelogram whose adjacent sides are determined by the vectors $\vec{a} = \hat{i} - \hat{j} + 3\hat{k}$ ***and*** $\vec{b} = 2\hat{i} - 7\hat{j} + \hat{k}$.

SOLUTION : **Given :** Vectors representing two adjacent sides of a parallelogram are

$$\vec{a} = \vec{i} - \vec{j} + 3\vec{k}$$

$$\text{and } \vec{b} = 2\vec{i} - 7\vec{j} + \vec{k}$$

$$\therefore \quad \vec{a} \times \vec{b} = \begin{vmatrix} \hat{i} & \hat{j} & \hat{k} \\ 1 & -1 & 3 \\ 2 & -7 & 1 \end{vmatrix}$$

$$= \hat{i}(-1+21) - \hat{j}(1-6) + \hat{k}(-7+2) = 20\hat{i} + 5\hat{j} - 5\hat{k}$$

We know that **area of parallelogram** $= |\vec{a} \times \vec{b}|$

$$= \sqrt{400+25+25} = \sqrt{450} = \sqrt{25 \times 9 \times 2}$$

$$= 5(3)\ \sqrt{2} = 15\sqrt{2} \text{ square units.}$$

Note. Area of parallelogram whose **diagonal vectors** are $\vec{\alpha}$ and $\vec{\beta}$ is $\frac{1}{2}|\vec{\alpha} \times \vec{\beta}|$.

11. Let the vectors $\vec{a}$ ***and*** $\vec{b}$ ***be such that*** $|\vec{a}| = 3$, $|\vec{b}| = \dfrac{\sqrt{2}}{3}$, ***then*** $\vec{a} \times \vec{b}$ ***is a unit vector, if the angle between*** $\vec{a}$ ***and*** $\vec{b}$ ***is***

    (A) $\dfrac{\pi}{6}$ (B) $\dfrac{\pi}{4}$ (C) $\dfrac{\pi}{3}$ (D) $\dfrac{\pi}{2}$

SOLUTION : **Given :** $|\vec{a}| = 3$, $|\vec{b}| = \dfrac{\sqrt{2}}{3}$ and $\vec{a} \times \vec{b}$ is a unit vector.

$$\Rightarrow \quad |\vec{a} \times \vec{b}| = 1$$

$$\Rightarrow \quad |\vec{a}||\vec{b}|\sin\theta = 1$$

Where θ is the angle between vectors $\vec{a}$ and $\vec{b}$

Putting values of $|\vec{a}|$ and $|\vec{b}|$, $3\left(\dfrac{\sqrt{2}}{3}\right)\sin\theta = 1$

$$\Rightarrow \quad \sqrt{2}\sin\theta = 1$$

$$\Rightarrow \quad \sin\theta = \frac{1}{\sqrt{2}} = \sin\frac{\pi}{4} \quad \Rightarrow \theta = \frac{\pi}{4}$$

Option (B) is the correct answer.

12. *Area of a rectangle having vertices* A, B, C *and* D *with position vectors* $-\hat{i} + \dfrac{1}{2}\hat{j} + 4\hat{k},$ $\hat{i} + \dfrac{1}{2}\hat{j} + 4\hat{k},$ $\hat{i} - \dfrac{1}{2}\hat{j} + 4\hat{k}$ *and* $-\hat{i} - \dfrac{1}{2}\hat{j} + 4\hat{k},$ *respectively, is*

(A) $\dfrac{1}{2}$ (B) 1   (D) 2   (C) 4

SOLUTION :   **Given :** $ABCD$ is a rectangle.

We know that $\overrightarrow{AB} = P.V.$ of point $B - P.V.A.$ of point A

$$= \hat{i} + \frac{1}{2}\hat{j} + 4\hat{k} - \left(-\hat{i} + \frac{1}{2}\hat{j} + 4\hat{k}\right)$$

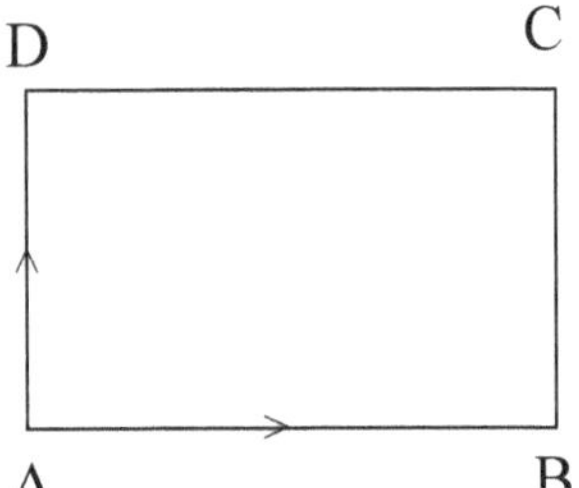

$$= \hat{i} + \frac{1}{2}\hat{j} + 4\hat{k} + \hat{i} - \frac{1}{2}\hat{j} - 4\hat{k}$$

$$= 2\hat{i} + 0\hat{j} + 0\hat{k}$$

$$\therefore \quad AB = |\overrightarrow{AB}| = \sqrt{4+0+0} = \sqrt{4} = 2$$

and $\overrightarrow{AD} = P.V.$ of point $D - P.V.$ of point A

$$= -\hat{i} - \frac{1}{2}\hat{j} + 4\hat{k} - \left(-\hat{i} + \frac{1}{2}\hat{j} + 4\hat{k}\right)$$

$$= -\hat{i} - \frac{1}{2}\hat{j} + 4\hat{k} + \hat{i} - \frac{1}{2}\hat{j} - 4\hat{k} = -\hat{j} = 0\hat{i} - \hat{j} + 0\hat{k}$$

$$\therefore \quad AD = |\overrightarrow{AD}| = \sqrt{0+1+0} = \sqrt{1} = 1$$

$\therefore$ Area of rectangle $ABCD = (AB)(AD) \qquad (= Length \times Breadth)$

$$= 2(1) = 2\, sq.\,units$$

$\therefore$ Option (C) is the correct answer.

or Area of rectangle $ABCD = \left| \overrightarrow{AB} \times \overrightarrow{AD} \right|$

NCERT SOLUTION

(v) MISCELLANEOUS EXERCISE

1. Write down a unit vector in XY-plane making an angle of 30^0 with the positive direction of x-axis.

SOLUTION : Let $\overrightarrow{OP}$ be the unit vector in XY-plane such that $\angle XOP = 30^0$

Therefore, $|\overrightarrow{OP}| = 1$

i.e., $OP = 1 \qquad ... (i)$

By Triangle Law of Addition of vectors,

In $\triangle OMP,\ \overrightarrow{OP} = \overrightarrow{OM} + \overrightarrow{MP}$

$$= (OM)\hat{i} + (MP)\hat{j}$$

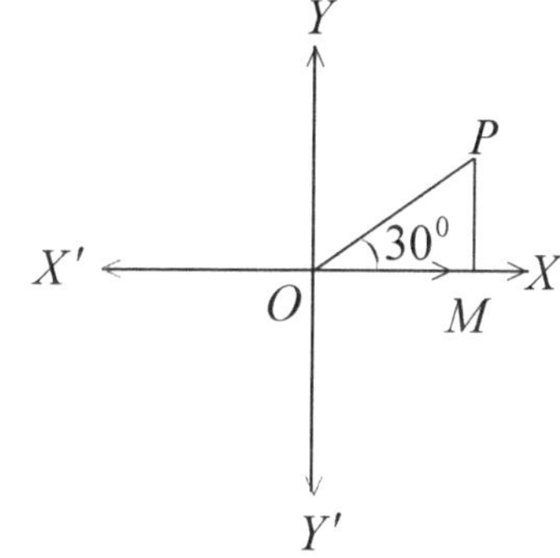

$$\left[\because \quad \hat{a} = \frac{\vec{a}}{|\vec{a}|} \Rightarrow \vec{a} = |\vec{a}|\,\hat{a} \text{ and unit vector along } OX \text{ is } \hat{i} \right.$$

$$\left. \text{and along } OY \text{ is } \hat{j} \right]$$

$$\Rightarrow \quad \overrightarrow{OP} = OP\frac{OM}{OP}\hat{i} + OP\frac{MP}{OP}\hat{j}$$

(Diving and multiplying by OP in R.H.S.)

$$= (1)(\cos 30^0)\,\hat{i} + (1)(\sin 30^0)\,\hat{j} \quad [\because\ By\,(i),\ OP = 1]$$

$$\Rightarrow \quad \text{unit vector } \overrightarrow{OP} = (\cos 30^0)\,\hat{i} + (1)(\sin 30^0)\,\hat{j} \qquad ... (ii)$$

$$\Rightarrow \quad \overrightarrow{OP} = \frac{\sqrt{3}}{2}\,\hat{i} + \frac{1}{2}\,\hat{j}$$

Remark : From Eqn. (*ii*) of above solution, we can generalise the following result.

A unit vector along a line making an angle with positive x-axis is

$$(\cos\theta)\hat{i} + (\sin\theta)\,\hat{j}$$

2. Find the scalar components and magnitude of the vector joining the points $P(x_1, y_1, z_1)$ and $Q(x_2, y_2, z_2)$.

SOLUTION : Given points are $P(x_1, y_1, z_1)$ and $Q(x_2, y_2, z_2)$

$$
\begin{array}{ll}
P\cdot\!\!\!\!\xrightarrow{\hspace{4cm}}\!\!\!\!\cdot Q \\
(x_1, y_1, z_1) \qquad\qquad (x_2, y_2, z_2)
\end{array}
$$

$\Rightarrow$ P.V. (Position vector) of point P is

$$(x_1, y_1, z_1) = x_1\,\hat{i} + y_1\,\hat{j} + z_1\,\hat{k}$$

and P.V. of point Q is $(x_2, y_2, z_2) = x_2\,\hat{i} + y_2\,\hat{j} + z_2\,\hat{k}$

$\therefore$ Vector $\overrightarrow{PQ}$, the vector joining the points P and Q.

$$= P.V. \text{ of terminal point } Q - P.V. \text{ of initial point } P$$

$$= x_2\,\hat{i} + y_2\,\hat{j} + z_2\,\hat{k} - (x_1\,\hat{i} + y_1\,\hat{j} + z_1\,\hat{k})$$

$$= x_2\,\hat{i} + y_2\,\hat{j} + z_2\,\hat{k} - x_1\,\hat{i} - y_1\,\hat{j} - z_1\,\hat{k}$$

$$\Rightarrow \quad \overrightarrow{PQ} = (x_2 - x_1)\hat{i} + (y_2 - y_1)\hat{j} + (z_2 - z_1)\hat{k}$$

$\therefore$ Scalar components of the vector $\overrightarrow{PQ}$ are the coefficients of $\hat{i}$, $\hat{j}$, $\hat{k}$ in

$\overrightarrow{PQ}$ i.e., $(x_2 - x_1)$, $(y_2 - y_1)$, $(z_2 - z_1)$

and magnitude of vector $\overrightarrow{PQ}$

$$= \sqrt{(x_2 - x_1)^2 + (y_2 - y_1)^2 + (z_2 - z_1)^2}\ |\ \sqrt{x_2 + y_2 + z_2}$$

3. A girl walks 4 km towards west, then she walks 3 km in a direction 30^0 east of north and stops. Determine the girl's displacement from her initial point of departure.

SOLUTION :   Let us take the initial point of departure as origin.

Let the girl walk a distance $OA = 4$ km towards west.

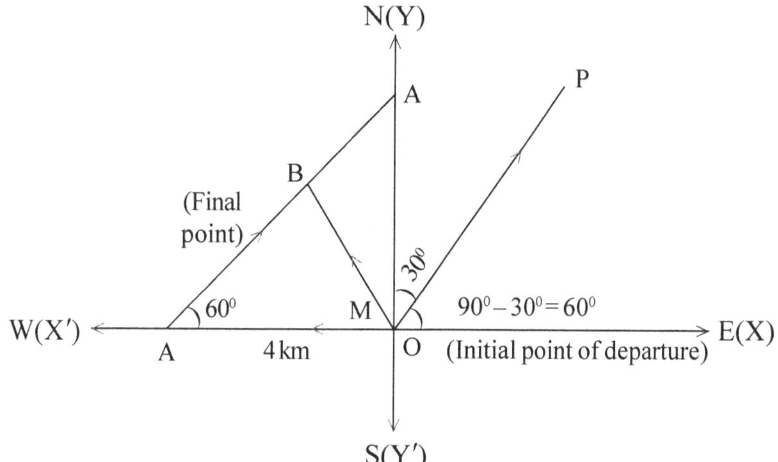

Through the point A draw a line AQ parallel to a line OP which is 30^0 east of North *i.e.*, in East-North quadrant making an angle of 30^0 with North)

Let the girl walk a distance $AB = 3$ km (given) along this direction $\overrightarrow{OQ}$ (given).

$\therefore \quad \overrightarrow{OA} = 4(-\hat{i})$ [$\because$ *Vector* $\overrightarrow{OA}$ *is along OX'*)]

$$= -4\hat{i} \qquad \qquad \dots (i)$$

We know that (By Remark QN. 1 of this miscellaneous exercise)

a unit vector along $\overrightarrow{AQ}$ (or $\overrightarrow{AB}$ making an angle $\theta = 60^0$ with positive x-axis

is $(\cos \theta)\,\hat{i} + (\sin\theta)\,\hat{j} = (\cos 60^0)\,\hat{i} + (\sin 60^0)\,\hat{j}$

$$= \frac{1}{2}\hat{i} + \frac{\sqrt{3}}{2}\hat{j}.$$

$\therefore \quad \overrightarrow{AB} = |\overrightarrow{AB}|$ (A unit vector along $\overrightarrow{AB}$) $|\because \vec{a} = |\vec{a}|\hat{a}$

$$= 3\left(\frac{1}{2}\hat{i} + \frac{\sqrt{3}}{2}\hat{j}\right) = \frac{3}{2}\hat{i} + \frac{3\sqrt{3}}{2}\hat{j} \qquad \qquad \dots (ii)$$

Girl's displacement from her initial point O of departure (to final point B)

$= \overrightarrow{OB} = \overrightarrow{OA} + \overrightarrow{AB}$ (By Triangle Law of Addition of vectors)

$$= -4\hat{i} + \left(\frac{3}{2}\hat{i} + \frac{3\sqrt{3}}{2}\hat{j}\right) = \left(-4 + \frac{3}{2}\right)\hat{i} + \frac{3\sqrt{3}}{2}\hat{j}$$

[By (i)] [By (ii)]

$$= \frac{-5}{2}\,\hat{i} + \frac{3\sqrt{3}}{2}\,\hat{j}$$

4. If $\vec{a} = \vec{b} + \vec{c}$, then is it true that $|\vec{a}| = |\vec{b}| + |\vec{c}|$? Justify your answer.

SOLUTION : The result is not true (always).

Given : $\vec{a} = \vec{b} + \vec{c}$

$\therefore$ Either the vectors $\vec{a}, \vec{b}, \vec{c}$ are collinear or vectors $\vec{a}, \vec{b}, \vec{c}$ form the sides of a triangle.

Case I. Vectors $\vec{a}, \vec{b}, \vec{c}$ are collinear.

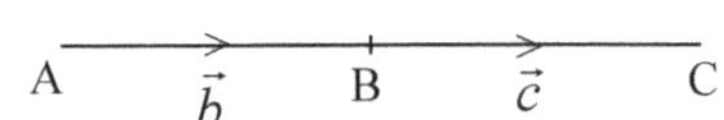

Let $\vec{a} = \overrightarrow{AC}, \vec{b} = \overrightarrow{AB}$ and $\vec{c} = \overrightarrow{BC}$,

then $\vec{a} = \overrightarrow{AC} = \overrightarrow{AB} + \overrightarrow{BC} = \vec{b} + \vec{c}$

Also, $|\vec{a}| = AC = AB + BC = |\vec{b}| + |\vec{c}|$

Case II. Vectors $\vec{a} = \vec{b} + \vec{c}$ form a triangle.

Here also by Triangle Law of vectors,

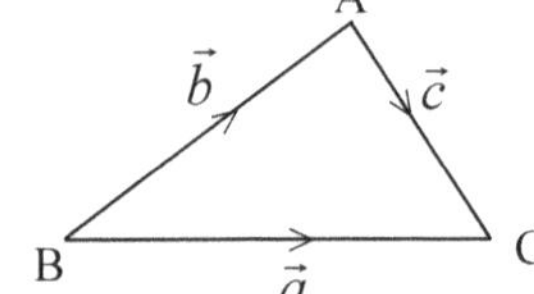

$$\vec{a} = \vec{b} + \vec{c}$$

But $|\vec{a}| < |\vec{b}| + |\vec{c}|$

($\because$ Each side of a triangle is less than sum of the other two sides)

$\therefore |(\vec{a}) = \vec{b} + \vec{c}| = |\vec{b}| + |\vec{c}|$ is true only when vectors and are collinear vectors

$\vec{b}$ and $\vec{c}$ are collinear vectors.

5. Find the value of for which $x(\hat{i} + \hat{j} + \hat{k})$ is a unit vector.

SOLUTION : Because $x(\hat{i} + \hat{j} + \hat{k}) = x\hat{i} + x\hat{j} + x\hat{k}$ is a unit vector (given)

Therefore, $|x\hat{i} + x\hat{j} + x\hat{k}| = 1$

$\therefore$ $\sqrt{x^2 + x^2 + x^2} = 1$

$[\because\ x\hat{i} + y\hat{j} + z\hat{k} = \sqrt{x^2 + y^2 + z^2}\,]$

Squaring both sides $3x^2 = 1$ or $x^2 = \dfrac{1}{3}$

$\therefore$ $x = \pm\dfrac{1}{\sqrt{3}}$

6. Find a vector of magnitude 5 units an dparallel to the resultant of the vectors.

$$\vec{a} = 2\hat{i} + 3\hat{j} - \hat{k} \ \text{ and } \ \vec{b} = \hat{i} - 2\hat{j} + \hat{k}.$$

SOLUTION : **Given :** Vectors $\vec{a} = 2\hat{i} + 3\hat{j} - \hat{k}$ and $\vec{b} = -\hat{i} - 2\hat{j} + \hat{k}$

Let vector $\vec{c}$ be the resultant of vectors $\vec{a}$ and $\vec{b}$.

$$\therefore \quad \vec{c} = \vec{a} + \vec{b} = 2\hat{i} + 3\hat{j} - \hat{k} + \hat{i} - 2\hat{j} + \hat{k}$$

$$= 3\hat{i} + \hat{j} + 0\hat{k}.$$

$\therefore$ Required vector of magnitude 5 units and parallel (or collinear) to resultant vector $\vec{c} = \vec{a} + \vec{b}$ is

$$5\vec{c} = 5\frac{\vec{c}}{|\vec{c}|} = 5\left(\frac{3\hat{i} + \hat{j} + 0\hat{k}}{\sqrt{9 + 1 + 0}}\right)$$

$$= \frac{5}{\sqrt{10}}(3\hat{i} + \hat{j}) = \frac{5}{\sqrt{10}} \frac{\sqrt{10}}{\sqrt{10}}(3\hat{i} + \hat{j})$$

$$= \frac{5}{10}\sqrt{10}(3\hat{i} + \hat{j}) = \frac{\sqrt{10}}{2}(3\hat{i} + \hat{j}) = \frac{3}{2}\sqrt{10}\,\hat{i} + \frac{\sqrt{10}}{2}\,\hat{j}$$

7. If $\vec{a} = \hat{i} + \hat{j} + \hat{k}, \ \vec{b} = 2\hat{i} - \hat{j} + 3\hat{k}$ and $\vec{c} = \hat{i} - 2\hat{j} + \hat{k}$, find a unit vector parallel to the vector $2\vec{a} - \vec{b} + 3\vec{c}$.

SOLUTION : **Given :** Vectors $\vec{a} = \hat{i} + \hat{j} + \hat{k}, \ \vec{b} = 2\hat{i} - \hat{j} + 3\hat{k}$

and $\vec{c} = \hat{i} - 2\hat{j} + \hat{k}$

Let $\vec{d} = 2\vec{a} - \vec{b} + 3\vec{c}$

$$= 2(\hat{i} + \hat{j} + \hat{k}) - (2\hat{i} - \hat{j} + 3\hat{k}) + 3(\hat{i} - 2\hat{j} + \hat{k})$$

$$= 2\hat{i} + 2\hat{j} + 2\hat{k} - 2\hat{i} + \hat{j} - 3\hat{k} + 3\hat{i} - 6\hat{j} + 3\hat{k}$$

$\therefore \quad \hat{d} = 3\hat{i} - 3\hat{j} + 2\hat{k}$ $\therefore$ A unit vector parallel to the vector

$\vec{d} = 3\hat{i} - 3\hat{j} + 2\hat{k}$ is

$$\hat{d} = \frac{\vec{d}}{|\vec{d}|} = \frac{3\hat{i} - 3\hat{j} + 2\hat{k}}{\sqrt{9 + 9 + 4} = \sqrt{22}} = \frac{3}{\sqrt{22}}\hat{i} - \frac{3}{\sqrt{22}}\hat{j} + \frac{2}{\sqrt{22}}\hat{k}$$

8. Show that the points $A(1, -2, -8)$, $B(5, 0, -2)$ **and** $C(11, 3, 7)$ **are collinear and find the ratio in which B divides Ac.**

SOLUTION :   **Given:** Points $A(1, -2, -8)$, $B(5, 0, -2)$ and $C(11, 3, 7)$.

i.e., Position vectors of points A, B, C are

$$\overrightarrow{OA} (= A(1, -2, -8)) = \hat{i} - 2\hat{j} - 8\hat{k}$$

$$\overrightarrow{OB} (= B(5, 0, -2)) = 5\hat{i} + 0\hat{j} - 2\hat{k} = 5\hat{i} - 2\hat{k}$$

and $\overrightarrow{OC} (= C(11, 3, 7)) = 11\hat{i} + 3\hat{j} + 7\hat{k}$

$\therefore \ \overrightarrow{AB} = P.V.$ of point $B - P.V.$ of point A

$$= 5\hat{i} - 2\hat{k} - (\hat{i} - 2\hat{j} - 8\hat{k})$$

$$= 5\hat{i} - 2\hat{k} - \hat{i} + 2\hat{j} + 8\hat{k})$$

or $\quad \overrightarrow{AB} = 4\hat{i} + 2\hat{j} + 6\hat{k}$

$\therefore \ AB = |\overrightarrow{AB}| = \sqrt{16 + 4 + 36} = \sqrt{56} = \sqrt{4 \times 14} = 2\sqrt{14}$

and $\overrightarrow{BC} = P.V.$ P.V. of point $C - P.V.$ of point B

$$= 11\hat{i} + 3\hat{j} + 7\hat{k} - (5\hat{i} - 2\hat{k})$$

$$= 11\hat{i} + 3\hat{j} + 7\hat{k} - 5\hat{i} + 2\hat{k}$$

$$= 6\hat{i} + 3\hat{j} + 9\hat{k}$$

$\therefore \quad BC = |\overrightarrow{BC}| = \sqrt{36 + 9 + 81} = \sqrt{126} = \sqrt{9 \times 14} = 3\sqrt{14}$

$\overrightarrow{AC} = P.V.$ of point $C - P.V.$ of point A

$$= 11\hat{i} + 3\hat{j} + 7\hat{k} - (\hat{i} - 2\hat{j} - 8\hat{k})$$

$$= 11\hat{i} + 3\hat{j} + 7\hat{k} - \hat{i} + 2\hat{j} + 8\hat{k}$$

$$= 10\hat{i} + 5\hat{j} + 15\hat{k}$$

$\therefore \quad AC = |\overrightarrow{AC}| = \sqrt{100 + 25 + 225} = \sqrt{350} = \sqrt{25 \times 14} = 5\sqrt{14}$

Now, $\overrightarrow{AB} + \overrightarrow{BC} = 4\hat{i} + 2\hat{j} + 6\hat{k} + 6\hat{i} + 3\hat{j} + 9\hat{k}$

$$= 10\hat{i} + 5\hat{j} + 15\hat{k} = \overrightarrow{AC}$$

$\therefore$ Points A, B, C are either collinear or are the vertices of $\triangle ABC$.

Again $AB + BC = 2\sqrt{14} + 3\sqrt{14} = (2 + 3)\sqrt{14} = 5\sqrt{14} = AC$

$\therefore$ Points A, B, C are collinear.

Now to find the ration in which B divides AC

Let the point B divides AC in the ratio $\lambda : 1$

$\therefore$ By section formula, $P.V.$ of point B is $\dfrac{\lambda \vec{c} + 1\vec{a}}{\lambda + 1}$

$\Rightarrow (5, 0, -2) = \dfrac{\lambda(11, 3, 7) + (1, -2, -8)}{\lambda + 1}$

Cross-multiplying,

$$(\lambda + 1)(5\hat{i} + 0\hat{j} - 2\hat{k}) = \lambda(11\hat{i} + 3\hat{j} + 7\hat{k}) + (\hat{i} - 2\hat{j} - 8\hat{k})$$

$$\Rightarrow 5(\lambda + 1)\hat{i} - 2(\lambda + 1\hat{k}) = 11\lambda\,\hat{i} + 3\lambda\,\hat{j} + 7\lambda\hat{k} + \hat{i} - 2\hat{j} - 8\hat{k}$$

$$\Rightarrow (5\lambda + 5)\hat{i} - (2\lambda + 2)\hat{k} = (11\lambda + 1)\hat{i} + (3\lambda - 2)\hat{j} + (7\lambda - 8)\hat{k}$$

Comparing coefficients of $\hat{i},\ \hat{j},\ \hat{k}$ on both sides, we have

$$5\lambda + 5 = 11\lambda + 1,\quad 0 = 3\lambda - 2,\quad -(2\lambda + 2) = 7\lambda - 8$$

$$\Rightarrow -6\lambda = -4,\ -3\lambda = -2,\ -2\lambda - 2 = 7\lambda - 8\ (\Rightarrow -9\lambda = -6)$$

$$\Rightarrow \lambda = \dfrac{4}{6} = \dfrac{2}{3},\ \lambda = \dfrac{2}{3},\ \lambda = \dfrac{6}{9} = \dfrac{2}{3}$$

All three values of λ are same.

$\therefore$ Required ration is $\lambda : 1 = \dfrac{2}{3} : 1 = 2 : 3$.

9. Find the position vector of a point R which divides the line joining the two points P and Q whose position vectors are

$(2\vec{a} + \vec{b})$ and $(\vec{a} - 3\vec{b})$ externally in the ration 1 : 2. Also, show that P is the middle point of line segment RQ.

SOLUTION : We know that position vector of the point R dividing the join of P and Q externally in the ratio $1 : 2 = m : n$ is given by

$$\vec{c} = \frac{m\vec{b} - n\vec{a}}{m - n} = \frac{1(\vec{a} - 3\vec{b}) - 2(2\vec{a} + \vec{b})}{1 - 2}$$

$$= \frac{\vec{a} - 3\vec{b} - 4\vec{a} - 2\vec{b}}{1 - 2} = \frac{-3\vec{a} - 5\vec{b}}{-1} = 3\vec{a} + 5\vec{b}$$

Again position vector of the middle point of the line segment RQ

$$= \frac{P.V.\ of\ point\ R + P.V.\ of\ point\ Q}{2}$$

$$= \frac{3\vec{a} + 5\vec{b} + \vec{a} - 3\vec{b}}{2} = \frac{4\vec{a} + 2\vec{b}}{2}$$

$$= 2\vec{a} + \vec{b} = P.V.\ of\ point\ P.\ \text{(given)}$$

$\therefore$ Point P is the middle point of the line segment RQ.

10. Two adjacent sides of a parallelogram are $2\hat{i} - 4\hat{j} + 5\hat{k}$ and $\hat{i} - 2\hat{j} - 3\hat{k}$. Find the unit vector parallel to its diagonal. Also, find its area.

SOLUTION :   Let $ABCD$ be a parallelogram.

Given: The vectors representing two adjacent sides of this parallelogram are say

$$\vec{a} = 2\hat{i} - 4\hat{j} + 5\hat{k}$$

and $$\vec{b} = 2\hat{i} - 4\hat{j} + 5\hat{k}$$

Formula: $\therefore$ Vectors along the diagonals $\overrightarrow{AC}$ and $\overrightarrow{DB}$ of the parallelogram are

$$\vec{a} + \vec{b}\ \text{ and }\ \vec{a} - \vec{b}$$

$i.e.,$ $\vec{a} + \vec{b} = 2\hat{i} - 4\hat{j} + 5\hat{k} + \hat{i} - 2\hat{j} - 3\hat{k}$

$$= 3\hat{i} - 6\hat{j} + 2\hat{k}$$

and $\vec{a} - \vec{b} = 2\hat{i} - 4\hat{j} + 5\hat{k} - (\hat{i} - 2\hat{j} - 3\hat{k})$

$$= 2\hat{i} - 4\hat{j} + 5\hat{k} - \hat{i} + 2\hat{j} + 3\hat{k} = \hat{i} - 2\hat{j} + 8\hat{k}$$

$\therefore$ Unit vectors parallel to (or along) diagonals are

$$\frac{\vec{a} + \vec{b}}{|\vec{a} + \vec{b}|}\ \text{ and }\ \frac{\vec{a} - \vec{b}}{|\vec{a} - \vec{b}|} = \frac{3\hat{i} - 6\hat{j} + 2\hat{k}}{\sqrt{9 + 36 + 4} = \sqrt{49} = 7}\ \text{ and }\ \frac{\hat{i} - 2\hat{j} + 8\hat{k}}{\sqrt{1 + 4 + 64} = \sqrt{69}}$$

Let us find area of parallelogram

$$\vec{a} \times \vec{b} = \begin{vmatrix} \hat{i} & \hat{j} & \hat{k} \\ 2 & -4 & 5 \\ 1 & -2 & -3 \end{vmatrix} = \hat{i}(12+10) - \hat{j}(-6-5) + \hat{k}(-4+4)$$

$$= 22\hat{i} + 11\hat{j} + 0\hat{k}$$

We know that area of parallelogram $= |\vec{a} \times \vec{b}|$

$$= \sqrt{(22)^2 + (11)^2 + (0)^2} = \sqrt{484 + 121} = \sqrt{605}$$

$$= \sqrt{5 \times 21} = \sqrt{121 \times 5} = 11\sqrt{5} \text{ sq. units.}$$

11. Show that the direction cosines of a vector equally inclined to the axes OX, OY and OZ are

$$\frac{1}{\sqrt{3}}, \frac{1}{\sqrt{3}}, \frac{1}{\sqrt{3}}.$$

SOLUTION : Let l, m, n be the direction cosines of a vector equally inclined to the axes OX, OY, OZ.

$\therefore$ A unit vector along the given vector is

$\hat{a} = l\hat{i} + m\hat{j} + n\hat{k}$ and $|\hat{a}| = 1$

$$\Rightarrow \sqrt{l^2 + m^2 + n^2} = 1 \quad \therefore \ l^2 + m^2 + n^2 = 1 \qquad \ldots(i)$$

Let the given vector (for which unit vector is $\hat{a}$) make equal angles (given) θ, θ, θ (say) with $OX(\Rightarrow \hat{i})$, $OY(\Rightarrow \hat{j})$ and $OZ(\Rightarrow \hat{k})$

$\therefore$ The given vector is in positive octant $OXYZ$ and hence θ is acute. $\ldots(ii)$

$\therefore$ For angle θ between $\hat{a}$ and $\hat{i}$,

$$\cos\theta = \frac{\hat{a} \cdot \hat{i}}{|\hat{a}| \, |\hat{i}|} = \frac{(l\hat{i} + m\hat{j} + n\hat{k}) \cdot (\hat{i} + 0\hat{j} + 0\hat{k})}{(1)(1)}$$

or $\cos\theta = l(1) + m(0) + n(0) = l$

or $l = \cos\theta$ $\hfill \ldots(iii)$

Similarly, for angle θ between $\hat{a}$ and $\hat{j}$, $m = \cos\theta$ $\hfill \ldots(iv)$

Similarly, for angle between $\hat{a}$ and $\hat{k}$, $n = \cos\theta$ $\hfill \ldots(v)$

Putting these values of l, m, n from (iii), (iv) and (v) in (i), we have

$$\cos^2\theta + \cos^2\theta + \cos^2\theta = 1 \qquad \Rightarrow 3\cos^2\theta = 1$$

$$\Rightarrow \; \cos^2\theta = \frac{1}{3} \qquad\qquad \Rightarrow \; \cos\theta = \pm\sqrt{\frac{1}{3}} = \pm\frac{1}{\sqrt{3}}$$

$$\therefore \; \cos\theta = \frac{1}{\sqrt{3}} \; (\because \text{ By } (ii) \; \theta \text{ is acute and hence } \cos\theta \text{ is positive})$$

Putting $\cos\theta = \dfrac{1}{\sqrt{3}}$ in (ii), (iii) and (iv), direction cosines of the required vector

are $l, m, n = \dfrac{1}{\sqrt{3}}, \dfrac{1}{\sqrt{3}}$ and $\dfrac{1}{\sqrt{3}}$.

12. Let $\vec{a} = \hat{i} + 4\hat{j} + 2\hat{k}$, $\vec{b} = 3\hat{i} - 2\hat{j} + \hat{k}$ **and** $\vec{c} = 2\hat{i} - \hat{j} + 4\hat{k}$. **Find a vector** $\vec{b}$ **which is perpendicular to both** $\vec{a}$ **and** $\vec{b}$, **and** $\vec{c}.\vec{d} = 15.$

SOLUTION :   **Given :** Vectors are $\vec{a} = \hat{i} + 4\hat{j} + 2\hat{k}$

and $\vec{b} = 3\hat{i} - 2\hat{j} + 7\hat{k}$

By definition of cross-product

of two vectors, $\vec{a} \times \vec{b}$ is **a**

vector perpendicular to both

$\vec{a}$ and $\vec{b}$.

Hence, vector $\vec{d}$ which is also

perpendicular to both $\vec{a}$ and $\vec{b}$

is $\vec{d} = \lambda(\vec{a} \times \vec{b})$ where $\lambda = 1$ or some other scalar.

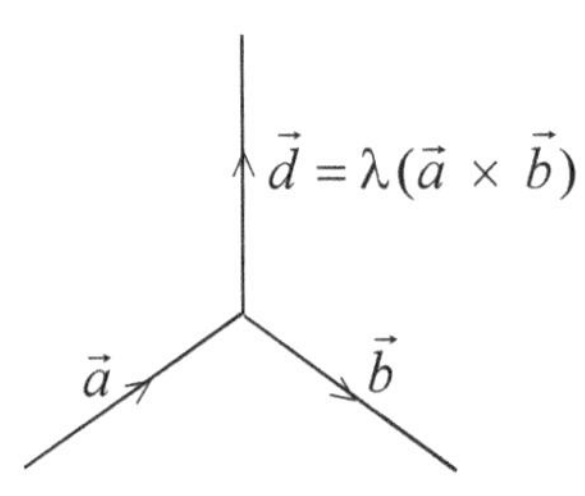

Therefore, $\vec{d} = \lambda \begin{vmatrix} \hat{i} & \hat{j} & \hat{k} \\ 1 & 4 & 2 \\ 3 & -2 & 7 \end{vmatrix}$

Expanding along first row, $= \lambda[\hat{i}(28+4) - \hat{j}(7-6) + \hat{k}(-2-12)]$

or $\vec{d} = \lambda[32\hat{i} - \hat{j} - 14\hat{k}]$ ...(i)

or $\vec{d} = 32\lambda\hat{i} - \lambda\hat{j} - 14\lambda\hat{k}$

To find λ **: Given:** $\vec{c} = \hat{i} + \hat{j} + \hat{k}$

Also given $\vec{c} \cdot \vec{d} = 15$

$$\Rightarrow\ 2(32\lambda)+(-1)(\lambda)+4-14\lambda)=15$$

$$\Rightarrow\ 64\lambda+\lambda-56\lambda=15\ \Rightarrow 9\lambda=15\ \Rightarrow \lambda=\frac{5}{3}$$

Putting $\lambda=\dfrac{5}{3}$ in (i), required vector

$$\vec{d}=\frac{5}{3}\,(32\hat{i}-\hat{j}-14\hat{k})=\frac{1}{3}(160\hat{i}-5\hat{j}-70\hat{k})$$

13. The scalar product of the vector $\hat{i}+\hat{j}+\hat{k}$ with a unit vector along the sum of the vectors $2\hat{i}+4\hat{j}-5\hat{k}$ and $\lambda\hat{i}+2\hat{j}+3\hat{k}$ is equal to one. Find the value of λ.

SOLUTION : **Given :** Let $\vec{a}=\hat{i}+\hat{j}+\hat{k}$ ... (i)

$\vec{b}=2\hat{i}+4\hat{j}-5\hat{k}$ and $\vec{c}=\lambda\hat{i}+2\hat{j}+3\hat{k}$

$\therefore\ \vec{b}+\vec{c}(=\vec{d}\ \text{(say)})=(2+\lambda)\hat{i}+6\hat{j}-2\hat{k}$

$\therefore\ \hat{d}$, a unit vector along $\vec{b}+\vec{c}=\vec{d}$ is

$$\hat{d}=\frac{\vec{d}}{|\vec{d}|}=\frac{(2+\lambda)\hat{i}+6\hat{j}-2\hat{k}}{\sqrt{(2+\lambda)^2+36+4}=\sqrt{4+\lambda^2+4\lambda+40}}$$

or $\quad\hat{d}=\dfrac{(2+\lambda)\hat{i}+6\hat{j}-2\hat{k}}{\sqrt{\lambda^2+4\lambda+44}}$

$$=\frac{(2+\lambda)}{\sqrt{\lambda^2+4\lambda+44}}\,\hat{i}+\frac{6}{\sqrt{\lambda^2+4\lambda+44}}\,\hat{j}-\frac{2}{\sqrt{\lambda^2+4\lambda+44}}\,\hat{k}\qquad ...\,(ii)$$

Given : Scalar (*i.e.*, Dot) Product of $\vec{a}$ and $\hat{d}$ *i.e.* $=\vec{a}\cdot\hat{d}=1$

$\therefore$ From (i) and (ii),

$$\frac{1(2+\lambda)}{\sqrt{\lambda^2+4\lambda+44}}+\frac{1(6)}{\sqrt{\lambda^2+4\lambda+44}}+\frac{1(-2)}{\sqrt{\lambda^2+4\lambda+44}}=1$$

Multiplying by L.C.M. $=\sqrt{\lambda^2+4\lambda+44}$,

$$2+\lambda+6-2=\sqrt{\lambda^2+4\lambda+44}\ \ \Rightarrow\lambda+6=\sqrt{\lambda^2+4\lambda+44}$$

Squaring both sides $(\lambda+6)^2=\lambda^2+4\lambda+44$

$$\Rightarrow\ \lambda^2+12\lambda+36=\lambda^2+4\lambda+44$$

$$\Rightarrow \; 8\lambda = 8 \; \Rightarrow \lambda = 1.$$

14. If $\vec{a}, \vec{b}, \vec{c}$ **are mutually perpendicular vectors of equal magnitude, show that the vector** $\vec{a} + \vec{b} + \vec{c}$ **is equally inclined to** $\vec{a}, \vec{b}, \vec{c}.$

SOLUTION :   **Given:** $\vec{a}, \vec{b}, \vec{c}$ are mutually perpendicular vectors of equal magnitude.

$$\therefore \; \vec{a}.\vec{b} = \vec{b}.\vec{a} = 0, \; \vec{b}.\vec{c} = \vec{c}.\vec{b} = 0,$$

$$\vec{a}.\vec{a} = \vec{a}.\vec{c} = 0 \qquad\qquad\qquad \dots (i)$$

and $|\vec{a}| = |\vec{b}| = |\vec{c}| = \lambda$ (say) $\qquad\qquad\qquad \dots (ii)$

Let vector $\vec{d} = \vec{a} + \vec{b} + \vec{c}$ make angles $\theta_1, \theta_2, \theta_3$ with vectors $\vec{a}, \vec{b}, \vec{c}$ respectively.

$$\therefore \; \cos\theta_1 = \frac{\vec{d}.\vec{a}}{|\vec{d} + \vec{a}|} = \frac{(\vec{a} + \vec{b} + \vec{c}).\vec{a}}{|\vec{a} + \vec{b} + \vec{c}||\vec{a}|} \left.\right\}$$

$$= \frac{\vec{a}.\vec{a} + \vec{a}.\vec{b} + \vec{a}.\vec{c}}{|\vec{a} + \vec{b} + \vec{c}||\vec{a}|} = \frac{|\vec{a}|^2 + 0 + 0}{|\vec{a} + \vec{b} + \vec{c}||\vec{a}|} \qquad\qquad \text{[By } (i)\text{]}$$

$$\Rightarrow \; \cos\theta_1 = \frac{|\vec{a}|^2}{|\vec{a} + \vec{b} + \vec{c}||\vec{a}|} = \frac{|\vec{a}|}{|\vec{a} + \vec{b} + \vec{c}|} \qquad\qquad \dots (iii)$$

Let us now find $|\vec{a} + \vec{b} + \vec{c}|.$

We know that $|\vec{a} + \vec{b} + \vec{c}|^2 = (\vec{a} + \vec{b} + \vec{c})^2$

$$= \vec{a}^2 + (\vec{b} + \vec{c})^2 + 2\vec{a}.(\vec{b} + \vec{c})$$

$$[\because \; (\vec{A} + \vec{B})^2 = \vec{A}^2 + \vec{B}^2 + 2\vec{A}.\vec{B}]$$

$$= \vec{a}^2 + \vec{b}^2 + \vec{c}^2 + 2\vec{b}.\vec{c} + 2\vec{a}.\vec{b} + 2\vec{a}.\vec{c}$$

$$= |\vec{a}|^2 + |\vec{b}|^2 + |\vec{c}|^2 + 2\vec{b}.\vec{c} + 2\vec{a}.\vec{b} + 2\vec{a}.\vec{c}$$

Putting values from (i) and (ii)

$$|\vec{a} + \vec{b} + \vec{c}|^2 = \lambda^2 + \lambda^2 + \lambda^2 + 0 + 0 + 0 = 3\lambda^2$$

$$\therefore \; |\vec{a} + \vec{b} + \vec{c}| = \sqrt{3\lambda^2} = \lambda\sqrt{3}$$

Putting this value of $|\vec{a} + \vec{b} + \vec{c}| = \lambda\sqrt{3}$ and $|\vec{a}| = \lambda$

from (ii) in (iii), $\cos\theta_1 = \dfrac{\lambda}{\lambda\sqrt{3}} = \dfrac{1}{\sqrt{3}} \qquad \therefore \; \theta_1 = \cos^{-1}\dfrac{1}{\sqrt{3}}$

Similarly, $\theta_2 = \cos^{-1}\dfrac{1}{\sqrt{3}}$ and $\theta_3 = \cos^{-1}\dfrac{1}{\sqrt{3}}$

$\therefore \quad \theta_1 = \theta_2 = \theta_3 \left(= \cos^{-1}\dfrac{1}{\sqrt{3}}\right)$

$\therefore \quad$ Vector $\vec{a} + \vec{b} + \vec{c}$ is equally inclined to the vectors $\vec{a},\ \vec{b}$, and $\vec{c}$.

15. Prove that $(\vec{a} + \vec{b}).(\vec{a} + \vec{b}) = |\vec{a}|^2 + |\vec{b}|^2$, if and only if $\vec{a}$, $\vec{b}$ are perpendicular, given $\vec{a} \neq \vec{0},\ \vec{b} \neq \vec{0}$.

SOLUTION : We know that $(\vec{a} + \vec{b}).(\vec{a} + \vec{b})$

$$= \vec{a}.\vec{a} + \vec{a}.\vec{b} + \vec{b}.\vec{a} + \vec{b}.\vec{b}$$

$$= |\vec{a}|^2 + \vec{a}.\vec{b} + \vec{a}.\vec{b} + |\vec{b}|^2$$

$$= |\vec{a}|^2 + |\vec{b}|^2 + 2\vec{a}.\vec{b}$$

For If part: Given: $\vec{a}$ and $\vec{b}$ are perpendicular

$\Rightarrow \quad \vec{a}.\vec{b} = 0$

Putting $\vec{a}.\vec{b} = 0$ in (i), we have

$$(\vec{a} + \vec{b}).(\vec{a} + \vec{b}) = |\vec{a}|^2 + |\vec{b}|^2$$

For only if part:

Given: $(\vec{a} + \vec{b}).(\vec{a} + \vec{b}) = |\vec{a}|^2 + |\vec{b}|^2$

Putting this value in L.H.S. eqn. (i), we have

$$|\vec{a}|^2 + |\vec{b}|^2 = |\vec{a}|^2 + |\vec{b}|^2 + 2\vec{a}.\vec{b}$$

$\Rightarrow \quad 0 = 2\vec{a}.\vec{b} \qquad \Rightarrow \quad \vec{a}.\vec{b} = \dfrac{0}{2} = 0$

But $\vec{a} \neq \vec{0}$ and $\vec{b} \neq \vec{0}$ (given).

$\therefore \quad$ Vector $\vec{a}$ and $\vec{b}$ are perpendicular to each other.

16. Choose the correct answer:

If θ is the angle between two vectors $\vec{a}$ and $\vec{b}$, then $\vec{a}.\vec{b} \geq 0$ only when

$(A)\ \ 0 < \theta < \dfrac{\pi}{2}$ $\qquad (B)\ \ 0 \leq \theta \leq \dfrac{\pi}{2}$ $\qquad (C)\ \ 0 < \theta < \pi$ $\qquad (D)\ \ 0 < \theta \leq \pi$

SOLUTION :   **Given:** $\vec{a} \cdot \vec{b} \geq 0$

$$\Rightarrow \; |\vec{a}| \, |\vec{b}| \cos\theta \geq 0 \qquad \Rightarrow \cos\theta \geq 0$$

$[\; \because \;\; |\vec{a}|$ and $|\vec{b}|$ being lengths of vectors are always ≥ 0 and this is true only for option out of the given

options $\left(\because \; \text{For option (A)} \;\; 0 < \theta < \dfrac{\pi}{2},\; \cos\theta > 0 \right)$.

17. Choose the correct answer:

Let $\vec{a}$ and $\vec{b}$ be two unit vectors and θ is the angle between them. Then $\vec{a} + \vec{b}$ is a unit vector if

(A) $\theta = \dfrac{\pi}{4}$ *(B)* $\theta = \dfrac{\pi}{3}$ *(C)* $\theta = \dfrac{\pi}{2}$ *(D)* $\theta = \dfrac{2\pi}{3}$

SOLUTION :   **Given:** $\vec{a},\; \vec{b}$ and $\vec{a} + \vec{b}$ are unit vectors

$$\Rightarrow |\vec{a}| = 1,\; |\vec{b}| = 1 \;\; \text{and} \;\; |\vec{a} + \vec{b}| = 1$$

Now, squaring both sides of $|\vec{a} + \vec{b}| = 1$, we have

$$|\vec{a} + \vec{b}|^2 = 1 \qquad \Rightarrow (\vec{a} + \vec{b})^2 = 1$$

$$\Rightarrow \; \vec{a}^2 + \vec{b}^2 + 2\vec{a}.\vec{b} = 1$$

$$\Rightarrow \; |\vec{a}|^2 + |\vec{b}|^2 + 2\,|\vec{a}|\,|\vec{b}|\cos\theta = 1$$

where θ is the given angle between vectors $\vec{a}$ and $\vec{b}$.

Putting $|\vec{a}| = 1$ and $|\vec{b}| = 1$, we have

$$1 + 1 + 2\cos\theta = 1$$

$$\Rightarrow \; 2\cos\theta = -1$$

$$\Rightarrow \; \cos\theta = \frac{-1}{2} = -\cos 60^0$$

$$\Rightarrow \; \cos\theta = \cos(180^0 - 60^0)$$

$$\Rightarrow \; \cos\theta = \cos 120^0$$

$$\Rightarrow \; \theta = 120^0 = 120 \times \frac{\pi}{180} = \frac{2\pi}{3}$$

$\therefore$ Option (D) is the correct answer.

Very Important Results :

(1) $\hat{i}.\hat{i} = |\hat{i}|^2 = 1,\ \hat{j}.\hat{j} = 1,\ \hat{k}.\hat{k} = 1.$

(2) $\hat{i}\times\hat{i} = \vec{0},\ \hat{j}\times\hat{j} = \vec{0}$ and $\hat{k}\times\hat{k} = \vec{0}.$

(3) $\hat{i}.\hat{j} = 0 = \hat{j}.\hat{i},\ \hat{j}.\hat{k} = 0 = \hat{k}.\hat{j},\ \hat{i}.\hat{k} = 0 = \hat{k}.\hat{i} = \vec{0}$

(4) $\hat{i}\times\hat{j} = \hat{k},\ \hat{j}\times\hat{k} = \hat{i}$ and $\hat{k}\times\hat{i} = \hat{j}$

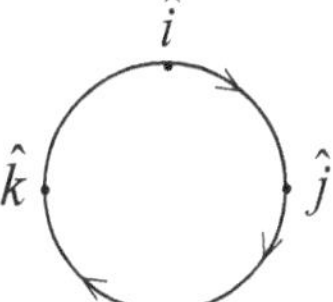

18. *Choose the correct answer:*

The value of $\hat{i}.(\hat{j}\times\hat{k}) + j.(\hat{i}\times\hat{k}) + k.(\hat{i}\times\hat{j})$

(A) 0   **(B)** –1   **(C)** 1   **(D)** 3

SOLUTION : $\hat{i}\times\hat{j} = \hat{k},\ \hat{j}\times\hat{k} = \hat{i}$ and $\hat{k}\times\hat{i} = \hat{j}$

$$\hat{i}.(\hat{j}\times\hat{k}) + j.(\hat{i}\times\hat{k}) + k.(\hat{i}\times\hat{j})$$

$$\hat{i}.(\hat{j}\times\hat{k}) + j.(\hat{i}\times\hat{k}) + k.(\hat{i}\times\hat{j})$$

$$= \hat{i}.\hat{i} + \hat{j}.(-\hat{j}) + \hat{k}.\hat{k}$$

$$(\because\ \hat{i}\times\hat{k} = -\hat{k}\times\hat{i} = -\hat{j})$$

$$= 1 - 1 + 1 = 1$$

$\therefore$ Option (C) is the correct answer.

19. *If* θ *be the angle between any two vectors* $\vec{a}$ *and* $\vec{b}$, *then* $|\vec{a}.\vec{b}| = |\vec{a}\times\vec{b}|$, *when* θ *is equal to :*

(A) 0   **(B)** $\dfrac{\pi}{4}$ **(C)** $\dfrac{\pi}{2}$ **(D)** π

SOLUTION :   **Given:** $|\vec{a}.\vec{b}| = |\vec{a}\times\vec{b}|$

$$\Rightarrow |\vec{a}||\vec{b}||\cos\theta| = |\vec{a}||\vec{b}|\sin\theta$$

$$(\because\ \vec{a}.\vec{b} = |\vec{a}||\vec{b}|\cos\theta$$

$$\Rightarrow |\vec{a}.\vec{b}| = |\vec{a}||\vec{b}||\cos\theta|)$$

Dividing both sides by $|\vec{a}||\vec{b}|$, we have $|\cos\theta| = \sin\theta$

and this equation is true only for option (B) namely $\theta = \dfrac{\pi}{4}$ out of the given options.

$$\left[\because \ \cos\frac{\pi}{4} = \frac{1}{\sqrt{2}} \ \text{and also} \ \sin\frac{\pi}{4} = \frac{1}{\sqrt{2}} \right]$$

∴ Option (B) is the correct option.

www.ingramcontent.com/pod-product-compliance
Lightning Source LLC
Chambersburg PA
CBHW040208110726
48005CB00019B/2941